The Manchester Outrage
– a Fenian tragedy

Jack Doughty has had a varied and interesting career. He played professional Rugby League with Oldham, but following a serious injury he moved into amateur acting before graduating to television and a few appearances at Oldham Repertory Theatre. From this he went on to performing song and dance routines in Music Hall. This was followed by a dramatic change in direction when he became involved in professional boxing, opening at gym in Bacup, Lancashire in the mid-eighties. In 1988, Jack opened a new gym at Rochdale, before leaving there in 1993 to open a boxing gym at Shaw, Oldham.

For the past fourteen years Jack has managed and trained fighters, producing several champions. Though he also stages regular small hall shows in order to develop young boxers, he has always been far more interested in training techniques and spends much of his time in the gym.

Apart from the theatre and sport Jack was always interested in reading and studying crime and his first venture into print reflected this with *Come at once – Annie is dying* (1987). This was followed by *The Rochdale Thunderbolt* (1991), a biography of the boxer Jock McAvoy. He had a marked success with another biography *The Rochdale Hangman and his victims* (1998). He has also written a radio play for the BBC, *The Shadow of Slim*, and a stage play, *The Cato Street Conspiracy*, which was performed at The Little Theatre, London. Jack is now working on his autobiography.

The Manchester Outrage
– a Fenian tragedy

Jack Doughty

◇JADE◇

Jade Publishing Limited,
5, Leefields Close, Uppermill, Oldham, Lancashire, OL3 6LA.

This first impression published by Jade Publishing Limited 2001.

ISBN 1–900734–15–X
The Manchester Outrage
– a Fenian tragedy.

Printed in Great Britain by
Esparto Digital Limited

Typeset by
Jade Publishing Limited, Uppermill, Oldham, Lancashire.

British Library cataloguing in Publication Data
Doughty, Jack
The Manchester Outrage
– a Fenian tragedy.

I. Great Britain.
2. – Great Britain
I. Title II.
355.1'342'0941

ISBN 1–900734–15–X

Dedication

To Marianne

Other titles by Jack Doughty

Come at once – Annie is dying (1987). Pentaman Press. Murder at the Workhouse, in Victorian Oldham.

The Rochdale Thunderbolt (1991). Pentaman Press. The biography of the boxer Jock McAvoy.

The Rochdale Hangman and his victims (1998). Jade Publishing Limited. The story of Jack Ellis, Executioner from 1901 to 1923.

The Shadow of Slim, a radio play for the BBC.

The Cato Street Conspiracy. A stage play performed at the Little Theatre, London.

Contents

Acknowledgments

I would like to thank the following people for various forms of assistance I received while working on this book.

The late John Lavin, former Registrar at Moston Cemetery, Manchester, who first pointed out the Manchester Martyrs' monument to me while I was in the process of researching another book, and set me off on a trail which covered over five years' research and writing. My thanks are due also to the present Registrar, Mr. B.H. Stott; to Mr. H. Richardson of Belmont Gardens, Donnybrook, Dublin; the staff of the National Library of Ireland, Dublin and Mr. Kynaston, Deputy Registrar at Philips Park Cemetery, Manchester.

When I first became interested in the subject I visited St. Patrick's Roman Catholic Church, Livesey Street, Manchester and spent some time with the Parish Priest, the late Monsignor Early. More recently, I spoke with the present Parish Priest, Father O'Mara. Both were extremely helpful.

My gratitude also to Jack Ireland, and Gordon Turner, both excellent photographers, who were keenly interested in the Fenian story, to my sons Richard and Danny for their enthusiastic and painstaking work at the Oldham and Manchester Public Libraries, and to Editor Pamela Daniels for her keen attention to detail.

Jack Doughty
November, 2001.

Illustrations

Preface

On the 18 September, 1867, the City of Manchester was shaken to its foundations by the news that a police van had been attacked in broad daylight on the Hyde road, only a couple of miles from the City centre, by a bunch of wild Irishmen armed with guns, hammers, hatchets and various other implements, the van broken into, two prisoners released and a policeman shot dead.

The rescued prisoners were Colonel Thomas J. Kelly and Captain Timothy Deasy, American Civil War veterans and leading figures in the Fenian Brotherhood, a revolutionary movement dedicated to the overthrow of the British Government in Ireland.

The episode, in which a very brave police officer, Sergeant Charles Brett, gave his life rather than surrender his prisoners, was to cause a great public furore and result in further tragic loss of life, when three young Irishmen were hanged at the New Bailey Prison, Salford, near Manchester, on 23 November of the same year.

The story of the Manchester Martyrs, as they came to be known, cannot effectively be told without first examining its background, the Fenian Movement, and the roots from which that movement sprang.

Though the Fenians can in no way be equated with present-day terrorists and so-called 'freedom fighters' in terms of viciousness and total disregard for human life, it would be most unwise to view them as heroes. What may be said on their behalf is that they strove to help free a nation which at that time was, without doubt, severely oppressed and poverty-stricken. Also, there appears to be little, if any, evidence that they deliberately set out to kill or maim. Yet, inevitably, innocent people lost their lives. For apart from the killing of Sergeant Brett, a terrible tragedy was to occur at Clerkenwell, London, not many months later.

The Manchester Fenians convicted of Brett's murder were described at the time by some newspapers as the ignorant dupes of a ruthless conspiratorial organisation, hell-bent on wholesale destruction.

Yet they saw themselves as patriots, totally committed to the cause of Irish independence. Others saw them as swashbuckling heroes and dubbed them 'the boys who smashed the van'.

The case of the Manchester Martyrs has remained surrounded by controversy since the day of the outrage, and the question of whether they came to the Hyde Road bridge prepared to commit murder, if necessary, to free their leaders, is explored in detail here, as is also the identity of the man who fired the fatal shot, for it has never been accepted in some quarters that the killer was among those executed.

The Fenian story and, in particular, the saga of the Manchester Martyrs, is indeed a fascinating one, packed with drama and tinged with the warmth, humour and innate vulnerability of the Irish character.

The principal players are more colourful than would be found in the pages of any novel or adventure tale; from that fiercely determined band of U.S. Army officers, real fighting men such as Kelly, Deasy, McCafferty, Condon, O'Neill, Burke and Mackey; to big John Francis Nugent; McAuliffe, the fighting preacher; and the three poor Irish lads who died on the scaffold in Manchester on a damp, foggy, November morning in 1867.

CHAPTER 1

The roots of Fenianism

The Fenian Movement, otherwise known as the Irish Republican Brotherhood, was a secret society formed around the middle of the nineteenth century. Of course, it was not the first time that Irishmen had plotted to break the shackles of English rule, and it would be by no means the last, but it can truly be said that though the Movement was eventually crushed, its inspiration led directly to the successful rising half a century later.

From the remnants of the Young Ireland Movement, summarily snuffed out by the authorities in 1848, was built a fighting force strong in spirit and manpower, though certainly lacking in resources. It was to become the greatest single threat to British domination in Ireland since the far off days of 1798, when Wolfe Tone landed on the West coast with 2,000 Frenchmen, ready to wipe the English from the face of Ireland for ever.

Unlike the Fenians, who would follow him many years later, Theobald Wolfe Tone had never intended, in the beginning, to gain his objectives by the use of force. His initial aim had been to unite his countrymen, Catholic and Protestant, under one flag, while at the same time striving for the rights of Ireland by political rather than militant means.

Wolfe Tone's United Irishmen did not form themselves into an undercover organisation, their meetings being held quite openly in public places. It was a mistake that would not be repeated by the Fenians when their turn came. The United Irishmen's gatherings were continually broken up by the police, even though they could not really have been considered seditious.

Faced with the decision either to disband or become a secret society, the members took the latter course. From then on, hounded by the authorities, they became increasingly militant in their attitude, until finally, in 1798, the conflict exploded into open rebellion.

About two years prior to all this Wolfe Tone had visited the New World, in the belief, no doubt, that with their own fight for independence not long past, the Americans might be inclined to support him. He certainly found a great deal of sympathy, but little else. Tangible aid would only come from across the Atlantic after the population of

1

America had been swollen by the great Irish exodus, which was still to take place. When that aid arrived it would be the Fenians who would benefit, after Wolfe Tone and his United Irishmen were no more than a memory.

From America Tone went to France, at a time when the revolutionaries there were in the throes of creating a republic. After much negotiation the new rulers of France agreed to an invasion of Ireland, and on 22 August, 1798, General Humbert sailed into Killala Bay and landed his troops at Killala, on the County Mayo side of the bay. The fight, however, was already lost, thousands of poorly-armed peasants having been slaughtered in the weeks preceding the arrival of the French force. But the invaders did not turn back, and in fact were the victors in several minor clashes with British troops. Eventually they were surrounded and defeated by Cornwallis at Ballinamuck. Wolfe Tone, now a French officer, arrived in a following vessel, was captured and sentenced to be hanged. When his request to be placed in front of a firing squad, so that he might die like the soldier he had become, was refused, he took his own life by cutting his throat. Several leaders of the '98 rising died on the scaffold. They included the brothers Sheares, McCann, Perry and Bagenal Harvey. Lord Edward Fitzgerald died of his wounds in an Irish gaol, while another prominent United Irishman, Oliver Bond, died in Newgate. Wolfe Tone is buried some twenty miles from Dublin, in the tiny churchyard at Bodenstown.

The brave but foolhardy attempt at revolt led by Robert Emmet in Dublin some five years later was little more than a gesture of defiance, and another name was added to the ever-growing list of Irish martyrs when Emmet was publicly executed in 1803. The hanging was accompanied by the barbarous murder of an Irish judge, who was dragged from his carriage in the streets of Dublin and killed in the presence of his daughter.

The plight of the Irish people at this time was indeed desperate. Successive governments in London had virtually crushed the life out of the country by the imposition of crippling taxes and tithes. To make matters worse, a law was passed which prohibited the export of wool to any country other than England, where it was subject to excessively high import duties. Such a move could hardly have been calculated to put the economy on its feet and, not surprisingly, it declined rather than developed.

Over the centuries major wars and minor skirmishes had led to the annexation of land, most of which was now owned either by the descendants of English settlers or by absentee landlords in England.

2

Such people collected their dues from tenants, who themselves often sub-let small sections to peasants so impoverished that they had barely the means to stay alive.

At this time the voice of the great Daniel O'Connell was beginning to make itself heard. The young lawyer, born in County Kerry in 1775, was to dominate Irish politics for the first half of the nineteenth century. O'Connell at his peak held mass political rallies throughout Ireland as he campaigned for Catholic emancipation. At that time Catholics were barred from membership of Parliament. In 1829, after a long battle, the Emancipation Bill was passed. A wonderful orator, O'Connell believed always in the power of the spoken word, never in violence and bloodshed.

But poverty was still the scourge of the Irish, and the failure of the potato crop in the eighteen-forties brought widespread famine. People already living from hand-to-mouth were now literally starving to death. Families were evicted as they could not pay their rents. Many were foresaking their native land in droves to seek a better living elsewhere, with thousands crossing the Atlantic to settle in America. Over one million people left Ireland between 1847 and 1857. *'In a few years'* stated a writer in *The Times, 'a Celtic Irishman will be as rare in Connemara as is the Red Indian in Manhattan.'*

Unseasonably inclement weather conditions in the late summer of 1845 was believed to have been responsible for the failure of the potato crop, on which the already severely impoverished Irish people relied, almost entirely, for sustenance. By the end of August in that year it had become clear that the crop in most counties was so badly diseased as to be considered inedible. Subsequently, it was established that a killer fungus was the cause of the problem, resulting in most of the potatoes grown being soggy, pulplike and rotten.

The blight also affected England, but as the potato was nowhere near as heavily relied upon there, it did not have the same devastating effect on the population as it did in Ireland.

Over the next four or five years the situation hardly improved at all, and it was during this period that the mass exodus to America and England really intensified. Thousands of those left behind turned to the authorities for help, but though the desperate plight of the Irish was constantly discussed in Parliament and a 'Soup Kitchen' Act belatedly passed, it did little to alleviate the suffering. In many areas free food was handed out. These meagre rations, however, proved totally inadequate and the workhouses were soon full up and incapable of taking in all who came to their gates.

3

Many of those who had managed to reach England found themselves destitute and were to be seen begging in the streets of Liverpool, Manchester and other towns in the North-west, ragged, barefoot children among them.

For those remaining in Ireland the future appeared bleak indeed. To such desperate people the rantings of the politicians were utterly meaningless, and for once the advice of O'Connell went unheeded. For while the great reformer urged the turbulent element to continue the fight for their rights only within the framework of the law, a number of his own closest followers were in the process of forming the Young Ireland Movement, their vowed intention being nothing less than armed insurrection.

William Smith O'Brien, leading light in the movement, and a politician of the highest integrity, made his move in 1848, an ill-conceived affair which the authorities had little trouble in putting down. Most of the leaders were sentenced to be hanged, a verdict later commuted to transportation for life, with Smith O'Brien eventually being granted a full pardon.

The '48 rebellion threw up many interesting characters, some of whom were to become important figures in Irish revolutionary history: John Mitchel and Terence Bellew McManus [both of whom were sent to the convict settlement in Van Diemen's Land, from which they later escaped], John O'Mahoney, Philip Grey and James Fintan Lalor. Lalor, who led an equally abortive insurrection the following year, lodged at 39, Great Britain Street, [now known as Parnell Street] Dublin, about three doors on the west side of Coles Lane. He died at the end of 1849. Among Lalor's associates at that time were Thomas Clarke Luby and John O'Leary, both of whom would later play prominent parts in the birth of the Fenian Movement.

Also to the fore among the '48 insurgents was a young man named James Stephens, who was to become one of the founders of Fenianism and is perhaps the best known of all those connected with it.

Born in Kilkenny in 1824, Stephens received a good education, though his parents were far from well-to-do, and eventually became an engineer. In the eighteen-forties he worked on the new Limerick-Waterford railway, later moving to Dublin to seek further employment. Already a man of high principles and deep national fervour, Stephens very quickly became involved with the Young Irelanders and was wounded in the attempted rising. After some weeks in hiding he managed to escape to France, where in Paris he renewed contact with another '48 fugitive, John O'Mahoney, the two of them spending a number of years in the French capital. Stephens managed to eke out a meagre existence by teaching English, while O'Mahoney taught Gaelic at the Irish College. Much time was spent in the company of other revolutionaries and assorted outcasts from various countries, and there can be no doubt that Stephens drew much knowledge from these contacts which was mentally filed away to be used at a later date. O'Mahoney, who appears not to have been possessed of Stephens's fanaticism, eventually left, in 1853, to try his luck in America.

It was around this period also that John Mitchel and Terence Bellew McManus arrived in America, following their escape from the penal settlement in Van Diemen's Land. McManus travelled on west to settle in California, while Mitchel, a man of strong political views, stayed in New York, where he later published a newspaper, *The Citizen.*

Stephens waited for the furore to abate before returning to Ireland at some time in the mid-eighteen-fifties. He was soon involved again in the old conspiracy game, attaching himself to an organisation calling itself the 'Phoenix Literary Society' of Skibbereen. This innocuous title hid the group's true function, for in effect the club was a secret society. All who joined were required to swear an oath to renounce all allegiance to the Queen and be prepared to take up arms when called upon, in the fight to make Ireland an independent republic.

When members were observed drilling, whispers of a new rising began to circulate and the authorities became very jumpy. Arrests were made and the movement appeared to have shot its bolt. But from the ashes of the Phoenix Society, Stephens formed a new organisation, the Irish Republican Brotherhood, known as the I.R.B. Throughout the late eighteen-fifties and early 'sixties a great many new members were recruited. They swore an oath of allegiance, were formed into companies or circles, and drilled in secret. Most of the swearing-in was done at Donnelly's, in Magennis Place, not far from the present Fenian Street in Dublin.

At the same time a number of small 'munitions factories' came into being. Not far from Lalor's old lodgings in Great Britain Street, near the corner of King's Inn Street, a man named Michael Moore made pikes. In nearby Loftus Lane was another factory, and at 4, Halston Street, one of the drill halls. It had originally been Robert McKenzie's forge, and the owner, Martin Henley Carey, was later imprisoned for allowing his premises to be used by the Fenians. At 63, Mary Street, Charles Hopper, who became Stephens' brother-in-law, kept a cigar store, which was used as a meeting place. At 16, Lombard Street, was Peter Langan's timberyard. Langan was another of the

5

links between the '48 rising and the birth of Fenianism, and it was at his yard that Stephens met for the first time a number of the men who would later occupy prominent positions in the organisation.

Meanwhile things were slowly beginning to happen in America, where John O'Mahoney, Michael Doheny and other '48 exiles had formed, in 1855, what they called the Emmet Monument Association. Their aim, when strong enough, was to invade Ireland, a wild scheme by any reckoning, even if one disregards the fact that they possessed at that time very little in the way of arms, money or men in the required numbers.

Joseph Denieffe, a Kilkenny man who had been in New York since 1851, joined the new movement some months after its inception. In the spring of 1856 he was recalled home because of his father's illness, and asked the leaders of the Emmet group where he should report to on arriving in Ireland. To his amazement he was told by Michael Doheny that the organisation did not as yet even have an agent across the Atlantic. He was commissioned therefore to establish contact with revolutionary-minded men in Ireland as soon as possible.

In Kilkenny he was introduced to John Haltigan, foreman printer on the *Kilkenny Journal*, and over a number of weekends the two of them worked hard to spread word of the planned 'invasion' throughout neighbouring towns. After staying for some months Denieffe went to Dublin, carrying with him a letter from Haltigan to Peter Langan. He was also given the address of Matthew Farrell of Creighton Street, a chimney sweep, with whom Denieffe found lodgings. Farrell took him along to Langan's yard. At a meeting there, Langan and two of his friends, Garrett Shaughnessy and Philip Grey, were sworn in as members of the Emmet Monument Association.

It was also at Langan's that Denieffe was first introduced to James Stephens. Having received no word from New York since his arrival he had become discouraged and was about to return when he was informed that Stephens wished to meet him. Stephens was described, at this period, as 'seedily attired, long-haired and rather bohemian'. Nevertheless, Denieffe was impressed by him and did not need much persuading to remain in Ireland. Following their meeting, a correspondence with the American Irishmen began, and towards the end of 1857 Owen Considine of Nenagh arrived from New York with communications from O'Mahoney and Doheny.

Denieffe, who had been working as a tailor's cutter in Carrickmacross, was now sent by Stephens to New York with a reply. On arriving, he found that the Emmet Association had been wound up and a new committee formed.

Joseph Denieffe was soon on his way back, with £80 and a promise of more to come. Stephens, accompanied by Thomas Clarke Luby, embarked on organising tours throughout Ireland, swearing in men as he went.

In 1861, Terence Bellew McManus died in poverty in San Francisco. His family in Ireland was keen that his wish to be buried in his native soil be granted, and responsibility for the funeral was assumed by members of the St. Patrick's Brotherhood, a debating society founded earlier that year. A committee was set up which included members of the I.R.B., who, though in the minority, seemed to hold sway, with Stephens apparently dominating.

The body arrived at Kingsbridge station from Cork on Monday 4 November, 1861, and, permission for its lying in state at the Pro-Catholic Cathedral having been refused, was escorted by members of the St. Patrick's Brotherhood to the Mechanic's Institute. There it lay all that week while a constant stream of people filed past.

There was much squabbling over the funeral arrangements, a trait that was to characterise almost every Fenian activity over the coming tempestuous years. At the request of Miss McManus, Terence's sister, Father Kenyon had consented to deliver the funeral oration. Several evenings prior to the funeral, he rehearsed the text before Stephens at 17, St. James's Terrace, Dolphin's Barn, the house of Luby's mother. Stephens was far from happy with it and next day high-handedly announced that the speech would instead be read by Captain Smith, leader of the American delegation. This naturally led to arguments, also involving Smith O'Brien, who had been invited to join in the proceedings and felt that he was not being accorded the prominence due to him. Many bitter remarks were made before the arrangements could finally be settled. The speech was read by Captain Smith, Stephens having sat up all the previous night to rewrite it, following which he retired discretely into the background.

On the day of the funeral, Sunday 10 November, a massive crowd turned out despite the cold, wet weather. McManus in his youth had been one of the boldest fighters in the Young Ireland Movement, and many thousands marched with him to his final resting place at Glasnevin, every one uncovering his head at the spot where Robert Emmet had died. At the graveside, the prayers were intoned by Father Patrick Lavelle of Ballinrobe, while Captain Smith read Stephens's speech by torchlight, as it was then dusk. It was a scene highly-charged with emotion, which evoked in the mass of spectators deep feelings of sympathy and fierce patriotism.

That day a new spirit came into being in Ireland. The funeral of Terence Bellew McManus proved a great shot in the arm for the I.R.B., for it was followed by a tremendous upsurge in the number of recruits keen to join the ranks. It was a masterstroke by Stephens, cleverly planned and executed, which gave the movement the credibility and support it had lacked up to that time.

CHAPTER 2

The 'Yankee Boys'

In 1863, James Stephens founded his own newspaper, the *Irish People*. Its office was at 12, Parliament Street, just a short distance from Dublin Castle, though the actual printing was done at the works of Pattison Jolly in West Essex Street.

The *People* was excellently written and highly seditious. On its staff were Thomas Clarke Luby, the registered owner; John O'Leary, the editor; Jeremiah O'Donovan Rossa, publisher; Cornelius O'Mahoney, bookkeeper; James O'Connor, bookkeeper-cashier and Charles Kickham. John Haltigan, brought to Dublin from Kilkenny, was in charge of the typesetting. All were leading members of the I.R.B., with the exception of O'Leary, who, although he refused to take the oath was, nonetheless, as loyal to the cause as any of his colleagues.

In the main they were men of good education. Before becoming involved with the Young Irelanders and playing a part in the rising of '48, Luby, Dublin-born, had studied law, and no doubt sacrificed a good career for his political beliefs.

O'Leary, a Tipperary man, had studied medicine before taking up with the '48 men, Lalor and Grey. After Lalor's death in 1849, O'Leary, contrary to some reports, had little contact with undercover movements or secret societies of any kind until his appointment to the *Irish People*, a post he was somewhat dubious about accepting at first.

Jeremiah O'Donovan Rossa. a native of Rosscarbery, County Cork, was the man who had founded the Phoenix Society of Skibbereen. Charles Kickham, born at Mullinahone, in 1828, was another Young Irelander and something of a scholar, who later in his life published several novels, songs and poems.

In Dublin, O'Leary lodged at 16, Palmerston Place; O'Donovan Rossa and his wife at 18, Middle Mountjoy Street, where another prominent I.R.B. member, William Francis Roantree of Leixlip, County Kildare, occupied a room.

There was also a police informer on the *Irish People* staff, but this would not come to light until a much later date.

Stephens, highly enthusiastic at the paper's inception and with big ideas and plans for his own intended journalistic contributions, quickly lost interest in the new venture and wrote no more than a handful of articles for the early issues. Yet under the management of his

9

extremely able staff the new publication quickly established a wide circulation. Copies regularly found their way to England and even further afield, for Irishmen were by now scattered all over the globe, particularly in America, where O'Mahoney's movement had become firmly established, operating quite openly and apparently without fear of suppression.

O'Mahoney is said to have been responsible for adopting the name 'Fenian', which is believed by most historians to derive from the Fianna or Fiann warriors of ancient Ireland, but according to the Oxford English Dictionary originates from *féne*, the ancient Irish people. Once the name became known it captured the imagination of the public and was thereafter much more widely used than the official title of the organisation, the Irish Republican (or Revolutionary) Brotherhood.

John O'Mahoney was born at Clonkilla, County Cork, in 1815, into a wealthy land-owning family, and received a good education, being in particular a keen student of ancient Irish history. Some measure of his ability as a scholar may be judged from the fact that while in America he translated *The History of Ireland from the earliest period to the English Invasion* by the Reverend Geoffrey Keating, from the original Gaelic into English, a massive undertaking and a major contribution to nineteenth century Irish literature.

Throughout the early eighteen-sixties Fenian circles were formed all over America. In New York a central H.Q. had been established and conventions were held in several major cities, including Chicago, Pittsburgh and Philadelphia. In Washington and New York, offices were opened for the sale of Irish Republican bonds. It was claimed that upwards of 30,000 people were engaged in attending meetings and raising funds.

There was even a Fenian Sisterhood, with a Head Centress [sic] named Ellen O'Mahoney, a Chicago school teacher. Contrary to popular belief she was not a relative of John O'Mahoney. For many years she had been principal of the high school in Quincy, Illinois, before moving to Chicago in 1863 to take up a similar post. While there she involved herself in Fenian affairs and ultimately became leader of the organisation's sorority.

As in Ireland, each circle had an 'A', or Centre, in charge. Under him came nine Sub-Centres. These were given the rank of Captain and each controlled nine sergeants, each of whom controlled nine privates. The idea behind it all was that, for security reasons, no man should know the identity of anyone outside his own section. In practice, these elaborate precautions did not usually work out. Each circle would, if every level reached its full complement of members, comprise 820 men.

10

John O'Mahoney was official Head Centre for America, and under his control came the many Centres and Sub-Centres who led the various circles throughout the country. Though well aware of all that was going on, the American authorities seemed content to turn a blind eye, even when rumours began to circulate about vast stores of arms and plans for the purchase of ships in which to carry the intended revolutionaries.

In America the Civil War was raging at that time. Among the ranks of fighting men were hundreds of Irish, and, ludicrous as it may seem, or perhaps characteristically, they fought on both sides. There were even Irish regiments, an example being the famous Corcoran Legion. By all accounts the Irish were among the bravest and most reckless engaged in that tragic and bitter struggle. Yet despite their preoccupation with the job in hand very few of the American Irishmen had forgotten the plight of their countrymen back home, and when hostilities finally came to an end in 1865, large numbers of them, including many officers, were ready and eager to place their military training and battle experience at the disposal of the fast-growing Fenian Brotherhood.

As well as recruiting civilians the Fenians in Ireland were also making great efforts to enrol military men by secretly approaching serving soldiers. One of the first to take on this hazardous assignment was the notorious 'Pagan' O'Leary, a man with a highly colourful background. O'Leary, whose correct Christian name was Patrick, was born at Macroom in 1825 and was studying to become a priest in America when the war with Mexico broke out. A sudden desire for a life of excitement caused him to abandon his calling and enlist in the forces. During the fighting he received a head wound, which was believed to account for much of his subsequent behaviour. It was said to have affected his mind strangely, completely altering his views on religion. He developed a strong aversion to St. Patrick and was thereafter invariably referred to as 'The Pagan'.

After the Mexican war O'Leary settled in New York and joined up with the Fenians, going to Dublin in 1863, where he was given the task of attempting to entice British soldiers into the organisation. He was arrested the following year in Athlone, his work being taken over by Roantree. Roantree himself was to be arrested in 1865, and John Devoy, one of the more prominent Fenians, took his place.

It was not long before Irish-Americans began turning up in the old country, at first in odd ones and twos, later in quite large numbers. Leading members of the organisation's American arm came to make contact with Stephens and assure themselves that preparations for some sort of positive action, were in the pipeline. They were treated to some

11

of the sermonising leader's loftiest speeches and left the *Irish People* office with the firm conviction that the projected new republic would become a reality before the year 1865 was out.

One of the early arrivals in Ireland was Captain Thomas J. Kelly. A Galway man and hero of the American Civil War, Kelly was to become one of the leading Fenian figures and would later play a major role in the tragic affair of the Manchester Martyrs. Other prominent military men to arrive from across the Atlantic that year were Generals Halpin and Millin, who had also fought in the Mexican war.

A major worry at this time was the comparatively poor response to fund-raising in America, for only a fraction of the money promised – £100 per week – had materialised. Nevertheless, the coming of the Irish-Yankees gave a great lift to the movement in Ireland. They were a jaunty, aggressive bunch, and after making contact with them, many of the more hot-headed native Fenians became restless, and ready to take up arms at a moment's notice. But despite his rantings, Stephens was by nature a cautious man, also extremely dominant and well able to contain the reckless element. His influence at this period was at a peak it would rarely reach later.

All was running as smooth as clockwork. There was, as planned, a gradual build-up on both sides of the Atlantic. While pikes were being made in Ireland, money and guns were being shipped in secretly from America. Drilling and instruction in the use of firearms was being carried out under the supervision of American officers, while recruitment was still brisk, and the *Irish People* was gaining new readers every week, with the presses working overtime.

However, all was not as rosy as it appeared on the surface. The British Government was receiving regular intelligence reports from informants in New York, and actually had a spy in the *Irish People* office in Dublin. He was Pierce Nagle, a native of Tipperary and a former teacher, who lodged at 3, Chapel Lane while working on the *People* as a folder. Despite his rather menial position he was quite close to Stephens and had sworn in a number of recruits, although he later denied in court that he had ever taken the Fenian oath himself. For many months Nagle fed the authorities as much information as he could lay his hands on, which was considerable.

The appearance of the Americans and the effect they were having on native Fenians was causing the British Government to become very edgy indeed. In the autumn of 1865 Stephens finally gave them what they needed to make their move, when he placed in Nagle's hands a letter to be read out to members of the Clonmel circle. Within a very short time the document was being studied at Dublin Castle. Its contents were clearly treasonable and indicated that the date of the intended rising was not far off. The time was ripe to put a stop to the flood of seditious propaganda pouring from the presses of the *Irish People*. In mid-September, 1865 the premises were raided by the police, who seized many more incriminating documents plus most of the staff. James Stephens, however, was not one of those unfortunate enough to have been in the building at the time. As soon as he heard of the raid he left his lodgings, went to ground, and could not be found anywhere.

Suspected persons were being picked up all over the country, and some newspapers, believing that the revolt was over before it had begun, were congratulating the authorities on having effectively nipped in the bud a movement which had come very close to staging an open rebellion.

By Saturday 23 September, the number of Fenians under lock and key in Dublin totalled 35. In Cork 13 men were in custody and arrests had also been made in Louth, Mayo, Tipperary and several other counties, the total number of prisoners amounting to 187.

In Cork the government forces made a find of considerable importance. Among documents seized was a roll book containing the names of members of Her Majesty's forces stated to be willing to defect to the Fenian ranks in the event of a rising. The list included the name of a certain Sergeant-Major of the 99th Foot stationed at Cork Barracks. On the day following the seizure of the book, the Colonel of the Regiment sent for the man in question and placed the damning piece of evidence before him. The Sergeant-Major was very much taken aback and denied everything. Eventually, however, he admitted that the signature was his. He was immediately placed under arrest along with a private in his command.

Among the *People* staff arrested were Luby, O'Leary, Nagle, Roantree, Cornelius O'Mahoney, James O'Connor and O'Donovan Rossa, who was picked up as he left the tailor's shop owned by George Hopper at 80, Dame Street. This George Hopper was either another brother-in-law of James Stephens, or his father-in-law.

Pierce Nagle was extremely angry at being arrested. He was told by detectives that he was being taken into custody because of the company he was keeping, but of course, was later used as the chief prosecution witness.

Quite a number of Irish-Americans were among those picked up, including a man named Murphy, who was set at liberty after representations had been made to Dublin Castle on his behalf by the American Consul, on the grounds that he was an official connected

13

with the War Department in Washington. Several other Americans were also later released, but some were less fortunate. In Queenstown, (now Cobh), at the beginning of October, 1865, two men with Yankee accents were apprehended on suspicion of being Fenian emissaries, and brought up at the police court. They were John McCafferty, a former Captain in the Confederate Army, and a man named O'Riorden, also an ex-Captain, whose Fenian rank was said to be that of Colonel.

It was stated in the newspapers on the day following the arrests that McCafferty had served in Morgan's Cavalry*, but had deserted and joined the Brotherhood. A number of books and Fenian pamphlets were found on his person, along with several inflammatory speeches obviously intended to incite discontent and arouse the people's anger against their landlords and the Government. He was also found to be carrying a pair of formidable-looking revolvers.

His companion was committed on the information of a man named Warner, who stated that O'Riorden was the officer who inspected the Fenians at the premises of a member named Geary, in Cork, and lectured them on the use of the rifle.

A detective who had operated in the Queenstown area for some months gave evidence that O'Riorden had been back to America and returned again within this period. He always associated with known Fenians, and his latest trip to Ireland was believed to be connected with the contemplated rising. O'Riorden denied that he had any ties with the Brotherhood, and claimed that his comings and goings were to do with family matters. Papers found in his possession, however, clearly indicated that he was a leading member of the Fenian circle in Detroit, Michigan.

The two were sent for trial, the American Consul refusing to give any aid to the prisoners or to intercede on their behalf. McCafferty, nonetheless, was released not long afterwards, an action the authorities would live to regret.

*Morgan's Cavalry, or Morgan's Raiders, as they were sometimes known, came into being in 1863, when the Southern armies were gradually being driven South. Confederate General, John Morgan, was sent to set up a diversion – until expected reinforcements were brought up – by engaging the enemy at Louisville. Deliberately disregarding instructions to restrict his activities to Kentucky, Morgan pressed on to launch a series of daring and highly successful raids behind enemy lines in Indiana and Ohio. After being captured, Morgan later escaped from the Ohio Penitentiary and re-organised his forces, making further raids in Kentucky and Tennessee. On a misty September morning in 1864 he was killed by a bullet from the rifle of Private Andrew Campbell of the Union Army, outside the house of Mrs. Williams in Greenville, Tennessee, where he had spent the night, prior to embarking on another of his famous raids.

CHAPTER 3

The Movement in disarray

There followed a great hue and cry for James Stephens, although it was strongly rumoured that he had already left the country. The Fenian Head Centre was, in fact, still in Dublin, though not more than a handful of people knew exactly where.

A reward of £200 was being offered for the apprehension of Geary, the Cork grocer and prominent Fenian, whose house had been used to hold meetings. Geary had come within an ace of being caught, making his escape through a back window while the police were searching his premises.

Arrests were also being made in England after Fenian demonstrations in Leeds, Liverpool, Salford and Sheffield, and the Fenians of Springfield, Illinois issued an appeal to Americans for funds to aid 'an uprising people', announcing that the date had already been set for the establishment of a provisional government.

In Belfast, four casks containing arms were seized on board a Fleetwood steamer. The casks, which were bound for merchants in Londonderry and Dungannon, were found to be packed with rifles and revolvers of a very high quality. Following this find, an extensive search was carried out at the English fishing port of Fleetwood, where fifteen cases containing arms were discovered.

Despite all the precautions being taken and the extra vigilance of the police, robberies, particularly at jewellers' shops, were being perpetrated with increasing frequency in an effort to raise money on behalf of the Brotherhood.

In September, 1865, an audacious and ingenious raid was carried out on the premises of Mr. Yorke, watchmaker and jeweller of St. George's Crescent, Liverpool. A stranger called at the shop and made a selection of several articles amounting to the value of £200 or so. He promised to return on the following day to pay for and collect the goods. In the meantime, he said, he would be obliged if Mr. Yorke would allow him to leave a large trunk, which, he confided, contained silver plate, and into which he also intended to pack his purchases. The jeweller, anxious to accommodate such a free-spending customer, gladly agreed to the request, and before the shop closed for the night the trunk was duly deposited, on the understanding that it would be opened on the following morning.

As it turned out, the box, which proved to be unusually weighty, did not contain silver plate, but a burglar, who emerged from his strange hiding place during the night and proceeded to pack several hundred pounds' worth of watches and jewellery into the trunk. He was in the act of making his escape when he had the misfortune to walk straight into the arms of a patrolling police constable. According to newspaper reports, it was no leprechaun that had hidden in the trunk, but a rather under-sized Irishman.

In spite of having to suffer the indignity of being driven into hiding, James Stephens was still regarded as unchallenged head of the organisation in Ireland and the man who would ultimately lead the revolt. Across the water things were not nearly so clear-cut, the Fenians of America having now split into two quite distinct factions, with O'Mahoney controlling one of them. The other half, known as the Senate wing, was jointly led by William Roberts and Thomas Sweeney. The Fenian Senate was constituted on similar lines to the American system, Roberts having been declared President. Sweeney, whose Fenian rank was that of General, was named as Commander-in-Chief of the Armed Forces, and was second only to Roberts in order of importance. This faction was known to be rather more reckless than the O'Mahoney mob, and could hardly wait to get into action.

The split had, in the main, been brought about because of what Roberts considered to be the vacillating attitude of John O'Mahoney, whom they now believed would talk and plan for another ten years and still not make any positive move. O'Mahoney himself was of the opinion that all was going according to plan, and that patience and caution must be observed at all costs if the ultimate objective, the invasion of Ireland, was to be carried through successfully. Roberts and Sweeney, on the other hand, were hell-bent on invading Canada at the earliest possible date, the idea being to move in on a relatively unprotected portion of British territory, a move calculated not only to give the Brotherhood a base of its own from which to launch the planned offensive on Ireland, but in addition, a great moral boost. Also, it was firmly believed that such a bold and decisive step would help give credibility to the new republic in the eyes of the world and, particularly, the United States' Government.

O'Mahoney's apparent unwillingness to light the fuse was no doubt the result of bitter experience. As one of the small band of American Fenians who had taken an active part in the '48 rising, he was well aware of the utter foolishness of plunging headlong into a conflict for which the rebels were nowhere near prepared. Moreover, he had observed in many of his colleagues a dangerous inclination to underestimate the power of the British Armed Forces.

The Fenian Movement was at that time, quietly but steadily, gaining a foothold in England, and the leaders were hopeful of the support, not only of Irish immigrants, but of the English working classes. France too, it was believed, would look upon the cause with approval, and possibly even offer some sort of tangible aid once the revolt was under way. In fact, there were scant grounds for such a supposition. As one French newspaper put it:–

Fenianism had made no converts save amongst the dregs of the population; shopkeepers, small farmers, artisans, bricklayers and vagabonds of every description form the personnel of the movement. They are said, however, to be desperate and ripe for mischief, but having no definite object in view they conspire at random and are kept together solely by delusive promises, too readily credited by their unsuspecting ignorance. Thus they have been persuaded that they can rely on the early arrival of an American fleet with 50,000 soldiers and 200,000 muskets. Others believe in the aid of France.

With people so credulous it is easy to produce a sudden explosion which the great number of those affiliated might consider dangerous, but it is impossible to believe that the English Government can possibly entertain any serious apprehensions. Moreover, it cannot but derive some comfort from the fact that the Catholic clergy are to a man against Fenianism. No movement has ever existed in Ireland that the priests did not discourage by their example and denunciations in the pulpit. This time they not only abstain from, but actually condemn, this insurrectionary movement.

There may have been some merit in the foregoing argument, but quite clearly there were also many flaws. To refer to shopkeepers, farmers and bricklayers as the dregs of the population was as senseless a statement as could be imagined. It was perhaps true, up to a point, to say that the Fenians did 'conspire at random', but whether the promises from America were delusory or not still remained to be seen. Was the Catholic clergy to a man against Fenianism? The French reporter had obviously never heard of Father Lavelle, and there were certainly other priests of a similar mind in Ireland, although it should be emphasised that the Catholic Church itself was, and still is, against all secret societies, and openly denounced Fenianism.

17

There is no doubt that the British Government did entertain serious apprehensions regarding the Brotherhood, which was why, in addition to the many arrests being made, the Irish coastline was at that moment being extensively patrolled by warships under instruction to keep a sharp lookout for any vessel suspected of being hostile, which might even be flying the Fenian flag – a blaze of sunlight on a green background.

Surprisingly, the French press was not alone in regarding the Fenian conspiracy with contempt. One English newspaper felt that the closure of the *Irish People* office and the wholesale arrests had effectively put an end to what could have developed into a nasty situation.

'The rebellion', it stated, 'reputedly supported by 200,000 well-drilled warriors and led by American war veterans, has not even made a beginning. It has been frightened to death by a policeman or two, and most of the leaders are now in custody on charges of treason.'

The Movement had in fact suffered something of a set-back, but as events of the next two years would show, the obituary notices were just a little premature.

CHAPTER 4

Escape from the Bridewell

I n mid-November, 1865 came bad news for Fenians everywhere. James Stephens had been arrested at a house in Newbridge Avenue*, Sandymount, on the south bank of the Dodder, where he had been living for some time as 'Mr. Herbert'. Taken into custody with him were three other Fenians, Charles Kickham, Edward Duffy and Hugh Brophy. Stephens is said to have behaved with great coolness when arrested, though the other prisoners were 'very downhearted'. The Fenian leader was locked up in the Richmond Bridewell, but was not destined to remain there for very long.

Soon after the arrests, Thomas J. Kelly, who, despite the pretensions of a fellow American officer, General Millin, had taken charge of things while Stephens was in hiding, called a meeting of all top Fenians then in the city to consider the next move. This meeting was held over a barber's shop at 25, Wicklow Street, near the junction of St. Andrew Street and William Street.

The result was a daring escape plan, apparently masterminded by Kelly, in which John Devoy was one of the prime movers. In the early hours of 24 November Stephens was taken out of the Bridewell in an operation so well-organised and executed that no alarm was raised until many hours later. On the previous night the prisoner had been locked up as usual. Next morning his cell was empty. It was as smooth as that. Too smooth in fact, for the cell door had not been forced, but opened with a key. The prison authorities quickly concluded that the rescuers had received help from within, and two warders were subsequently placed under arrest.

Later it was revealed that both were Fenian sympathisers, and that one of them had in fact been involved some time previously in a revolutionary war in Italy. How this man had obtained such a post as prison warder, entrusted with the guarding of political offenders, was never satisfactorily explained.

A reward of £1,000 was offered for the recapture of Stephens, but despite strenuous efforts, neither the police nor the military could unearth the slightest clue as to the whereabouts of the fugitive.

* Newbridge Avenue is now Herbert Road.

19

If the arrest of Stephens had had a deflationary effect on the Fenians, his ultimate repatriation now proved a great tonic for the Movement, and though many Irish-Americans still knocking about the streets of Dublin, and their adherents among the natives, were perhaps a little more discrete than previously, there was again a feeling of expectancy and muted excitement in the air. As far as the authorities and the general public were concerned, both in Ireland and in England, there was now, more than ever, a general feeling of unrest.

The situation though, was not without its humourous side – with Irishmen involved, how could it be otherwise? Many occurrences reported at the time, though not directly connected with the rumoured uprising, concerned Fenians, with drink in most circumstances playing its inevitable part.

On a November evening in 1865 Mr.G——, a man engaged in the business of Mercantile Insurance in Liverpool, was on his way home to Edge Hill when he decided to make a brief call at a public house in Dale Street.

On entering, Mr. G—— was seen to be carrying a double-barrelled fowling piece, which he had just collected after having had repairs done to the stock. A few minutes later a tall gentlemanly-looking stranger came into the bar and ordered a drink. He was in his middle-thirties and from his manner and speech was obviously American. On seeing the gun and noting that Mr. G—— spoke with a distinct Irish accent, the stranger approached him and said,

'I suppose you are a Fenian?'

'I am not', was the reply. 'I am a loyal Irish subject of our Gracious Queen, and I despise Fenians and Fenianism.'

'Then you despise me', said the American.

'I don't know you, but if you are a Fenian or a Fenian leader, then yes, I do despise you', stated Mr. G——, very positively.

The stranger now slowly and deliberately took from his pocket a handkerchief, applied it to his nose, then threw it full into Mr. G——'s face, saying,

'My name is William Brown, and I am a Fenian General. I was born in New York, but my father was one of the Browns of County Mayo, and thus I treat anyone who deprecates Fenianism.'

'I'm an Irishman too sir, also, as it happens, a native of Mayo', replied Mr. G——, 'and thus I treat anyone who declares himself and acts in so crude a manner as you do.' And with one blow he laid the 'General' flat on his back amid cheers and shouts of applause from the company.

20

When the Yankee eventually regained his feet he appeared to have cooled down somewhat, but in true gentlemanly fashion he presented his card to Mr. G—— and some time was spent in negotiating a meeting with pistols.

Nothing definite was settled that evening, but several nights later, at an hotel in Ranalagh Street, both belligerents agreed to place themselves in the hands of a London commercial traveller, who had undertaken to see that fair play was observed when the 'affair of honour' was finally resolved.

Accordingly, at 12 noon on the following Thursday, three men were seen to enter a field a little south of Bidstone Hill. The Fenian General carried a small case containing two revolvers, one of which was handed to Mr. G——. Brown said that the pistols would kill at 50 yards' distance, but Mr. G—— objected to being more than the required 25 paces from his opponent, and after some discussion gained his point. The referee, having placed the protagonists in their positions, now produced a pistol himself and addressed them very seriously.

'Gentlemen, you are both in my hands, and I believe you to be honourable men. I am also sure that you are brave men and will therefore not attempt to take advantage of each other. Nevertheless, I shall watch your movements very carefully, and if one man should fall as a result of foul play I shall not hesitate to shoot the other.'

So, under the threat of sudden death from two sides, the protagonists waited tensely for the referee's signal. On receiving it, each man paced out the distance, turned, took aim and fired. However, the report of only one pistol was heard and both men remained upright. The referee examined the weapons and found that both had been discharged, although he had heard only one shot. It was something of a mystery, but he declared that the two Irishmen should now be satisfied and shake hands. He produced a flask of brandy and all three took a nip before leaving the field and proceeding towards Birkenhead. But before reaching the ferry the General turned pale and almost fainted. The fact was that the ball from Mr. G——'s pistol had struck him over the hip, and although he had not so much as flinched at the time, the wound was now bleeding profusely and his clothing was saturated.

The General was laid down on the ground, and, no doubt alarmed at the amount of blood he had lost, appeared to fear for his life, for he reached inside his coat pocket and brought out a letter which he requested his companions to forward to New York should he fail to recover. He then began to wax philosophical regarding Ireland's cause, in which he passionately believed. He did not, however, appear very proud of the part he had played in the American Civil War, stating that his one regret was that, along with his brother, he had inveigled hundreds of poor Irishmen into joining the Northern Army. No doubt many of them had lost their lives, and the thought of this obviously weighed heavily on his conscience.

As it turned out, the gallant General was in very little danger of expiring. For after the flow of blood had been staunched, close examination by the versatile commercial traveller revealed nothing more than a flesh wound.

Once on his feet, and fortified by a further shot of brandy, Brown hurriedly retrieved his letter and the journey was resumed.

Before taking his leave the General made a further request: that nothing should appear in the newspapers regarding the duel until after the coming Saturday, by which time he would have sailed by mail steamer for New York. After being assured of this, the American parted from his new friends a rather subdued and certainly a much wiser man.

––––––––––––––––

Early in December, 1865 several leading Fenians came up for trial and were summarily dealt with, John O'Leary being sentenced to twenty years' penal servitude. A similar term was meted out to Thomas Clarke Luby, while Roantree received ten years. Others sentenced around this period were O'Donovan Rossa, twenty years, and Charles Kickham, fourteen years. Pierce Nagle appeared as chief prosecution witness in these trials. Though the severity of the sentences came as something of a shock, only an average of five years or so was served, every last one of the prisoners having been freed by 1871.

There was great excitement in Queenstown, County Cork, in consequence of a rumour that a Fenian cruiser had been sighted outside the harbour, and a large party of police was sent out in a government boat to investigate. They found no sign of the reported vessel. In Limerick a ballad singer was prosecuted and fined for singing seditious songs in public, and in County Tipperary a Fenian funeral made head-lines when a cooper named Maher died at his home in Louth Street, Carrick-on-Suir. He had held the honourable post of Sub-Centre to the Fenians of the district, and his fellow members were determined to escort him to his last resting place in a manner befitting his position.

A grand demonstration was therefore planned. First in the procession came one of the Brotherhood leaders attired in sable weeds and bearing in his hands a black flag, furled and tied with a white ribbon. Next came the hearse. followed by four men also carrying black flags,

22

and behind them upwards of 200 men walking two abreast and wearing white hatbands. Thus, slowly and sadly, they laid the poor cooper away. The burial itself took no more than a few minutes, for the mourners, being understandably thirsty after their march through the streets, soon turned away from the grave and converged on the nearest taverns, where they spent the afternoon drowning their sorrows.

With the turn of the year, the Fenians seemed no nearer to staging the much-vaunted revolution than did the authorities to recapturing Stephens, who was still in hiding in Dublin. Rumours were rife that he was in the process of planning raids on various army fortresses, and might even be expected to make an attempt at rescuing his colleagues still held in prison. But though he was constantly in touch with the organisation, Stephens was thankful for the time being merely to lie low and retain his own freedom.

Ships arriving at all major ports were being closely watched in case the Head Centre attempted to leave the country. Early in March, 1866 a number of men from Dublin were observed boarding an American steamer lying in Kingstown harbour. None of them went below deck and all could clearly be seen from the quayside. As it turned out there was nothing untoward about the visit to the ship, apart from the fact that they began distributing drink among the sailors, singing Fenian songs and drinking toasts to the Brotherhood's cause. The commander, on discovering the scene, at once sent them ashore and gave orders that no further visitors would be welcome aboard his ship while it was in Kingstown (Dun Laoghaire).

That week the 92nd Highlanders, with 24 officers and 673 N.C.O.s and men arrived at Kingstown on the troopship *Simoom* from Portsmouth. The gunboat *Nightingale* and the cutter *Racer*, with detectives on board, were on special duty in the bay, several ships being boarded and searched as the hunt for Stephens intensified. Later in the week, 803 officers and men of the 71st Regiment arrived in Kingstown as the American corvette *Canadaigua* left the port.

Considering the number of soldiers in the area it is not surprising that Kingstown was relatively quiet and untroubled at that time, most reported incidents occurring elsewhere. Four men named Coper, Sullivan, Condon and Murphy were arrested at Bantry, while in Dublin police proceeded to Scatty's public house in Exchange Street as the result of a tip-off and arrested 27 people. They were nearly all strangers in the city and included nine deserters from the armed forces.

23

Up to this time 176 had been arrested in Dublin alone on charges relating to Fenianism. Of these, 42 were Americans, hardly any of whom could convincingly account for their presence in Ireland. Only four prisoners had been discharged, leaving 172 still in custody.

CHAPTER 5

Habeas Corpus

A fter a session lasting two months, the Fenian Senate in New York had adjourned as the year 1865 drew to a close. Weeks of ranting and inflammatory speeches had brought them no nearer to their avowed objective. They were still determined though, and as a gesture of defiance the Fenian flag was proudly hoisted above the Brotherhood's headquarters in Union Square.

The O'Mahoney Fenians held a mass meeting in New York in February, 1866 in an attempt to enlist the sympathy of the American people, the speakers bitterly denouncing England as the enemy of both Ireland and the United States, and calling upon the Federal Government openly to support the campaign for Irish independence.

At a meeting in Washington a deputation was appointed, consisting of B. Doran Killian, a lawyer and high-ranking Fenian, Major Wallach, Congressmen Rodgers and Hogan, and was subsequently granted an interview with President Andrew Johnson to protest at the alleged outrageous treatment of American citizens in Ireland. This, of course, referred to the many arrests involving Irish-Americans following the suspension of the Habeas Corpus Act, which made it legal for the authorities to make arrests merely on suspicion. The Bill was denounced by Fenians throughout the United States. For some reason they seemed to feel that their agents in Ireland should be allowed to go about the country unmolested, free to create all sorts of problems for the Government; organising, drilling and instructing, and openly talking of insurrection and even invasion.

On receiving news of the Act's suspension, O'Mahoney issued a circular from the 'military department' to the effect that the people should now stand ready for action and 'secret orders'.

At the same time, the Roberts Fenians were planning to send their own deputation to Washington to ask for the concession of belligerent rights to the Irish forces, on the grounds that the British Government's recent actions had established a state of martial law in Ireland.

That the Fenians still had designs on a piece of Canada was clearly confirmed when 600 Spencer rifles were seized by the Canadian authorities after they had been smuggled across the border.

At a time when unity should have been of paramount importance, the two rival Fenian factions were more than ever at loggerheads, constantly threatening 'excommunications' and referring to each other as 'the enemy'.

By early March the Senate faction was again in session, this time in Pittsburgh. Delegates from all over the country heard General Sweeney make a most impassioned speech. He declared:

'I am opposed to making speeches. We have been talking for years now and what have we done? It's time to drop the orator and take up the soldier. We must fight, or our names will go down to posterity as nothing more than braggarts. With arms in our hands we will meet our hereditary enemy again, and if we fall we shall fall with dignity, in the most honest cause that ever the tongue or pen of man worked for.

'I have been preparing for the last twenty years for this struggle. I have sworn to break my country's chains or die in the attempt.

'We have now a better prospect than ever a people had before. We have not been idle. We have made large purchases of arms and war material. If you are prepared to stand by us we promise that before the summer sun kisses the hilltops of Ireland a ray of hope will gladden every true Irish heart.

'By that time we shall have conquered and taken hostages for our brave patriots at home. The green flag will be flying independently in freedom's breeze and we will have a base of operations from which we can not only emancipate Ireland, but also annihilate England. If you will support us I pledge my income, fame, property and my life to this holy cause.'

The general sat down amid thunderous applause and the stage was set for the great adventure. From that day earnest preparations were made for the attack on Canada. Fenians from all over America turned up in New York daily in response to the General's call.

The Canadian authorities, recognising the seriousness of the situation, also began to make a few preparations. A Cabinet council was held in March, 1866, at which it was determined to call out 10,000 volunteers as well as the military. It was believed that the Fenians would make their move on St. Patrick's Day, and it was therefore planned to suspend the Habeas Corpus Act in Canada before 17 March.

Britain meanwhile had requested the American Government to compensate for its hitherto passive attitude to Fenianism by taking such precautions as might be necessary to prevent its territory being used as a base from which to launch an attack on a British dominion, but St. Patrick's Day came and went without any invasion taking place.

On 31 March, the Fenians again held a mass meeting presided over by Roberts and Sweeney, attended by over 10,000 followers, when further plans were laid. Large quantities of ammunition and uniforms had been purchased, it was announced, and were being stored in numerous American towns along the frontier. Sweeney was repeatedly asked to name the date of the invasion, but had to admit that he did not know himself exactly when and where the first blow would be struck.

While the American Fenians continued to indulge themselves in seemingly endless planning, the pattern in Ireland was also unchanged, with minor intrigues and skirmishes being reported almost weekly.

On a Saturday evening in April, 1866, a mysterious attempt was made to murder a British soldier, the incident being inevitably connected with the Fenian Conspiracy. Shortly after nine o'clock on the night in question, a private of the 8th Regiment named Walter Maher, rushed into the detective office in Exchange Court, Dublin, crying out that he had just been shot and wounded in a public house. The man, in a state of terror and weak from loss of blood, collapsed in the hall leading to the office and half-fainted. After being carried inside and recovering himself somewhat, Maher told his story.

He had been invited by a man he met in Thomas Street to go into Hoey's public house in Bridgefoot Street. On entering, the soldier saw that a number of men were drinking at the bar. He and his companion had been there only a matter of minutes when one of the men produced a revolver and deliberately discharged it at him. The ball missed him however and struck a man who happened to be standing in the doorway of the grocery shop, which was part of the same business. As the unfortunate spectator dropped to the floor Maher made a dash for the exit, followed by a hail of lead, some of which found its mark.

The soldier, who refused to mention any names, was in no state for further questioning, and was immediately conveyed to the Arbour Hill Military Hospital, where he was found to have been shot in the hand, neck and leg, the latter being the only serious wound. On entry, the ball had traversed the thigh and come out at the knee.

Acting-Inspector Hughes, with several men of G Division, immediately proceeded to Hoey's Bar. They found a police constable already there. On hearing shots he had entered the premises to find a man named Dowling lying on the floor. Also in the bar were Mary Ann and Annie Hoey, daughters of the proprietor. Hoey himself was an invalid confined to his room. In addition to the women, four men were also present, plus two others who were found ill in bed upstairs. Next on the scene came Inspector Armstrong, who directed that all those

27

found on the premises should be detained. It is doubtful if the would-be assassin was ever apprehended, but if he was a Fenian he was certainly acting on his own account and was probably drunk. The incident was not typical, for unlike many secret societies and revolutionary movements which came later, the Fenians did not usually set out to murder individuals, even British soldiers.

With the Roberts–Sweeney clan still making aggressive noises and the holders of Fenian War Bonds growing ever more impatient, John O'Mahoney suddenly decided to take the initiative. His invasion force was not, however, directed towards Ireland, where he had always insisted the first blow should be struck, but to Canadian territory, in a complete about-face which could only be interpreted as a bid to out-do the rival faction.

In mid-April, 1866 Doran Killian led a Fenian force of several hundred men north to Eastport, a border town in the State of Maine, the objective being to seize the Island of Campobello in the Bay of Fundy, which runs between Nova Scotia and the Canadian mainland. The expedition was doomed to failure, for as usual the Fenians' actions were well advertised. When a flotilla of British warships made their appearance in the bay it became clear that there would be no landing on Campobello.

Worse was to follow. A large quantity of arms, delivered by steamship to Eastport, was impounded by the authorities. The desperadoes, without guns to fight with, were quickly dispersed, and though not one Fenian was killed or even arrested, there could be no denying that the entire project had been a fiasco, and a great waste of time and valuable funds.

At this period it was rumoured that another Fenian force had set out to attack Bermuda. This was, however, untrue, and is believed to have been put about to pacify the bond holders.

O'Mahoney, bitterly disappointed at the result of the Campobello non-event, learned that James Stephens was in Paris, having made his escape from Ireland by boat via England, accompanied by Kelly. The belief was that Stephens intended to sail for America, where he hoped to re-unite the two opposing factions. O'Mahoney at once issued a circular to the effect that Stephens could be expected within the month.

Sure enough, on 10 May, 1866 the great man arrived in New York by steamer. He was enthusiastically received by the Irish, most of whom acknowledged him as General Head Centre. Stephens put up at the Metropolitan Hotel, where he received visitors daily in great numbers. He assured them all that he had left the organisation in Ireland in good shape and that the reins were in competent hands during his temporary absence. He was at pains to point out that he had gone to Paris on important business, and not because the enemy had forced him out of Ireland. His avowed intention now, he said, was to restore harmonious relations among all Fenians in America.

This, however, was to prove beyond him. or anyone else for that matter. Soon after Stephens' arrival, John O'Mahoney removed Killian from office, despite the latter's protests that he was in no way to blame for the failure of the Campobello expedition and that in any case it was only a temporary set-back.

After talks with Stephens, who was very critical of him, O'Mahoney resigned, stating, that having given his consent to the Campobello venture – the failure of which had damaged the cause – he felt obliged to accept responsibility for it. No one argued with him, many being of the opinion that he had been forced to resign by Stephens, who acknowledged the resignation by a letter, in which he approved of O'Mahoney's action as being both wise and patriotic, while at the same time condemning his weakness in sanctioning an operation which had diverted attention from the true objective – Ireland.

The Roberts–Sweeney faction, which had already made contact with Stephens, was naturally elated to hear of O'Mahoney's downfall. Not that Stephens sided with them, for he was strongly opposed to any venture into Canada. After a meeting in Stephens' suite at the Metropolitan, Roberts is reported to have stated that the two factions had become reconciled under the leadership of the General Head Centre. This, however, could hardly have been true, for Sweeney let it be known that he and Roberts had found Stephens singularly unimpressive as a leader. The General even went so far as to suggest that the Head Centre of all Fenianism might well be a British spy! He had, after all, escaped from Richmond gaol with remarkable ease. It was almost as if he had been let out. Perhaps he had been allowed to escape from prison by the authorities for the sole purpose of making his way to America to work for their interests and his own pardon. Sweeney had apparently believed this even before Stephens' arrival, and nothing had occurred since then to alter his opinion.

Sweeney himself was under scrutiny at this time – by the United States' military authorities. For though he still held a commission in the Union Army, he had been absent for lengthy periods due to his Fenian activities. It was not long before he was informed by the War Office that his services were no longer required.

On 25 May, 1866 James Stephens addressed a mass meeting of Fenians in Brooklyn, and declared that the object of their attentions was not Canada, Japan, or anywhere else, but Ireland. He urged a reconciliation of the opposing factions, confidently informing his audience that he could smuggle 10,000 rifles safely into Ireland, where there were men 'in the gap' ready and waiting to use them.

'Unless our country is liberated', he told them, 'the Irish race will be absorbed in this country, in England, and in many other places. We will lose our identity, and will eventually disappear from the face of the earth.'

He said his intention was to remain in America only a short time, and ended by declaring that if Fenians would only discontinue their internal squabbling they could be fighting the British troops on solid fronts within that very year.

The speech was received with wild enthusiasm and Stephens was assured that most Fenian circles were in whole-hearted agreement with the views he had expressed. This did not, however, prevent Roberts and Sweeney going ahead with their own plans.

CHAPTER 6

The invasion of Canada

In the last days of May, 1866 came news that large groups of men were moving north towards the Canadian frontier. Others were *en route* by rail from various parts of the United States, some from as far away as Tennessee. Rumour had it that they would rendezvous at Buffalo in upstate New York, a town on the banks of the Niagara river, close to the famous Falls.

The majority of the townspeople seemed disinclined to believe this story and received a nasty shock when a number of 'rowdies of the Irish class' were seen strutting around the streets in small but noisy groups, throwing their weight about and challenging anyone who dared confront them.

They had been in town only a matter of hours when a policeman was shot and wounded. The Fenian responsible was arrested, but before he could be removed to the local gaol his rescue was attempted by a companion, who pulled out and opened up a large, ugly-looking knife. He did not get the opportunity to use it, however, being promptly pounced upon and lodged in the lock-up with his mate.

Shortly after this incident a batch of over 300 Irish-Americans came into town on foot. That night the dram shops or 'groceries' as they were often termed, on account of the fact that food supplies could be obtained in them as well as liquor, were filled to overflowing. The houses of Irish residents were also crowded with visitors, practically all of whom were young men in their twenties and thirties. As public agitation increased the press took up the cause and every few hours extra editions were published, condemning the Fenians and their aims.

An auctioneer trading in the town's main thoroughfare, and significantly named O'Day, advertised that he had for sale a 'considerable number of muskets', which would be disposed of on the following day to the highest bidder. The advertisement was prefaced with the words 'Peremptory Sale Of Munitions Of War – On Account Of Whom It May Concern'.

Surprisingly, the authorities made no attempt to stop the sale, which attracted a considerable crowd, the majority of whom were the strangers, who were reported to be 'in great good humour' throughout the proceedings.

31

The auctioneer produced a number of muskets and passed them around, explaining that the purchasers could take one single gun, a case, or even the whole lot. They were all knocked down to a Mr. Gallagher at 3 dollars, 80 cents for each musket. A couple of haversacks were handed out next , the crowd being informed that there were a thousand to be sold, all in one lot. A Mr. James Loomey bought them at 25 cents apiece. Five large boxes, described by O'Day as 'mixed munitions of war', were put up and disposed of, thus concluding the sale. The buyer of these was a Mr. Hugh Glifferson, whom the auctioneer referred to as 'Captain'. Glifferson paid 12 dollars per case.

O'Day complained afterwards that a number of firearms which he had on his premises, for sale at a later date, had mysteriously disappeared during the proceedings.

Armed to the teeth, the desperadoes were ready to make their move. Many hundreds more had by now arrived on the scene, various estimates claiming their number to be between 500 and 2,000. They were raring to go and confident that nothing could stop them.

To prevent the belligerents from crossing the Niagara river, the U.S. war steamer *Mitchegaw* was anchored at the river's mouth, officially to enforce the laws of neutrality. Although it was known all over Buffalo that an attempt was to be made by the Fenians to cross on the Thursday night, the vessel inexplicably remained where it was, while a little further upstream the crossing was made in three cargo boats.

The Captain of the warship alleged later that he did not go up river to intercept the Fenians because his pilot went missing and could not be found. As the banks were dangerous and the current strong, he had not dared to move from the mouth of the river without him.

The muskets sold by O'Day were taken in large containers to the beach and distributed to the men, before they boarded the boats, which had been chartered in Buffalo. The crossing was made at a point where the river was about a mile wide – a little below Black Rock village. Between 60 and 70 policemen were said to have been positioned on the American side, with orders to prevent any organisation taking place, but they did not show themselves or offer any opposition whatsoever.

The Fenian force was commanded by Colonel John O'Neill, an Irishman who had fought with great distinction in the Civil War on the side of the Union. As a young lieutenant in the 5th Indiana Cavalry, O'Neill, described by his superiors as 'the ideal brave and impetuous Irish dragoon', had led a troop of fifty picked men with great effectiveness on many skirmishing expeditions against Morgan's Cavalry during the latter's daring raids in Indiana and Ohio.

Typical of O'Neill's exploits was an engagement which took place at a ford on the Ohio river in 1863. The ford was in the hands of the Confederates, who stubbornly refused to surrender it, having fought off repeated attacks over a period of several days. Lieutenant O'Neill, although he had only just returned to camp after a scouting mission, volunteered to lead the next assault. With the 14th Illinois bringing up the rear as a reserve force, O'Neill charged at the head of his company over fences and ditches straight on into the heart of the enemy's defences. The Confederates, taken by surprise at the audacity and suddenness of the attack, were driven back and scattered, leaving two field guns to O'Neill's men, as well as the ford.

The Fenians landed on Canadian soil shortly after midnight and immediately took possession of Fort Erie, a small, undefended village about three miles from Buffalo. They did not press on, but settled back to await reinforcements. It was reported later that in addition to Canadian Volunteers, British troops were moving in on Fort Erie to disperse them. In the meantime, Fenians were leaving Boston, New Haven, Portland and various other locations and making their way to the frontier to join the main force. They were well-armed in the main.

Fort Erie had been a British stronghold in 1812. From there British troops had crossed the river and virtually destroyed the town of Buffalo. Fort Porter, on the American shore opposite to Fort Erie, was garrisoned by U.S. troops at the time of the Fenian troubles, but, respecting the laws of neutrality, they took no steps to involve themselves.

On Friday morning, when it became generally known that the Fenians had made good their threat to invade Canada, intense excitement prevailed in Buffalo and thousands flocked to the banks of the river, which afforded a clear view of the Canadian shore. There were many Fenian sympathisers among the crowd, these, of course, being mainly of Irish extraction. Most Americans felt that the venture was sheer insanity, many expressing the view that the Canadians should not allow them to re-cross the river, but should shoot or hang them all, as they were 'always discontented, never satisfied with their lot, and probably never would be.'

But news of the bold venture into enemy territory had inflamed and excited thousands of Irish-Americans, many more of whom were now rushing to join the action. The Brotherhood's funds received a much-needed boost as further bonds were sold and more gifts of money contributed.

At Fort Erie the invaders had settled in to wait for the re-inforcements and also the expected defending army. The latter arrived first and immediately attacked. Though superior in numbers, they were in the main, untrained volunteers, and were soon put to flight. The Fenians, in contrast, were well-organised and led by O'Neill, who had a good sprinkling of Civil War veterans among his troops.

When news of the Irish army's success reached the American side there was great jubilation. Colonel John O'Neill was proclaimed the 'Hero of Fort Erie', and promoted to Brigadier-General 'for the gallant and able manner in which he handled the forces under his command, and for routing double the number of British troops at the Battle of Limestone Ridge, Canada, June 1st 1866'.

Unfortunately, this first success was also to be the last, for O'Neill's reinforcements were not, alas, destined to reach him. The intentions of many more Fenians to cross the river were seriously threatened when the Attorney-General's office in Washington issued the following proclamation, in mid-June, to all Attorneys and Marshals of the United States.

By order of the President, you are hereby instructed to cause the arrest of all prominent leaders or conspirators, persons called Fenians, whom you may have reason to believe have or may have been guilty of violations of the neutrality laws of the United States of America.
Signed James Speed
Attorney-General.

This proclamation caused many Fenians to change their minds about going on to join the invasion force. Hundreds, waiting for boats, left Buffalo to return home. Stragglers were arrested in large numbers by order of General George Mead, himself a Civil War veteran. Most of them were held for a short time before being sent on their way, but several Fenian officers, arrested at Malone, in upstate New York, were troublesome and refused to consider furnishing bail money. They were remanded for trial.

A number of Fenians returning home on the Hudson River Railroad became embroiled in a drunken quarrel amongst themselves which developed into a vicious brawl. Before tempers were quelled at least ten men had been thrown from the train whilst it was travelling at a good speed.

Despite part of the Fenian army still being firmly entrenched on Canadian soil, it was becoming clear that the end of the venture was in sight. Roberts belatedly issued orders for his men to return 'for the present', but not to accept transportation as he did not wish them to

34

compromise their convictions as Irish patriots. His orders, however, were largely ignored by men for whom the bubble had burst and who were now anxious to return to their families.

The Fenian forces in Canada did not attempt to re-cross the river. Neither did they engage British troops or Canadian volunteers again in open combat. Instead, realising that the long-overdue reinforcements would never arrive, and with supplies almost exhausted, they broke up into small groups, intent on plundering any undefended village they came to.

Foolishly, they also ventured into larger communities and paid the penalty for their rashness, 14 Fenians being arrested in Hamilton in one swoop. In the town of Cornwall several more were picked up and committed for trial on the evidence of a Colonel Wheeler, who himself had been arrested as a Fenian, but testified against them. The main body remained together, hiding in forests most of the time, raiding villages and farms for food and occasionally engaging in the odd skirmish with troops.

A French-Canadian reporter, sent by his newspaper to observe the movements of the intruders, was captured by them and later escaped. He had quite a story to tell on his return.

Setting off on horseback, he had run into a great many farmers and their families who were fleeing from the raiders. Most of them gave terrifying accounts of the savagery of the marauding Irishmen. The reporter pressed on, taking to the woods to escape observation. Eventually he came within sight of a community by the name of Primrose Hill, and saw a green flag flying over one of the larger houses. Close by in the fields he could see men chasing cattle in every direction. As the reporter ventured from the cover of the trees he was spotted, and instantly the alarm was raised by the repeated cry of 'British soldiers'. Immediately a bugle sounded and the plunderers made a rush towards their headquarters close at hand.

The reporter prudently turned his horse around, but was soon confronted by a small party of Fenians coming out of the woods laden with bundles of green elm-tree bark, which he assumed was intended to be used as rope for tying up prisoners or loot.

The Fenians relieved him of his horse, his papers and his purse, after which they ordered him to take off all his clothes, including his boots. One of the bandits stripped off and dressed himself in the stolen garments. Dressed in the Fenian's filthy ragged clothing, the journalist was escorted into the village, which was now the Fenian headquarters. There he saw whole sheep and oxen roasting on spits,

35

with dirty-looking cooks performing their tasks 'in an absolutely revolting manner'. One was parading the bowels of an animal up and down and proclaiming that this was the sort of fare they would feed to the British leaders in Canada once they had them as prisoners.

There appeared to be very little discipline in the camp, the Fenians quarrelling incessantly among themselves. The newspaperman gathered that they had no intention of facing up to the British soldiers in a straight fight, but planned to keep under cover as far as possible, continuing to pillage and destroy and keep the Canadian people in a state of fear. If necessary, they said, they would withdraw across the river, to re-organise and invade again. They would keep the game going all summer, until the Canadians could stand it no longer. They told the reporter that if any Irish prisoners were put to death they would certainly be avenged – by incendiarism and assassination. They boasted of having spies in Canada, and claimed that through them they were kept well informed, about troop movements in particular.

An officer named Captain Trestian appeared and tried to elicit information from the prisoner about the country, the roads, and any military information he might have. After being met with evasive answers, the Captain decided to change his tactics and ordered the reporter's belongings to be returned to him. This was done, even the purse being handed back. It was, however, quite empty. The Captain attempted to convince the journalist that the French-Canadians ought to favour the Fenians and even take their side, adding that General Sweeney had been in correspondence with high-ranking officials in Montreal.

Receiving no response, the officer left, and the reporter, along with two other prisoners, was placed under guard for the night in a room, the windows of which were reinforced by wooden bars. But by 10p.m. the guards had become so drunk that the prisoners were able to escape unmolested.

The invaders did not remain in Canada for very long. Those who did not fall into the hands of the authorities were glad to slink back across the river to the comparative safety of the United States.

36

CHAPTER 7

Relieved of command

The Movement now underwent a distinct period of decline. In late July, Stephens visited the hotel suite of a man named Sencott, who was attempting to claim 40,000 dollars for delivering lectures on Fenianism and for expenses incurred in connection with the Campobello fiasco. While there, Stephens was arrested, but later released on bail of 7,000 dollars.

Several days after this Roberts was also arrested and bailed at 5,000 dollars to appear in court later that year, charged with a breach of the neutrality laws. In spite of this, Roberts was reported to be planning a September raid on Canada, a project which never materialised. Throughout the remaining months of 1866 the Movement continued to show signs of disintegration. In Ireland, caches of arms were being seized almost every week, and their replacement caused a heavy drain on Fenian funds. In some quarters there was a loss of faith in the Brotherhood's leadership, and the number of informers seemed to be on the increase.

In September, a Fenian named Patrick Kearney was brought before the magistrates at Capel Street police court, Dublin, charged with the murder of one George Clarke on the banks of the Royal Canal. A bricklayer by trade and a Fenian himself, Clarke had lived in Jervis Street and had been suspected of giving information to the police which led to the seizure of arms and ammunition in Blackhall Row and Loftus Lane. A cabinet maker's shop in Loftus Lane had been converted into a munitions factory, complete with a smelting furnace. Bullets, hand grenades and pikes were turned out there in sizeable quantities. The factory was raided by police and put out of operation. The authorities had clearly received information from some quarter, and suspicion soon fell on Clarke, who had built the furnace. A secret meeting was held at which he was found guilty, and one dark night he was enticed to the fifth lock of the Royal Canal, at a mill known as Mallet's Folly, where he was shot.

The general depression was showing itself on both sides of the Atlantic. In New York, Roberts and Sweeney were constantly bickering, while Stephens was under heavy pressure from all sides to seize the reins firmly and take some sort of action. Many meetings were held, at which Stephens would insist that the time was not right, a view not shared by many of his leading officers, including Colonel Kelly, who had accompanied Stephens to America and remained in New York with him throughout that summer. On the Canadian issue he had supported the Head Centre, but was now becoming increasingly frustrated by the lack of activity. He was also rather perturbed that, for the first time, the authority of Stephens was being questioned by those who had previously lionised him.

There were many heated exchanges during this period at meetings held usually in Stephens' lodgings, or at his office at 19, Chatham Street. The Head Centre was even accused of cowardice by the outspoken Captain John McCafferty, who had come over from Ireland but was eager to return at the earliest opportunity. Also present at these meetings were officers Halpin, Gleeson, Cluseret, Mackey, Burke, Condon and Massey, the last four of whom were destined to gain great notoriety.

In November, 1866, it was rumoured that Stephens had been relieved of command and that his successor was Gleeson, a former U.S. army officer of massive proportions. Gleeson, who was said to be not far short of seven feet in height, was a former member of the Dublin police force. After emigrating to America he had joined the army, making rapid strides and attaining the rank of Colonel. Only the primitive manner in which he composed his dispatches prevented his rising even higher, for it was said that had he not been so devoid of education he would probably have progressed to Brigadier-General, so good a soldier did he become. Gleeson never did assume command of the Fenians. The reason why is not clear, but it was not long after Stephens' removal from office, that Colonel Kelly was generally accepted as the organisation's new leader.

Though now effectively deposed, Stephens never acknowledged, nor fully accepted the fact, and always vowed that he would be there when the great move was made in Ireland, a promise he did not, however, make the slightest attempt to keep.

Stephens left New York secretly sometime in late November, to return, it was believed, to Ireland. It was reported that he had embarked on a Bremen steamer, but this was not known for certain. During the following weeks a close watch was kept on all ports, but no sign of him was reported. Then, in mid-December, the Chief Constable of Hull received a communication from London, informing him that the authorities had learned that the fugitive might be expected to arrive in Hull, if he had not already done so. The message was quickly followed by a full description of the notorious Fenian chief, who did not, however, turn up at the Yorkshire port.

CHAPTER 8

A plausible Irish rogue

In early December, 1866, the police in London made an arrest which led them to suppose that Stephens might be hiding in the city. The detainee was an extremely interesting, if somewhat dubious character, by the name of Stephen Joseph Meany, a former newspaper reporter, who was said to be acting as secretary to Stephens.

A good-looking, flamboyant young Irishman of high intellect, Meany at one time appeared to have a brilliant career in front of him, thrown away it would seem, on account of his basic dishonesty, coupled with an inability to remain in any one place for very long.

Meany grew up in the town of Ennis, in County Clare, where as a young man he displayed abundant and varied talents. He was a leading light in local amateur dramatic circles, poet, and unpaid reporter on the *Clare Journal*, among other accomplishments.

At some time in the eighteen-forties the ambitious young Meany crossed the river Shannon to take up a full-time engagement on the *Limerick Chronicle*, a great chance for him, which he lost no time in making the most of, being an outstanding success from the very beginning. He had received a better than average education, in addition to which he was possessed of a fair measure of cunning, and a complete and utter disregard for the interests and feelings of those who crossed his path.

He was a first class journalist, and might have made a name for himself in the field of literature had he not been sent one fateful day to cover one of Daniel O'Connell's monster demonstrations, at Loughrea, for the repeal of the Act of Union between Great Britain and Ireland. There he met the great man, who was very much impressed by the tall, handsome, young reporter, as was also a certain young lady who had the misfortune to meet him at around the same time.

Not being overburdened by any feelings of loyalty to Pat O'Connor, the man who had given him his chance on the *Chronicle*, Meany needed little persuading to join the staff of the *Freeman's Journal*, a newspaper which supported O'Connell to the hilt. Making what amounted to an overnight switch, he became O'Connell's constant travelling companion, while reporting on the latter's hectic political activities.

During what was for him a lengthy spell of service, Meany proved himself a talented and industrious newspaperman. Within a short time he had risen to the highest position on the *Journal* and also married the girl from Loughrea.

He had been very well treated by O'Connell, who valued him highly. But all this was conveniently forgotten when Meany joined up with a group of clever men who broke the great repealer's heart and formed the Young Ireland movement, which had developed within the Repeal Association in the late eighteen-forties. Turning his back on the *Freeman's Journal*, Meany plunged headlong into a world of intrigue and sedition, and was soon languishing in Kilmainham gaol along with a number of his fellow conspirators.

Upon his release he found himself without funds or employment. It was from this point that his wanderings began in earnest. For short periods he worked on the old *Limerick Chronicle*, the *Banner of Ulster* and the *Drogheda Argus*, where he took over as editor. On the death of the proprietor, however, Meany decided to try his luck in England, accepting an offer to work on the *Liverpool Journal* and the *Liverpool Daily Post*, both owned by Mr. M.J. Whitty, who later described Meany as 'one of the best pressmen I ever knew'.

Old grudges seem to have been laid aside when, during the Crimean War, he wrote patriotic British songs, some of which were set to music by Harry Russell.

But his inability to settle down soon caught up with Meany again, and he left a good position with Whitty to inaugurate the *Lancashire Free Press*, in the interests of the Roman Catholics. This enterprise, coupled with his personal extravagances, quickly landed him in the bankruptcy court.

Following this unhappy venture, Meany held short-term engagements on various newspapers in the North and Midlands, spending several months in Nottingham. From there he returned to Lancashire, where he held, for a short period, the position of editor on the *Oldham Times*, a newspaper which did not survive for very long following his departure. While resident in Oldham Meany ran up his usual quota of bad debts, and when the demands for payment became pressing he departed suddenly one morning, leaving several tradesmen, including an hotel keeper, in a rather unpleasant position.

From Oldham he is believed to have made his way to London. He was now on the slippery slope and shortly afterwards was arrested for obtaining goods by false pretences and sentenced to eighteen months' imprisonment. Following his release he made his way to

Liverpool to look up old friends, whom he felt might help to give him a fresh start. They were more understanding than he deserved, and after remonstrating with Meany for his foolishness and irresponsibility in throwing away so much, they managed to raise enough money to cover his passage to America, where it was hoped that his sordid past would not catch up with him.

But after leaving the frying pan far behind him, Meany landed in New York and jumped straight into the fire, joining the Fenian Movement within a very short time of his arrival. Among the Brotherhood he was hailed as a wonderful new acquisition, and with his silver tongue and great force of character, soon became a Fenian senator, making violent speeches against British rule in Ireland and declaring that he had always been a rebel at heart.

In the year 1866 he was introduced to James Stephens during the latter's visit to New York, and quickly ingratiated himself with the Head Centre, spending a great deal of time in his company from then on and helping with certain secretarial duties. Meany was one of the very few among the Senate faction to declare his allegiance to Stephens.

But the wandering Irish boy was not destined to become one of the great figures of Fenianism. Before long there were whisperings about the misappropriation of the Brotherhood's funds, and when searching questions were asked it was discovered that Meany was nowhere to be found.

So it came about that Stephen Joseph Meany turned up again in Liverpool, where he let it filter out through public house acquaintances that he had been sent over from America on a secret mission, the details of which he naturally could not disclose. The fact was, that he had left the United States in a hurry, and was now considered expelled from the Brotherhood, the general opinion there being that should he ever have the nerve to turn up again in New York his safety could not be guaranteed.

From Liverpool he returned to Ireland, but eventually travelled to London, where he took lodgings in a street just off the Strand. During the following days he showed himself quite openly in places where he had been well-known a couple of years before. As a result the police were soon aware of his presence in the city. About two weeks after his arrival, he was pointed out in the Strand to Inspector Williams of the London Police, who approached him near the Lyceum Theatre and asked him if his name was Stephen Joseph Meany. Unable to prove otherwise, he was placed under arrest on a charge of conspiring

41

to overthrow Her Majesty's Government in Ireland. To this he pleaded innocence, insisting that he had had no part in any conspiracy. Whilst being escorted to Bow Street he never stopped talking, his conversation covering a variety of subjects, but never once touching on Fenianism.

At the police station Meany was formally charged. It was decided, however, that he should be dealt with in Ireland, and following an appearance before the magistrates in Dublin, he was committed for trial.

So the brief Fenian career of Stephen Joseph Meany came to an ignominious end. For when the long-threatened rising finally erupted, the man from County Clare was already safely lodged in gaol, where he would spend the next few years in bitter reflection on a life which had promised so much and amounted to so little.

In the summer of 1867 Meany was charged with being an accessory before the fact in connection with the rising which took place in March of that year. Had it not been for his love of notoriety, Meany, a man of great talent, might well have ended his career a revered and respected Irishman.

CHAPTER 9

The unrest continues

O n the other side of the Atlantic, where the Canadian escapade had finally blown itself out, many Fenians had been gaoled. After keeping them behind bars for a few months, it was decided to release those not charged with any of the more serious offences. In November, 1866, a large number of Irish-Americans were freed, being escorted from prison in Toronto by a guard of more than 20 men to the border suspension bridge, from where they would make their way home.

Before departing the gaol they took a hearty leave of the warders and officials, thanking them for the kindness they had received during their imprisonment. On arriving at the bridge each man was given five dollars by the Deputy-Sheriff to help him on his way.

Though the Canadian adventure was now just a memory, the Brotherhood's avowed aims were still firmly fixed in the minds of American Fenians. The links with Ireland were closely maintained, and though promises of a rising, first in 1865, then in the year following, had not been kept, hopes were high that 1867 would be the year for action.

In spite of the keenness with which seaports were watched, arms and ammunition continued to find their way into Ireland, although the authorities remained constantly on the lookout for information which would lead them to unearth more of the hidden arsenals which they knew existed.

In early January, 1867, the police received a tip that a number of mysterious-looking boxes had been delivered to a farm, owned by a man named Scanlon, at Killaloe on the River Shannon. A party of constables led by Sub-Inspector Bradshaw paid the farm a visit, finding only Scanlon's son on the premises. A search of the house proved negative, but when Bradshaw decided to turn his attention to the outbuildings, he was rewarded by the discovery of a cache of 17 beautifully-finished rifles, with bayonets attached, concealed in an excavation in the floor of one of the stables.

Encouraged by this find, the Sub-Inspector extended his search to the other farm buildings. In a barn, more firearms were found, along with several rifle belts and cases of ammunition. Scanlon's son was taken into custody and a search for the father instigated. He was picked up by the constabulary later the same day, and he and his son were subsequently committed for trial at the County Assizes.

During this very unsettled period, the Fenian conspiracy, as it was commonly referred to, continued to monopolise the attention of the Government in Ireland. The Lord Lieutenant, the Chief Secretary and the Attorney-General were almost overwhelmed by reports of drilling and other Fenian activities, and a great number of applications for protection were received by the authorities from country gentlemen who now lived in a constant state of apprehension.

The excitement was heightened by the arrival by boat of many more Irish-Americans. Several arrests were made in Dublin and elsewhere, and a box containing 14,000 percussion caps was seized in the town of Dundalk.

A report emanating from Dartmoor prison concerned one of the most prominent Fenians then in captivity, Jeremiah O'Donovan Rossa. Along with a fellow prisoner named Lynch, Rossa is said to have flatly refused to perform any duties when they arrived at the bleak, West Country gaol. The following morning they were ordered to scrub out their cells. They aggressively declined to do this and were locked up in a dark room where they cursed the Queen and execrated the tyranny of British rule at the tops of their voices.

Eventually they were taken out and each received twelve lashes across his bare back from a man described as 'a former Crimean practitioner', who was apparently well-schooled in finding the shortest cut to the sensitive part of the system. Under this treatment they gritted their teeth, winced and finally yelled out in agony.

Whether or not this punishment had the desired effect at the time is not known, but it certainly left its mark on O'Donovan Rossa, who later wrote of the shocking treatment he had received in English prisons.

In the year 1866, the emigration figures recorded that 101,251 men, women and children had left Ireland, a slight decrease on the preceding year. Since 1862 more than 100,000 had emigrated every twelve months. Even in the five years before this, when Ireland was relatively prosperous following the recovery of the potato crop, the emigration figures never fell below 65,000.

CHAPTER 10

The projected attack on Chester Castle

J ames Stephens did not turn up in England as expected, nor did he reappear in Ireland. By the end of 1866 he was back in Paris, having arrived at Le Havre by steamer. His stock was now at its lowest point, though some newspapers still referred to him as leader of the Fenian Movement. Yet though he undoubtedly entertained hopes of finding favour again in the Brotherhood, it was quite clear that he had been shunted aside by younger, more determined men, and was finished as Head Centre. During the last few months of his reign he had proved himself to be little more than a romantic idealist. When this had finally dawned on Kelly, Stephens was on his way out. Without the support of this highly respected fighting man he was no longer a credible figure as leader and would never be taken seriously again.

Colonel Kelly was in England. Having crossed the Atlantic in the company of several other officers, he made London his headquarters, and set about planning the rising in Ireland.

The stage was now set for the reappearance on the scene of Captain John McCafferty, who was then becoming one of the more prominent Fenians. Colonel Kelly was known to be strong, resolute and a believer in strict discipline. He also possessed the determination Stephens apparently lacked. McCafferty on the other hand was down-right reckless. After playing a leading role in the daring exploits of Morgan's Raiders during Civil War skirmishes in Ohio and elsewhere, he had deserted to join up with the Fenians. When the call came for men to go to Ireland he was one of the first to board ship. On arrival there he made little attempt to conceal his intentions, going about heavily armed and openly attempting to incite the natives to action. As already related, he was soon under lock and key after being arrested at Queenstown. However, the authorities failed to appreciate what a dangerous man they were holding, and within a matter of months McCafferty was free again and returned to America.

By the beginning of 1867 he was back, and spent time in Liverpool and also in London. Naturally aggressive, he was causing quite a stir in the Movement. Though a great ally of Colonel Kelly, he was himself a most impatient man, and while Kelly was planning the

45

rising in Ireland, McCafferty was busy with a little project of his own, which he felt would go a long way towards furthering the Fenian cause.

Though a large quantity of weapons and ammunition was by now in secret storage in readiness for the 'big day', McCafferty knew where he and his adherents could lay their hands on one of the biggest caches of arms in England – Chester Castle. There is no evidence that McCafferty had consulted his superior regarding his intentions, for Kelly does not appear to have played any part in the Chester affair.

It can truthfully be said that the Fenians were not noted for their thoroughness, but in this instance they had made a very close study of the city, first settled in AD79 by the Romans and, in particular, the Castle, which dates from 1070.

William the Conqueror defeated the English at the Battle of Hastings in 1066. On Christmas Day in the same year he was crowned King at Westminster Abbey. However, his rule was not accepted by everyone, and much unrest continued in various parts of the country, especially in the North.

In the winter of 1069, William put down a rebellion in Yorkshire, before riding over the Pennines and into Cheshire, where Norman rule was being strongly resisted. William's forces laid waste to the countryside and destroyed almost half of the dwellings in Chester, where he ordered a castle built, choosing a site overlooking a bend in the River Dee.

A castle has stood on the site since 1070, the first one being of timber construction. In the twelfth and thirteenth centuries the Castle was almost entirely rebuilt of stone.

In 1237 the Earl of Chester died without a male heir and the Earldom was seized by King Henry III. Chester then became a Royal Castle with new accommodation being built to house the King, Queen and their retinue on visits.

During the thirteenth century it was used first by Henry, and later by Edward I, as a military base for campaigns in Wales, and during the sixteenth century it served as a mustering place for troops bound for Ireland.

In the Civil War of 1642–46, Chester supported Charles I. After fierce fighting in Cheshire the tide of battle began to turn against the King. The Royalist forces withdrew to Chester and the siege of the city began in earnest. Lord John Byron commanded the Royalist army, while the Parliamentarians were led by Sir William Brereton.

Repeated attacks were valiantly resisted by the beleaguered Royalists, until, on 3 February, 1646, when it became clear that they could hold out no longer, the King's army surrendered.

With the Civil War over, a regular army was formed and a permanent garrison maintained at Chester Castle. In 1687 the garrison was provided with a new armoury in the Inner Bailey. In the latter part of the seventeenth century, during William III's campaigns in Ireland, Chester became the main military supply centre, and arms were transported from Woolwich Arsenal in North-East London to Chester Castle armoury for despatch to Ireland.

When Queen Anne died in 1714, and James Edward Stuart was passed over in favour of George I, a Protestant of the House of Hanover, there were uprisings in Scotland and the North of England. Stuart's supporters, the Jacobites, were eventually defeated and prisoners captured at Preston were taken to Chester Castle.

In 1745 a more determined rebellion, in support of James, was led by his son Charles Edward Stuart. This also failed and six cartloads of prisoners were imprisoned in Chester Castle.

In 1785, the architect Thomas Harrison was commissioned to design new buildings on the site of the old castle. Work lasted from 1785 to 1822 with much of the medieval castle being demolished, although parts of it still survive. The Agricola Tower, the Flag Tower, the Half-Moon Tower and part of the curtain wall of the Inner Bailey all date from the twelfth century.

Today, the Castle houses the Law Courts, the County Record Office, the County Council Offices and the Military Museum. It is still the Regimental Headquarters of the Cheshire Regiment.

At the time of the Fenian troubles a section of the Castle also served as the county gaol, but the greater part of the buildings were occupied by the military, with separate quarters for officers and men, and an armoury in which a 30,000 stand of arms was known to be stored.

It was the latter, of course, which interested McCafferty. Moreover, observation had shown that these arms were not particularly well guarded. Up to 1830 an entire regiment had been in occupation. The old Castle now housed a detachment of the 54th Foot, the second Battalion of the Dorsetshire Regiment, only 66 strong, under the command of Captain Edwards, the main body of the Regiment being stationed at Manchester. In addition to these, the only other military personnel were 27 Militiamen, whose barracks stood opposite the Castle gates.

In McCafferty's estimation the armoury was ripe for the taking. The main problem would be to transport the captured arms and ammunition either to some safe place of concealment in England, or better still, across the Irish Sea. To consider attempting to carry out the latter operation via nearby Liverpool would be out of the question, the port being too closely watched. But Holyhead on Anglesey offered far more promising possibilities. The country between it and Chester was wild and sparsely populated, and there was a direct rail and sea link to Ireland.

McCafferty's plan was to gain possession of the railway stations at Chester and Holyhead and possibly the main ones *en route*, such as Bangor, to ensure a clear run through for his men and the captured arms. As the train proceeded on its way, gangs of Irishmen would tear up the rails behind them to eliminate the possibility of pursuit. At Holyhead they would seize control of the mail boat, load it, and make the crossing to Ireland, where a landing would be made on a remote part of the coast.

But as always, the Fenians failed to keep their intentions secret. Apart from the fact that they had in their midst an informer by the name of John Joseph Corydon, the conspirators themselves were far from discrete in the way in which they carried out their preparations.

In early February, 1867, large numbers of Irish-Americans began to disembark from ships arriving in Liverpool. They were kept under close surveillance by detectives in the employ of Captain McHale of the Irish Constabulary, who was based in the city for the specific purpose of keeping an eye open for suspected Fenians landing in England.

The Yankees gathered together in public houses known to be the haunts of Fenians in Liverpool. It was at this point that the authorities began to get wind of the projected raid on Chester Castle. The Americans, among whom were a number of ex-Civil War officers, were said to be the vanguard of a large Fenian force which would shortly rendezvous in Chester. These men, under McCafferty, would be joined by several hundred of their followers from towns all over the north of England, who would assist them in gaining control of the railway stations prior to attacking the main objective.

Once the Castle was in the Fenian's possession they would hold it until even more reinforcements arrived, when they felt they would be in a strong enough position to proceed with the second part of their plan; transportation of the spoils to Holyhead.

Irishmen were soon arriving in Chester by the trainload. They came from Preston, Manchester, Oldham, Halifax, Birkenhead, Liverpool, Wallasey and other nearby towns known to have large Irish populations. Alarm was being caused in these communities as bands of men, mostly of the labouring class, gathered together at local railway stations, all buying tickets for the same destination – Chester.

A reporter getting into the Chester train at Victoria station, Manchester, at first noted nothing unusual. Then, just before the train was due to pull out, a gang of Irish labourers climbed aboard after

48

shaking hands with others who were evidently to remain behind. Those left on the platform were heard to call out, "Good luck to ye".

During the journey the reporter found himself in a compartment with 13 Irishmen, one of whom produced a fife, and at the request of his mates played "The Lakes of Killarney" and other Irish airs.

At Warrington, mysterious signs were passed between the occupants of the carriage and one of their brethren who was standing on the platform awaiting the train's arrival. He seemed most anxious to dissuade his friends from continuing their journey, although he appeared reluctant to approach too close to the train window.

From talk in the carriage it was evident that the man on the platform was at pains not to expose himself as a Fenian sympathizer, as he had been a Wigan policeman for some years. He was apparently a relative of several of the travellers.

On the morning of 11 February, more than 70 Irishmen crowded into Glodwick Road station in Oldham and boarded the train for Chester. It was rumoured that they had been furnished with funds to buy their tickets, but apparently not enough to cover the return journey, for when they reappeared in the town several days later, they came in twos and threes, mostly on foot. None of these men had bothered to give notice of their absence to their employers.

As well as the large Oldham contingent, between 15 and 20 men left nearby Lees station, travelling third class, and another 14 just missed the train there. They were told that another would follow, but as they would have to pay second class fare on this one, they rushed off to find some other means of transportation.

About 15 Irishmen booked from Ashton-under-Lyne, along with others from Stalybridge, Mossley and various stations in Saddleworth, just over the Yorkshire border.

During the day, between six and eight hundred men came into Chester from the Liverpool area alone. Trains began to arrive from more distant towns, over 100 men alighting in the early afternoon, while at least 400 detrained between 3 o'clock and 4-30. Later, about 50 Irishmen went on to Holyhead by the 5-30 train.

Most of the strangers lounged about on street corners in groups of a dozen or more, but during the course of the day many of them drifted into public houses located close to the Castle and the station. A number of them, described by one newspaper as 'dangerous-looking Irishmen'. elbowed their way into the station refreshment room, while others lay down in the first class waiting room, posting a couple of sentries by the door. They appeared to be acting under the direction of men having the accent and appearance of Americans.

In a vain attempt to keep the plot secret they continued to converse in guarded tones, almost whispers, and it was noticed that the majority tended to keep their hands in their coat pockets, as if trying to conceal something – possibly revolvers.

Apart from the fact that they had virtually commandeered the railway station and were all but blocking the pavements of the main thoroughfares, they were at pains to remain as inconspicuous as possible. There were, however, no breaches of the peace committed, so none of the newcomers was interfered with by the law. The citizens of Chester, nonetheless, were becoming more than a little alarmed at the situation, especially when rumour circulated that the Fenians intended to loot the city, then burn it to the ground. This was, of course, absolute nonsense.

A group of loiterers was approached by the Chief-Constable and questioned as to the nature of their business. They replied that they were iron-workers out on strike, and added rather cryptically that they had been paid to keep 40 miles away from Manchester.

Excitement in the city increased rapidly as groups of agitated citizens gathered together to discuss what steps should be taken to keep the peace. The magistrates held a meeting at which it was decided to communicate to the Home Secretary the alarming state of affairs at Chester. A large number of people came forward and were sworn in as deputy constables.

By this time the Fenians' efforts to disguise their intentions had become nothing short of ludicrous, for as they waited for their 'secret orders' details of the plot were even beginning to appear in the early editions of newspapers up and down the country.

The authorities, however, had been well aware of its existence even before the great movement of Irishmen to Chester began. Captain McHale's men, along with Liverpool detectives, were kept well-informed as to the Fenians' plans, thanks to Corydon, who was still going about unsuspected by his colleagues and had attended a meeting that week in Liverpool, when men were ordered to proceed to Chester to join up with McCafferty.

Upon receiving this information McHale passed it on to the Home Office, and, following verification, Divisional Superintendent Ride and Detective-Inspector Carlisle made the short journey from Liverpool to Chester, where they had talks with the Deputy-Mayor, the Chief-Constable and the garrison commander. The police were in full possession of the details of the plot, which, it was learned, was to be carried out under the direction of 27 Irish-American officers, all well-versed in the art of war, also a French officer, plus several other Americans with experience of engineering and railroads.

The citizens were in a very excited state, as indeed was the entire country. Although the plot was now out in the open and therefore had virtually no chance of succeeding, this had, in one sense, worked to the Fenians' advantage. There was great unrest everywhere, especially in the larger cities of the north, such as Manchester, Liverpool and Glasgow, with troops standing by in case of riots involving the Irish populations of these cities.

In addition to the Fenians already in Chester there were reports of many more either on their way or gathered together in groups on the outskirts of the city. A postman reported having seen as many as 500 of them assembled in a field.

That evening a meeting was held in the Music Hall, presided over by the mayor. The townspeople were told that information received from Liverpool confirmed fears that an attack was about to be made on the Castle, and that although the military were now taking steps to ensure that adequate precautions were put into operation, it was proposed to enlist the services of the citizens. This announcement was received with loud cheering, and a large number of people were at once enrolled as special constables.

A detachment of the 54th Regiment, under the command of Captain Stephenson and Lieutenant McCarthy, arrived shortly afterwards from Manchester, and the two 20lb cannons were removed from the front of the Castle into the militia barracks on the opposite side of Grosvenor Road. Sergeant-Major Stenston, of the Earl of Chester's Yeomanry, received orders to hold the Delamere Forest, Tabley, Tatton and Cholmondley troops in readiness to proceed to Chester on the following day, Tuesday, and Earl Grosvenor, M.P. and Lord Richard Grosvenor, M.P. were informed by telegraph of the state of affairs. Both left their duties in the House of Commons to travel north on the first available train.

In addition, the volunteer rifle and artillery brigades were under arms. They mustered at the Castle and were later allowed liberty, but for one hour only. At 7pm they were back at the Castle, where they were kept all night. On the following morning, as no attack had materialised, they were again dismissed, with orders to hold themselves in readiness should their recall be necessary.

Early on the Tuesday morning a detachment of the 1st Battalion Scots Fusiliers, commanded by Colonel H.P. Hepburn, left London by special troop train for Chester. They filled 27 carriages.

Still the Fenians made no move. A few isolated arrests were made, but after the men concerned had been questioned they were promptly released, as no crime or misdemeanour had actually been committed.

The situation had reached stalemate; the city literally swarming with police, soldiers, militiamen and vigilantes on the one hand, and the strangers, who ranged in appearance from well-dressed Yankees to roughly-clad labourers, on the other, each side watching the other like hawks.

It was becoming more and more apparent that the planned attack was not destined to take place. The Fenians were taken aback by the arrival of the police and the military, and the belligerent mood of the citizens. They had not expected such bold resistance, and were clearly disconcerted by it.

It had been the same old pattern of events. Leaks from within the organisation, coupled with a heavy-handed approach to the mission. With the element of surprise gone there was no point in proceeding with the plan.

By late Tuesday, only a few Fenians remained in the vicinity of Chester, hundreds of dejected Irishmen having set off for home, mostly on foot. Many Americans returned to Liverpool, while others made their way by train to Holyhead. It had been rumoured that two Fenian vessels had been sighted off the Welsh port. A gunboat was promptly dispatched from Liverpool, but no hostile ships were spotted.

Some of the would-be raiders had obviously left town in a hurry, for in a field close by the Chester railway station a number of haversacks with green shoulder straps, along with a large quantity of ball cartridges and revolver bullets, were found.

McCafferty himself disappeared rather hastily from the scene. He was in the Queen's Head Hotel and had ordered his dinner, when an American officer named Gibbons arrived from Liverpool with the news that the authorities were in full possession of the Fenians' plans. So sudden was McCafferty's departure that the meal was left on the table untouched.

Not all the Fenians had departed, however, for an arrest was made as late as Thursday. The man concerned was a Fenian by the name of McAuliffe, who had been going around Chester and neighbouring towns delivering lectures on 'the wrongs of Ireland'. He was a finely-proportioned young fellow, well over six feet in height, whose dress and appearance were those of a Catholic priest. Some four months previously the same man had addressed a meeting, composed mainly of Irish people, at the Temperance Hall in Oldham. On the advertising posters he described himself as a 'Knight of the Holy

Roman Empire, a former commander of the Federal American forces, and of the Papal Brigade'.

His professed intention was to speak on a matter connected with religion, but when, during the course of the proceedings, a policeman unexpectedly put in an appearance, the speaker suddenly became silent. An awkward pause followed, then several members of the audience rose to their feet and began addressing the assembly on the subject of the Catholic church and the Pope, in a rambling and far from convincing manner, causing the policeman to have grave suspicions as to the real purpose of the meeting.

Following his arrest in Chester, McAuliffe was remanded in custody to appear in court on the following Monday.

Apart from another stack of ammunition found in a field outside the city, there was very little evidence to suggest that the desperadoes had ever been there. The excitement was over. It had been another Fenian fiasco.

A week later, much alarm was caused at Warwick when Mr. Hickley, Chief Superintendent of Police, received a telegraph from London, informing him that a large group of suspicious-looking men had left Paddington station on the 6-15am train for Warwick. They would arrive at 9-15, and were said to include in their number none other than Head Centre James Stephens. Their supposed objective was Warwick Castle.

The Chief Superintendent immediately communicated with Captain Vaughton, commander of the militia barracks, who at once ordered his men under arms and issued them with ball cartridges. The local volunteers were also called out and two cannons loaded, ready to give the Fenians a warm welcome.

Great tension was evident as the 9-15 pulled slowly into Warwick station. As expected, a large body of men were among those seen to detrain. Upon investigation, however, it turned out that there was not a single Irishman among them. They were just a group of coursing enthusiasts bound for a meeting being held in a local park. This incident gives some indication of the general hysteria and apprehensiveness caused by the Fenian activities at that time.

As for McAuliffe, he was soon released, the police having very little evidence on which to hold him. But like John McCafferty, McAuliffe would prove to be a thorn in the side of the authorities in the months to come.

53

If the Chester affair was at an end, its aftermath was still to be felt throughout the country. Over the previous few years the mixed fortunes of the Fenian Brotherhood had been followed with great interest by most Irish people living in Britain. Some spoke the name with contempt, while others were ready and willing to give any support they could. Many gave sums of money in whatever amounts they could afford. This was passed on to Fenian circles already established in places as far apart as London, Liverpool, Manchester, Leeds, Birmingham and Glasgow. These contributors were referred to by newspapers as 'the misguided dupes of a detestable movement'.

In addition to the committed and those who simply didn't care, there were many Irish who wavered uncertainly in between. They were the ones who still dreamed of a free Ireland, yet harboured grave doubts as to the ability of the Brotherhood to make the dream a reality. The Fenians had done no more than flex their muscles in Chester, yet their appearance in such numbers had been worth a great deal in terms of publicity. The danger was that the 'don't knows' among Britain's Irish population would flock to join the more committed element, thereby placing an even greater strain on the forces of law and order.

There were already signs of increasing unrest in towns which hitherto had been trouble-free. In Leeds, a city from which some seventy-odd Irishmen had made the journey to Chester, a man named Thomas Fenton was arrested with 140 rounds of ammunition on his person, while a further quantity was found in the Morley tunnel. It was believed to have been thrown off the train by returning Fenians in fear of being searched by policemen at Wellington station.

In nearby Bradford, the magistrates decided to request the military authorities to increase the number of troops stationed at Bradford Moor. The Fenian circles of Leeds and Bradford were believed to be very strong indeed, causing fear in those areas. Fenton, a shoemaker, living in White Hart Yard, Briggate, claimed in court that the parcel of ammunition had been handed to him by a gentleman who had ordered him to take it to a house in York Street, which was in a locality principally inhabited by the Irish. The cartridges in the packet were obviously of a foreign make, being larger and more clumsily made than the British Government-issue bullets.

The most serious threat was without doubt to be found in Liverpool, where the Fenians had set up their headquarters in England, the chief fear being that, if roused, they might be reckless enough to set fire to the richly-stocked warehouses in the city. Banks arranged for greater security precautions, and there were fears that following the

54

failure of the Chester expedition the Fenians might attempt to raid the barracks and even the gunsmiths' shops.

Because of the possibility of break-ins, extra guards were posted at the various storehouses containing the volunteer arms, while many volunteers were called upon to stand by.

Following close on the heels of the Chester affair came news of an outbreak of trouble in Ireland. According to reports, bands of Fenians were concentrated in and around the Killarney Mountains. During the week of the Chester crisis, a coastguard station was ransacked and the arms taken. A mounted orderly carrying dispatches was captured, while the town of Killarney itself was threatened by large bodies of armed men.

The Government immediately dispatched a force of troops 1,000 strong from Cork, but by the time they arrived the Fenians had left, having gone back into the mountains. The troops were later strengthened by cavalry and artillery, and concentrated themselves at the Mallow Junction station.

The insurgents, believed to number several hundred, were commanded by Colonel John J. O'Connor, who could not have been in very close touch with his superiors, for he made his move three weeks in advance of the appointed date.

Many of the Fenians who had left Chester and made the crossing to Ireland were now being arrested as they stepped off the boat. At Drogheda, Head Constable Coghlan, with 24 constabulary men, boarded the steamer *Coleen Bawn* on its arrival from Liverpool and took into custody five men dressed in the garb of navvies. They were Thomas Paterson, John Egan and Thomas McLaughlin from Lancashire, and John Higgins and James Fegan from Leeds. They were remanded in custody until they could procure some reference as to their characters.

Captain John McCafferty had landed in Whitehaven on the Cumberland coast, from a Manx steamer, accompanied by John Flood, Head Centre for England. From there the two managed to arrange their passage to Dublin on a collier, the *New Draper*.

All ships arriving in Ireland were being searched by the police, a fact of which the fugitives were well aware. They had made plans to leave the boat before she actually docked, but unfortunately the port authorities had again been tipped off, and knew exactly which boat the fugitives would arrive on.

Police were stationed on each side of the quay, when, on the morning of 23 February, the *New Draper* was observed coming up the river. As she approached the quay an oyster boat was seen to go along-side. Two men left the collier and slipped on board. Immediately the police gave chase in a ferry boat.

Realising they had been spotted, the two Fenians pulled along-side a canal boat, clambered up the side and from there succeeded in climbing aboard another collier moored to the quay. But before any further progress could be made they were overtaken by the officers and placed under arrest, giving their names as William Jackson and John Phillips.

They were taken to Mountjoy Prison, where a warder, searching through 'Jackson's' clothing, found sewn up in a sleeve of his coat a gold ring box containing his portrait and bearing the inscription – 'Erin I love thee as one of thy patriots. Presented to Captain John McCafferty I.R.B. by the Detroit Circle, as a token of esteem – Detroit 1866'.

At around this time the following 'proclamation' was received by a number of newspapers in the name of the 'Irish Republic'. It had been enclosed in an envelope bearing the stamp of some bank, but great pains had evidently been taken to obliterate the name.

This extract is taken from the *Manchester Guardian* of Friday, 8 March, 1867:–

I.R.–Proclamation.–The Irish People to the World.

We have suffered centuries of outrage, enforced poverty, and bitter misery. Our rights and liberties have been trampled on by an alien aristocracy, who, treating us as foes, usurped our lands and drew away from our unfortunate country all material riches. The real owners of the soil were removed to make room for cattle, and driven across the ocean to seek the means of living, and the political rights denied to them at home, while our men of thought and action were condemned to loss of life and liberty. But we never lost the memory and hope of a national existence. We appealed in vain to the reason and sense of justice of the dominent [sic] powers. Our mildest remonstrances were met with sneers and contempt. Our appeals to arms were always unsuccessful. To-day, having no honourable alternative left, we again appeal to force as our last resource. We accept the conditions of appeal, manfully deeming it better to die in the struggle for freedom than to continue an existence of utter serfdom. All men are born with equal rights; and, in associating together to protect one another and share public burdens, justice demands that such associations should rest upon a basis which maintains equality instead [of] destroying it. We, therefore, declare that, unable longer to endure the curse of monarchial [sic] government, we aim at founding a republic, based on universal sufferage [sic], which shall ensure to all the intrinsic value of their labour. The soil of Ireland at present in the possession of an oligarchy, belongs to us, the Irish people, and to us it must be restored. We declare, also, in favour of absolute liberty of conscience, and the complete separation of Church and State. We appeal to the Highest Tribunal for evidence of the justice of our cause. History bears testimony to the intensity of our sufferings; and we declare, in the face of our brethren, that we intend no war against the people of England; our war is against the aristocratic locusts, whether English or Irish, who have eaten the verdure of our fields–against the aristocratic leeches who drain alike our blood and theirs. Republicans of the entire world, our cause is your cause, our enemy is your enemy. Let your hearts be with us. As for you, workmen of England, it is not your hearts we wish, but your arms. Remember the starvation and degradation brought to your firesides by the oppression of labour. Remember the past, look well to the future, and avenge yourselves by giving liberty to your children in the coming struggle for human freedom.

    Herewith we proclaim the Irish republic.

    [A harp]   *THE PROVISIONAL GOVERNMENT.*

CHAPTER 11

At last – the rising

D uring the early part of 1867 Colonel Kelly, along with a number of other American officers, was based in England. There were several reasons for this. First, the writ of habeas corpus had not been suspended there, so until after the rising at least, they were comparatively safe. Secondly, there was much work to be done in strengthening the Movement in England. In addition, Colonel Ricard O'Sullivan Burke, the officer entrusted with the task of buying guns and ammunition, had established an important connection with a dealer in Birmingham who had undertaken to supply all the Fenians' needs.

Kelly was in London, using the name Coleman, and living at 5 North Crescent, Tottenham Court Road.

Among the Americans who had volunteered to go to England was Godfrey Massey, who left New York on 11 January, 1867, carrying with him £550 in gold. This money was to finance the rising in Ireland. Massey landed at Liverpool, then made his way to London, adopting the name Cleburne for security reasons. In London the money was distributed among the other officers in sums of £15 to £20.

At a meeting held at Kelly's lodgings, Massey met several leaders from Ireland, including Mahoney (Cork), Byrne (Dublin) and Harbinson (Belfast). A Directory was constituted, headed by Kelly, 'to control the management of civil affairs in Ireland'. O'Sullivan Burke reported to the meeting that he had just returned from Birmingham, where he had managed to obtain arms on credit in the sum of £900.

General Gustave Cluseret, a French soldier of fortune, who had sold his services to various governments throughout the world, including that of the United States, was appointed Commander-in-Chief of the Fenian forces, with General Fariola, an Italian and former U.S. Federal Army officer, as his Chief of Staff.

Kelly, however, was acknowledged as head of the Movement, and it was on his orders that Godfrey Massey now prepared to travel to Ireland to make final preparations for the rising, the date having been finally fixed for 5 March. Before leaving, Massey conferred with Cluseret and Fariola at various addresses in London, including 5 Bedford Square and 137 Great Portland Street.

59

Massey, a native of County Tipperary, was illegitimate and had been raised as Patrick Condon [his mother's name]. Later he adopted the surname of the man known to be his father. In 1856 Massey went to America and served with distinction in the Civil War, leaving the army with the rank of Lieutenant-Colonel. In August 1865 he joined the Fenian Brotherhood in Houston, Texas, and went to New York in October of that year. Later he was given the rank of General.

On arriving in Ireland in February, 1867, Massey held a meeting in Dublin, when final plans were laid. In attendance was John Joseph Corydon, the still unsuspected traitor, through whom the authorities were appraised of the precise details of the rising, including the fact that the Fenians intended to take possession of Limerick Junction, which commanded the railway communications with Limerick, Cahir, Clonmel, Buttevant, Waterford, Fermoy, Mallow and Templemore. Bodies of constabulary, with Inspector Brownrigg in charge, were sent to Limerick Junction.

On Wednesday morning 4 March, the Inspector made a very important arrest indeed, when General Godfrey Massey was apprehended in the refreshment room at Limerick Junction station. In Mountjoy Prison Massey was offered his freedom. The price – full co-operation with the authorities. Eventually, he accepted and was used as a means of indentifying suspected Fenians and later as a witness at their trials.

Colonel O'Connor's troops having been dispersed without too much difficulty in Kerry, all was quiet for a time. Then American officers began arriving secretly from England and were sent to various parts of Ireland to organise the local circles and recruit as many of the peasants in the country districts as could be persuaded to join them.

On the appointed day the Fenians were to muster at Tallaght Hill, just outside Dublin, prior to the signal being given. The long-awaited rebellion would then be under way, with outbreaks occurring simultaneously all over the country. Thus it was hoped to draw troops away from Dublin itself, the real centre of operations. Because of the presence of informers in the ranks, however, this part of the plan was doomed to immediate failure.

Within the city itself the atmosphere was electric. Large numbers of policemen patrolled the streets, as did several detachments of cavalry, while in addition to the usual guard at the castle, a troop of Lancers from the Island Bridge barracks was placed on duty there at midnight.

In the several barracks around Dublin, the military had been given orders to turn out at a moment's notice, and all available members of the police force were kept at their stations, prepared to act if required.

Large groups of men were observed making their way along the roads from the early evening until late at night. Police Inspector O'Brien met what he assessed to be more than a hundred men in the course of a few minutes. Most carried haversacks. During the night the police stopped a horse and cart, and asked the driver, who was walking at the head, what he was carrying. He replied that it was just straw. The cart was, in fact, piled high with straw, which was found to be covering a large number of pike heads, also a quantity of ball cartridges and percussion caps. It was obviously one of the 'ammunition carts' being used by the insurgents.

A number of arrests were made even before hostilities commenced, one of the first being that of a shoemaker named Fitzpatrick of 27 Wicklow Street, who was found to have his own private store of ammunition. Five dozen ball cartridges, nearly 200 rifle bullets, 2 bullet moulds and about 2lb of gunpowder were taken from his premises. Thomas Reardon, believed to be a deserter from a cavalry regiment, was arrested in Capel Street carrying a highly-polished, five-barrelled revolver, capped and loaded. Two others, Murphy and Coulter, found drinking with him, were also taken in. About 500 Fenians gathered in Temple Road, Rathmines, a Dublin suburb. Many were mere youths, one of whom held aloft a green flag with a harp in the centre. They were in a threatening mood and carried rifles, revolvers, daggers and American swords.

When a military force under Lord Strathnairn arrived, consisting of detachments of the 52nd Regiment and the 9th (The Queen's Royal) Lancers, the Fenian mob took flight and were driven off in utter confusion. As they broke up into smaller groups, a bunch of 150 or so was confronted by a body of about 100 policemen, who called on them to surrender. Instead, they opened fire. The police, returning the shots, wounded five of the rebels, two mortally. Many prisoners were taken, plus several wagons containing ammunition.

A rising of several hundred Fenians also took place at Drogheda some three hours later. They cut the telegraph wires at midnight and seized the market house. They were then met by police, who wounded several and took at least 40 prisoners. Among ammunition captured were many bottles of Greek fire, intended for use as incendiary bombs. The night train from Cork was thrown off the rails at Limerick Junction; planks of wood were later found on the line in two places. There was no telegraph communication to Cork, the wires having been cut.

A Fenian force led by one William Cosgrove assembled at Milltown, near Dublin, before attacking the police barracks at Dundrum and Stepaside, forcing the constabulary to surrender, along with their arms, ammunition and bedding. The Fenians proceeded next to Glencullen police barracks, marching their handcuffed captives before them. At the barracks they ordered the five occupants to 'surrender to the Irish Republic'. They were met with a point blank refusal.

The prisoners were then paraded in front of the rebels, but before any shooting could commence the besieged policemen agreed to give up in order to save the lives of their colleagues, on condition that they should all be set at liberty. The Fenians, being content to settle for the arms and ammunition, agreed, and kept their side of the bargain.

In Dublin, detachments of the 2nd Dragoons (Royal Scots Greys) and Highlanders set off in pursuit of hundreds of insurgents fleeing from Temple Road. They had gone off in the direction of Tallaght, where the Fenians were estimated to number in excess of 1,000, all armed. The fugitives were followed by a large military force with artillery, and led by constables familiar with the terrain. On Tallaght Hill the Fenians found themselves virtually surrounded, with the cavalry and infantry moving in rapidly. Many managed to escape, but six wagon loads of ammunition were captured and a large number of prisoners taken.

That week, at least 150 Fenians were delivered to Dublin Castle. Around ten deaths were reported, with more than 50 wounded. Several of the prisoners were reasonably well-dressed, and these were assumed to be the ringleaders. The rest were a motley assortment of miserable-looking men and boys in a ragged and dishevelled state.

The revolt was not going according to plan at all and seemed to be lacking cohesion. Yet, despite the initial reverses, which came as something of a shock to the insurgents, there was still a great spirit of determination among them.

In Cork, a large band of men, observed moving towards the powder mills at Ballincollig, was intercepted by the military, from whom they fled, cheering and laughing defiantly. Most of the rebels up in the hills were clearly visible from Limerick Junction.

Several important arrests were now being made. General Thomas Bourke was captured in Tipperary, while in a clash between Fenians and the army at Limerick Junction, Captain Lane, leader of a group of the rebels, was taken. At Kilmallock, another Irish-American officer was discovered wounded, hiding in an ashpit. William Harbinson, Head Centre for Belfast, was also reported to be in custody.

Harbinson, whose memorial now stands at Dublin-in-the-Green, was in the south of Ireland, obviously fighting with the rebels, for there appears to be no record of any outbreak then taking place in what is now Ulster.

There were believed to be a number of houses in Belfast at which the Fenians stored arms, and acting on a tip-off, the police visited the home of a widow named Cassidy. After digging up the floor of an outhouse they discovered twenty Enfield rifles with fixed bayonets, wrapped in oilcloth, plus 2,000 percussion caps.

The rebels on the run from Tallaght were thought to have crossed into Kildare. In Killarney, where preparations were being made to resist a further rising, a thorough search was made of Toomie's Wood for Colonel O'Connor, but without result. O'Connor, who was reputed to treat any prisoner he took with kindness, ultimately managed to avoid arrest and escape to America.

Some 'gentlemen' were said to be arming their tenants, a risky business, one would have thought, under the prevailing circumstances, and farmers were drawing their money out of the local banks.

The village of Kilteely was occupied in force by the rebels, who took away all the arms they could find and compelled many of the young men to join them. Some of the newcomers got drunk, but paid for all the liquor they consumed and committed no acts of violence, being kept in some sort of order by their leader, who wore a green uniform. The villagers generally made the strangers welcome.

On hearing of their presence in the vicinity the authorities sent out troops from Limerick, but when they arrived the Fenians had disappeared. They were said to have made for Tipperary, 13 miles distant, taking with them food, arms and horses and carts.

That day, troop reinforcements under Colonel McNeil of the 48th Foot, the Northamptonshire Regiment, arrived from the Curragh and were sent on to Tipperary. Later it was reported that several bands of Fenians had taken to the mountains to escape arrest. At Mallow, many farm houses and other residences were entered and arms removed, although no other outrages were committed.

In Cork, groups of Fenians were seen congregating outside the city. Cavalry patrols kept watch all night in the suburbs, and in the early hours of the morning an American officer was arrested as he left the city to take command of a band of rebels in the hills to the north-west. Many young men left Cork in small groups to rendezvous in the suburb of Fairhill, then marched northwards, tearing up the rails of the Great Southern Railway as they went. They were believed to be making for Mallow Junction.

Shortly after 2am a large body of insurgents attacked the police barracks at Middleton, in County Cork, but were repulsed, leaving several dead in a field. Next they moved on to Castle Martyr, meeting on the way four policemen, one of whom was shot dead in the encounter, another wounded and the remaining two taken prisoner. The police station at Burnfort, between Blarney and Mallow, was ransacked and burnt to the ground.

The Fenians around Cork were breaking up into foraging parties, pillaging farms and villages, stealing weapons and harassing the constabulary and military night and day.

A house in Cork, owned by a man named O'Reilly, was entered one evening by a band of about a dozen men led by a well-dressed American. Again weapons were the only items taken. A farmhouse at Michelstown on the Limerick border was attacked by the desperadoes, who demanded arms. The farmer, who was obviously not one to be intimidated, opened fire on them, killing one man and wounding another. The remainder at once took flight. Three men were later arrested and committed for high treason.

In Dublin, the constabulary surprised 13 men in the process of holding a meeting. One of them, named Forrester, who had been involved in the Chester affair, put up a stubborn resistance, but was eventually overpowered. Several of the others carried revolvers, but were given no opportunity to use them. At Salne, near Drogheda, hundreds of Fenians assembled on a hill and many more young men from the district rushed to join them.

The British Government issued two proclamations, one offering a reward of £250 for the capture of Captain Dunne, an Irish-American who led the Fenians at Kilmallock, in Limerick; and the other offering rewards of £100 each for the leaders of the other outbreaks. At Kilmallock, Dunne had shaken the opposition by the ferocity of his attack on the police barracks; only the last-minute arrival of reinforcements preventing a total Fenian victory. The local authorities, anticipating the raid, had removed all weapons from gunsmiths, pawn-brokers and ironmongers, but the rebels, nevertheless, caused great havoc when they arrived. A doctor named Cleary was shot dead in the street, and the manager of the Union Bank, named Bourne, was also wounded, although the bank and its contents remained intact. Many more rebels were on the run, with army flying columns hot on their tracks. The weather was intensely cold, with heavy falls of snow. It was no time for men to be hiding in the mountains, inadequately clad and with very little food in their haversacks.

On Monday 11 March, two Fenians, identified as having taken part in the raids on Stepaside and Glencullen police barracks, were arrested as they came down from the mountains and committed for trial on a charge of high treason. They were in a pathetic condition, emaciated, exhausted and thoroughly dispirited.

In Dublin, the police visited many firms and elicited the names of those employees who had not reported for work during the rising. In some cases the absentees had still not returned. In Limerick, where a number of young men had been missing since the commencement of hostilities, the police made up a complete list and awaited their return to place them in custody.

A young man named Jourdan trudged into town and was promptly arrested. He had been gone for over a week and was in a very sorry state. As he was escorted to gaol the police were followed by a large angry mob, shouting and cursing at them. Outside the police barracks the crowd closed in threateningly and had to be driven back with bayonets. One particularly troublesome and aggressive individual was arrested and thrown into the cells along with the returned Fenian. There was turmoil in Limerick, where shopkeepers and other traders were beginning to feel the effects of the riots, many considering closing down their businesses.

Though the Fenians were weakening and reported raids becoming no more than spasmodic, the Government was determined to hunt down every last one of the rebels in the shortest possible time. It was feared that if the Movement was not stamped out conclusively the authorities would be plagued by protracted guerrilla warfare. There would be no easing off, therefore, until every known Fenian was ferreted out and put where he could do no further harm.

The influx of troops into Ireland continued, the 89th Regiment, the Royal Irish Fusiliers (Princess Victoria's) from Aldershot, were the next to arrive in Dublin on the night of 12 March. Her Majesty's armour-plated screw steamer *Caledonia* was under orders to transport detachments of the Royal Marines to Ireland, three gunboats to follow her, and troops and horses sailed by the paddle steamer *Trafalgar*, which returned later for soldiers of the 21st Foot, the Royal Scots Fusiliers. The fear of a major uprising had abated, but many troops had been in the field for days and nights on end, and were desperately in need of rest. There had also been isolated outbreaks in Kildare, where some of the fugitives from Tallaght were still hiding, and detachments of the newly-arrived troops were immediately sent there. Despite the hail and sleet, which had continued to beat down throughout the night,

65

there were still groups of Fenians to be seen on the mountains of Wicklow and Tipperary.

That week another important arrest was made when police at Boyle, County Roscommon, picked up a Fenian named Edward Duffy. Well known to the authorities, Duffy had been one of those arrested with James Stephens at Sandymount. He had later been released on the grounds of ill-health and had used his liberty to help further the cause of Fenianism.

While stragglers still held out stubbornly in the mountains, many young men were attempting to get out of the country. Large numbers of these were being stopped as they tried to book passage to America. Those who could give a satisfactory account of their movements were allowed to leave, but many were detained, the gaols being packed to overflowing.

The weather had not helped the rising. This was one of the most bitter winters for many years, with heavy snowstorms and biting winds. As the dust of battle began to settle it was seen that the Fenians had suffered a great number of casualties. Wounded men, blue with cold, were continually being picked up, and on the bleak hillsides many unburied bodies lay strewn about. Distraught mothers and wives searched frantically among the dead and dying for sons and husbands, desperately hoping not to find them. It was a harrowing and pitiful sight.

Some arrests were made of men employed by the Great Southern and Western Railways, one of whom claimed that he had been pressed into service by the Fenians. Many peasants, fearing a similar fate, had fled and hidden themselves in the fields when the desperadoes arrived in their communities. Realising that the danger was now passed, they returned to their homes and resumed work. Business began to revive and markets and fairs were again well attended.

All the troops stationed at the Royal Barracks in Dublin paraded under the direction of Brigadier-General McMurdo to hear sentence passed by a Court Martial on three defectors from the 85th Foot, the King's Shropshire Light Infantry. O'Brien, Cavanagh and Merthyr had been found guilty of having been involved in the Fenian conspiracy. The sentence was that O'Brien be transported for the period of his natural life, Cavanagh for seven years and Merthyr for five. At the conclusion of the proceedings, O'Brien shouted defiantly,

"Three cheers for the Irish Republic".

He was forcibly subdued by his escort.

Addressing a grand jury in Galway, Mr. Justice Christian expressed his relief that the taint of Fenianism had not spread to Connaught. This was not entirely true. There were Fenian circles in that province, but for some reason they did not take part in the rising, a fact which once again bears testimony to the inexpert manner in which the Fenians had organised themselves.

'Where', the Judge asked, 'were the thousands and tens of thousands of disciplined men awaiting the word of command? Where were the depôts of arms? Where were the Head Centres, the Generals and the Colonels who were to have swept into the ocean the handful of British troops opposing them? Instead of these there were hundreds of Irish youths, of the lowest class of society, assembling in scattered groups, without a definite plan of action and imperfectly armed.

'Why did these men flee like frightened sheep before a mere handful of men when they outnumbered them twenty to one? Because they found themselves betrayed and deceived! Led to expect that everything was set for a successful revolution. But they found that there were no leaders and no proper organisation. They were helpless for defence or offence, and so there was nothing left for them to do but slink back again to their homes, cowed and dishonoured.

'I believe', went on the Judge, 'that this Movement is nothing more than a gigantic pecuniary swindle, organised by smart Americans, or Irish-Americans, who have been playing off the lives and liberties of their dupes in Ireland in order that they might receive the money to supply their own excesses in America'.

A more ludicrous statement can hardly be imagined. The Judge's motives in making it may well have been of the best, but to attempt to turn the Fenians against their leaders by what clearly amounted to a pack of lies was not really the sort of comment one would expect from a presumably intelligent and fair-minded man such as a judge.

The whole affair could, of course, have been much better co-ordinated, but what the judge did not mention, if he was aware of it, was that the chief co-ordinator, General Massey, was in the hands of the opposition on the day before the rising actually began, and collaborating with them very soon afterwards. Also, that the other traitor, Corydon, had given the authorities full details of the plot prior to that.

The number of arms purchased and smuggled into the country was quite high, but exaggerated, and a good proportion of them were later seized. Where were the officers? These were, in fact, the very men who had acquitted themselves the best. Experienced soldiers such as Dunne, General Bourke, Colonel O'Connor, Captains Rodgers, O'Brien, Lane, Mackey and many others had fought valiantly, some having been killed or wounded, while others were locked up in prisons all over Ireland.

Had the Fenians run like sheep? If so, it was not from fright. The discipline and training instilled into the forces opposing them was legendary. A few sessions of drilling and lectures on the use of the rifle could never make up the difference. During the Second World War the Italians were said, many times, to have broken ranks and fled, but this certainly stemmed from a lack of the fiercely strict, unquestioning discipline to be found in the British forces. Taken man for man the Italians are not cowards, far from it, any more than the Fenians were.

It is an ironic truth that at that period sixty per cent of the British Army was composed of Irish or Scotsmen, thus emphasising the difference that training, discipline and the effects of having been under fire can make to soldiers of the same nationality.

Of one thing the judge could not have been more wrong. No one was in it to make money. The only ones to benefit financially were the traitors, and even they were ultimately disappointed by the size of the rewards they received. There was absolutely no question whatsoever of the Irish-Americans taking part for mercenary reasons. They were among the most fervent and loyal to be found in the Brotherhood's ranks, and fought for the love of Ireland – and possibly also for the love of a fight.

The only doubt regarding the whereabouts of Fenian leaders at the time of the actual fighting, surrounds, surprisingly enough, Kelly himself. It has been claimed that he had opposed a revolt at that particular moment on the grounds that the Fenians were not sufficiently prepared, but that other factions disagreed and went ahead against his advice, Kelly therefore remained in London. This cannot be so, for Kelly was the man who sent Massey to Ireland to make final preparations and get the revolt under way. The date of the rising was decided at a meeting in London presided over by Kelly. Having thus played a major role in the planning, Kelly fades from the scene. There appears to be no record of his part in the fighting, although reports at the time stated that the Irish constabulary was hunting for him in various parts of Ireland, which was understandable enough, yet he cannot be placed at any specific location during the action.

One possible explanation might be that, having sent his General ahead to make preparations, Kelly had fully intended to be there himself within a few days. But as Massey was arrested on 4 March, the day before hostilities were due to commence, the revolution was clearly doomed to failure, and was, in fact, crushed almost before it had begun. Any subsequent fighting amounted to no more than a few skirmishes. There was certainly nothing that might be described as a battle. It is therefore possible that Kelly never left London. If he was in Ireland at the time of the fighting he did not play a prominent part in it. Nor is there any record of his taking over command following Massey's arrest. There cannot be the slightest doubt though that he remained loyal to the cause, and his character was such that if he did not actually take part in the fighting it was through no fault of his own.

As for James Stephens, there is no doubt at all that he remained in Paris, for though he would quite likely have been welcomed by many of his followers among the native Irish, his presence would never have been tolerated by the men who had removed him from office.

In a small hotel close to the Rue St. Lazaire terminus, the former Head Centre rented a room for five francs a month. On arrival he was accompanied by a few loyal Fenian officers. The hotel was the one he had occupied several years previously, when John O'Mahoney had also stayed there before emigrating to America.

Although the Fenians had many sympathisers in Paris, they found very few friends among the more moderate French people and press. One newspaper, in fact, condemned the Irish rising as a criminal act, and accused America of having applied the torch, adding that 'it appeared very odd indeed that the outbreak should occur at a time when the United States and Russia were on very intimate terms, especially as each had an old account to settle with Britain'.

As he languished in the French capital, Stephens must have watched the situation in Ireland with a certain amount of cynical satisfaction, no doubt feeling, with some justification, that events had vindicated his judgement.

CHAPTER 12

'Erin's Hope'

Y ankee Fenians still in America were desperate to do their bit, and in April a schooner, the *Jacknell*, left Sandy Hook, New York, with officers, men and arms aboard. They could have had very little idea at that time of the true state of affairs in Ireland.

In mid-ocean, the *Jacknell* fired a salute and the Fenian flag was hoisted, a rising sun on a green background, the name of the vessel then being changed to *Erin's Hope*. One month later, she stood off the isle of Inishmurray off the Donegal coast. A pilot named Gallagher came out to meet her and to enquire if his services were needed. He was asked if he was a Fenian, and upon replying that he was not, was sworn in at gun point.

At four o'clock that day Gallagher steered the ship close to the coast of Sligo, in the direction of Streda Point. A small hooker then dropped towards her from the Donegal shore and a stranger of gentlemanly appearance came on board. He was Colonel Ricard O'Sullivan Burke, former officer in the 15th New York Engineers, of whom much more will be learned later.

Burke informed the new arrivals that the rebellion had long since been suppressed and that it would be highly dangerous for them to remain in the vicinity. He then went ashore. Three officers who accompanied him returned later with food and fresh water. Gallagher, worried about his own safety, attempted to jump into a small boat but was dragged back. Later, however, he was allowed to go ashore with two men who had been injured in a shooting accident during the voyage. Accompanying this party was a third Fenian, Patrick Nugent. On landing, Gallagher took to his heels, sought out a coastguard and informed him of all that was going on.

The two wounded men, who had been left on the beach, were taken into custody, while Nugent was picked up later. After cruising up and down the coast for some days the Fenians put a large party of men ashore in Waterford. They were soon under arrest. *Erin's Hope* could do little else but turn tail and head back across the Atlantic.

The Yankees were held in Mountjoy Prison for almost a year before being released and sent back to America.

Hundreds of Fenians were now scattered, either hiding or on the run, the search for the rebels ranging throughout Ireland and many parts of England. The families of arrested Fenians were shown little sympathy by the authorities. When the wife of a prisoner in Tipperary applied for outdoor relief it was refused on the grounds that the hardship was self-inflicted. The local people, however, took up a collection for the wives and children of men held in custody.

The Government was unrelenting in its determination to track down all who had taken part in the revolt, particularly the ringleaders, not all of whom were Americans. One person they were anxious to find was William Cosgrove, aged 32, who had led the Fenian attacks on police barracks at Dundrum, Stepaside and Glencullen. A native Irishman, Cosgrove lived at Windy Arbour in the County of Dublin, and for some time before the rising was strongly suspected of being deeply involved in subversive activities.

Cosgrove was a carpenter by trade, and word reached the ears of the police that he had manufactured a quantity of pikestaves and hidden them in a haystack with the intention of fixing on heads at his leisure, without exciting the curiosity of his neighbours. A search had failed to locate the weapons and it is possible that Cosgrove was able to complete the work in secret in time for the outbreak.

After the rising had been put down, Cosgrove's house was one of the first to be visited by the police, but they could ascertain only that the missing Fenian had not been seen since the fighting began.

This was quite true, for after enduring severe hunger and cold in the mountains, Cosgrove somehow managed to board a boat for England, making for the Lancashire town of Ashton-under-Lyne, where he had a number of good friends among the Irish community. After a few days he moved on to nearby Stalybridge in Cheshire, before crossing back over the border and travelling to Oldham, where he found lodgings in Back Rope Street near the town centre with a fellow countryman named Michael Leonard.

Within a short time he was joined by his wife and three children, and found a modest house to rent in Castle Mill Street. But before the Cosgroves could move in, their new-found freedom was snatched away, probably owing to the treachery of an informer.

In the middle of April, 1867, Police Constable Pinkerton of the Irish Constabulary was sent to England with a warrant for Cosgrove's arrest. He made straight for Oldham, where he enlisted the help of Inspectors Bell and Lowe, plus several constables. From information received, Pinkerton had not the slightest doubt that the fugitive was hiding somewhere in the town, although his exact whereabouts were still not known.

A number of beerhouses frequented by Irish people were visited, among them the Harp, in West Street, a notoriously rough part of the town where no policeman would dare venture alone after dark. In the Harp, a group of suspected Fenian sympathisers were playing cards. They were questioned closely, but naturally enough had no information to impart to the police. The pub crawl produced no results, nor did further enquiries over the following two days. It was then decided to make the rounds of all joinery firms in the town on the assumption that Cosgrove would try to find work in his trade. In actual fact, not wishing to be asked questions by a prospective employer, the fugitive Fenian had decided to work on his own account, and it was this unfortunate decision which was to lead to his capture.

The police, having already made a number of fruitless calls, arrived at the premises of A. Schofield and Sons, Timber Merchants, Lees Road, and enquired if they had in their employ a joiner answering to Cosgroves' description: 'Irish, aged thirty to thirty-four, with a slight stoop'. They had not, but a short time after the police left, the wanted man walked into the yard to buy some timber. The yard manager, a man named Brierley, immediately sent a message to nearby Townfield Police Station. Cosgrove was arrested as he was leaving the timberyard.

At first he denied he was the man they were seeking, stating that his name was William Long, but at length he admitted to being William Cosgrove and said he was amazed that the Irish Constabulary had taken the trouble to follow him all that distance, as he had done so little to warrant such attention. This was far from the truth, however, for he had caused quite a commotion at Stepaside and Glencullen, charging in at the head of his group, shouting threats to the beleaguered men inside the police barracks and calling for Greek fire with which to burn down the buildings.

Cosgrove was accommodated in the cells at Oldham Town Hall, then, a magistrate having endorsed the warrant, he was sent back to Dublin the same night to stand trial.

Also awaiting trial in Dublin was the now notorious Captain John McCafferty. Along with two other Irish-Americans, Thomas F. Bourke and Patrick Doran, he was brought up before a special commission early in May.

Around 29 years of age, McCafferty was described as 'dark complexioned and good-looking, though of very determined aspect'. He was also fashionably dressed, in a well-cut coat of black velvet and brown kid gloves.

The principal charge against McCafferty was that he had organised the intended attack on Chester Castle, which was frustrated only through information given to the police by Corydon, who was now obliged to remain under constant police surveillance for fear of reprisals The Attorney-General, before the jury was sworn, admitted that the prisoner was an alien, and in his opening address referred to the law on the subject.

An alien – not a natural-born subject of the Queen – when once he comes into the country, imposes upon himself a duty and an obligation of allegiance, which, so long as he remains, is as binding as if he had, in fact, been born here and never left. Having received the benefit of our laws he owes the duty of allegiance to the Sovereign.

It was revealed that after his acquittal in Cork, in 1865, McCafferty had sailed from Queenstown for America, where he reported back to the Brotherhood's leaders. He had attended a meeting at Jones's Wood in 1866, at which O'Mahoney, Stephens and Meany were also present, and had made an inflammatory anti-British speech. He sailed again across the Atlantic the following year, when he entered into communication with Fenian leaders in Liverpool and London.

Principal witness for the Crown was the traitor Godfrey Massey, who, on his appearance in court, was described by the *New York Times* as 'the most gentlemanly-looking person that has yet appeared in connection with the Fenian Movement'. *The Times* article went on: –

He was dressed in a suit of fine black cloth with a smart frock coat, which he wore open. His hair is black, with a lofty tuft surmounting a good forehead. He formerly wore a large black beard, which he has shaved off since his arrest, leaving an imperial and moustache. His complexion is rather sallow, his features regular and handsome. His voice is agreeable, but betrays an obvious brogue, modified by his American accent.

The former Fenian General, who gave his evidence under the name of Patrick Condon, his mother's maiden name, related how he had met 20 Centres in Dublin, to whom he gave orders for a rising in March. He had gone to Limerick Junction to mass his troops, and had himself been captured.

Regarding the affair at Chester, Massey told of having attended a meeting of all the American officers in Liverpool, held at the house in Edgar Street of a man named Walsh. McCafferty and Flood were there, the former taking it upon himself to lead the raid on Chester Castle.

74

The jury, after an hour's absence, returned a verdict of guilty. McCafferty was subsequently sentenced to death and advised by Mr. Justice Fitzgerald not to entertain any hopes of a reprieve.

George Reilly, another Crown witness, admitted that he had been a police spy since the previous October, receiving a total of £200 in small payments for his treachery in giving information against men who had regarded him as a friend. Like all other informers he would now go in fear for the rest of his life.

An incident recorded the following month bears testimony to the contempt with which such men were regarded by the general public in Ireland. On a Sunday afternoon a savage attack was made on two men in a public house in Drumcondra, one of whom had given evidence against McCafferty. The informers were escorted by a detective, but this did not prevent their being set upon by the other customers, who struck out at the two frightened men with pewter pint pots. In attempting to defend his charges, the detective was seriously wounded – a temple artery had to be cauterised later to stop haemorrhaging. Only the arrival of police reinforcements saved the informers from being beaten to death.

Thomas F. Bourke was defended by the well-known barrister, Isaac Butt, who admitted his client's treasonable conspiracy, but told the court,

> 'While the crime of treason is to be condemned, it should not be forgotten that George Washington, the most revered of men, was once stigmatised as a traitor, and that those illustrious men, who, with William the Third, founded English liberty, were themselves rebels'.

Having criticised severely the evidence of informers, Butt concluded by admitting that Fenianism had its emissaries, its treasury and its munitions of war in Ireland and in America. In this there was something for statesmen to consider, and he thought their time would be profitably employed in devising measures that would bring health, wealth and prosperity to a very unhappy country.

After two hours' deliberation the jury returned verdicts of guilty on Bourke and Doran. Both were sentenced to death. Among the Fenians sentenced at trials held in Limerick, Cork and Dublin over the following months were Edward Duffy, who got fifteen years' penal servitude, and John Flood, who, for his part in the Chester episode, received a similar term.

Michael Cody, referred to by some newspapers as James Cody, was described by the Attorney-General as one of the worst of all the characters involved in the conspiracy. Cody was the leader of a band of Fenians dedicated to dealing with informers and others against whom they bore a grudge. Following his arrest, a paper was found on him listing the names and private addresses of the three judges who had found Bourke and Doran guilty. Cody, who had been a member of the rescue party that engineered the escape of James Stephens, and had also assisted John Devoy in the work of enrolling Irish-born British soldiers into the Brotherhood, was given twenty years.

The condemned prisoners were placed in Kilmainham gaol to await their execution. Meanwhile, in America, President Andrew Johnson was bombarded with urgent pleas to intercede, by friends and relatives of the men, all of whom were Civil War veterans.

McCafferty and Bourke, in adjoining cells, were attended by the Reverend Kennedy. Bourke was due to be hanged on 29 May, McCafferty on 12 June, and the possibility of a reprieve for either seemed very slight indeed. Calcraft, the hangman, was standing by to travel to Ireland, and had made it known that he was claiming £50 for the job plus expenses, an outrageously high sum for those times and one that he would have had little chance of receiving.

The prisoners seemed resigned to their fate and did not appear sullen or downhearted. They conversed cheerfully enough with the prison officers and remained in good health, apart from the fact that Bourke suffered slightly from a disease of the knee joint. He was treated by Dr. Thornhill, the prison physician. Mr. Price, the Governor, and Mr. Fluett, his deputy, saw to it that the condemned men received the usual indulgences, including plenty of brandy, eggs and meat. Bourke constantly spoke in the most affectionate terms of his wife and children in America, and seemed infinitely more concerned about their fate than about his own.

The sentences, however, were never carried out, being commuted in each case to life imprisonment. Bourke though, was made to sweat it out, his reprieve coming through with only hours to spare.

———————————

Nearly every steamer arriving in New York from Europe at that time carried disappointed Fenians returning from the abortive rising, among them a Captain Powell, who referred to himself as 'secretary of the navy', a post which could only be described as a sinecure.

76

Kelly was also reported to have returned to the United States, and though some reports place him in Dublin at that period, it seems highly unlikely that he could have been there and evaded arrest. However, he would turn up next in Manchester, England, with disastrous consequences for three reckless young Irishmen and a very brave English policeman.

CHAPTER 13

Arrest in Shudehill

T he first half of 1867 had been a bitter time indeed for the Fenians. The general feeling throughout Britain was that the Movement had been brought to its knees and would now gradually fade out of existence. But though considerably dimmed, the defiant flame still flickered, and with men like Colonel Kelly at liberty the authorities could have no guarantee that the tribulations of the previous two years were at an end. Being acutely aware of this fact, they were still expending a good deal of time and manpower on attempting to ascertain his whereabouts.

The failure of the March rising in Ireland had left many Fenian circles in England virtually dormant. Without any clear purpose they would, no doubt, have disbanded within a matter of months, but the Irish-Americans still at large were determined that this should not be allowed to happen.

Not unnaturally, these circles were mainly to be found in the heavily industrialised north, at the heart of which lay the sprawling city of Manchester, whose wealth had been built from the sweat, suffering and misery of its labouring classes, among whom the Irish were now almost as numerous as would be the Jews in London's East End before the century was out. Manchester itself, for that matter, had a large and growing Jewish population, based mainly in Cheetham Hill and Hightown. Generally speaking, they were conscientious, industrious workers. As well as labourers, tailors and artisans, they included shop-keepers and small businessmen, a great number of whom prospered and became wealthy, respected members of the community.

The Irish on the other hand were a completely different proposition. Very few were tradesmen. Possessing neither the instinct nor the acumen for business, and sadly lacking in education, they generally took on the more menial jobs; labouring in iron foundries and cotton mills, or working as navvies.

The life was hard and the surroundings drab compared to those they had reluctantly left behind. The dingy warehouses and mean back streets of Manchester were a far cry indeed from the clear blue lakes of Killarney and the majestic green hills and mountain slopes of Wicklow and Kerry. They had come to the prosperous land of England to escape hunger and find employment. In return, they were forced to share the grinding poverty and loathsome existence of the English worker, which at that time was at its most wretched.

Manchester's Irish community had settled chiefly around the city centre and along the roads leading out to Oldham and Rochdale. Theirs was a world of vermin-ridden tenement and cellar dwellings. In a society in which the gap between rich and poor was almost beyond belief the Irish were at the very bottom of the heap.

Taking into account their numbers it is not surprising that Manchester had been one of the first English cities to have its Fenian circles, though it must be stated that many Irish immigrants were very much opposed to the Movement's principles and methods. A large contingent of Manchester Fenians had travelled to the Chester fiasco and returned disillusioned. Also, news of the crushing defeat of Fenianism in Ireland had not helped morale, but the Manchester circles, nine in all, still existed, though the number of men in them had dwindled somewhat, and those remaining were indifferent when it came to attending meetings.

All this was to change rapidly with the arrival of Captain Edward O'Meagher Condon, an American Civil War veteran, who was sent in the early summer of 1867 to rejuvenate the Manchester circles. Condon had fought with the Corcoran Legion and was a highly-respected member of the Movement's upper echelon.

Condon, writing in the *Irish World and American Industrial Liberator* in 1908, explains,

> *After the failure of the rising in Ireland, some of us, who had gone over there from this side [America], felt that in order to avert danger from friends whose hospitality to us would expose them to severe penalty, we should go to England, where observation was not so close, and await further developments. We had determined not to come home without making, if possible, another effort for Ireland's independence.*

On arriving in Manchester, Condon found Captain O'Rourke, an old comrade from the Corcoran Legion, in charge of the organisation in the North of England. It was agreed that while Condon would attempt to bolster the local circles, O'Rourke would return to America and endeavour to raise sufficient funds to enable the Fenians in England to embark on a more positive course of action, for by this time aid from across the Atlantic had just about dried up.

Within a matter of weeks Condon had effected a complete re-organisation in the north, cutting the number of circles in Manchester to three, eliminating the weaker ones while considerably strengthening those remaining.

As autumn approached the situation was beginning to look much healthier, and Condon decided to organise a convention in Manchester, to be attended by Fenian delegates from all over Britain, which would be graced, Condon informed the Manchester Irishmen, by Colonel Kelly himself, as well as several other high-ranking officers.

This meeting took place in August and was well attended, though mainly by local Fenians. In addition to Colonel Kelly, Captain James Murphy, formerly of the 20th Massachusetts and Head Centre for Scotland, was present, with several men from north of the border, also Colonel Ricard O'Sullivan Burke, who was now in charge of operations in the South of England, Captain Michael O'Brien and Captain Timothy Deasy. All had fought in the American Civil War and in the Irish rising, Deasy having led the insurgents at Millstreet, County Cork.

Colonel Kelly was confirmed as Chief Executive of the Irish Republic, while O'Meagher Condon was officially placed in control of operations in the North of England, from the Midlands to the Scottish border. At the same time it was decided to hold another convention of the entire organisation in Britain at the earliest opportunity.

After the meeting Colonel Kelly and several other officers remained in Manchester, keeping in close contact with Condon, who left the city periodically to visit Fenian circles throughout the North and Midlands.

Condon's 1908 account of the events leading up to the apprehension of Kelly and Deasy was prompted by the appearance of a newspaper article written by a certain P.J. Murphy. This was based on statements made to him by a former Manchester Fenian named O'Bolger, then living in America under the name of Bolger. According to Condon, there were so many omissions, mis-statements and perversions of fact in the account, that he felt it necessary to put the record straight 'in justice, both to the living and the dead'.

Condon remembered O'Bolger very clearly and considered him something of a trouble-maker, as will be gathered from the following extract from Condon's account:

I was walking down a Manchester street one night in September of the year mentioned [1867] and unarmed, when I saw approaching from the opposite direction two tall men, evidently Irish peelers, with a smaller individual between them. I stepped

81

aside in order to observe them without being noticed, and as they came closer recognised the middle party as Corridon [sic], the informer. Retracing my steps, I followed the three, meeting with a friend on the way, who came with me, and saw that they entered a police station not far off. Warrants were out, we knew, for the arrest of the Irish-Americans who were believed to be still in Britain or Ireland, and it was evident that Corridon had come to assist the police in ferreting out those who were supposed to be in Manchester.

On the next morning I dispatched men to various points throughout the city, to make known the fact that the informer was in town, and likely to visit his old resorts, sending William Melvin to notify among others, Bolger, or O'Bolger, who was a Sub Centre. When Melvin returned he told me that on going into Bolger's house he found several people there, and that being in a hurry to proceed further and deeming it difficult to convey the information without attracting attention, he had gone to this man's brother, who lived next door, and given him my message.

Bolger seemed to regard Melvin's omission to communicate with him directly as an intentional slight – there had been, I believe, some friction between them – and he came to see me later protesting against Melvin's action and demanding that he be allowed to make a complaint about it to Colonel Kelly. Under ordinary circumstances I would not have heeded this childish demand, but just then there were in the city or vicinity some envoys from the Roberts' party of the Fenian Brotherhood, who had been endeavouring to induce the organization in Britain to unite with them. I had refused to think of severing relations with the men on this side who had always clung to the policy of fighting in Ireland, but the Roberts' people had succeeded in getting a few men to confer with them on the subject during one of my frequent absences while organizing, though without persuading their hearers to take their side. I was naturally anxious to preserve peace and unity in our ranks, and prevent anything like a split among the men whom I was working so hard to keep together.

Under these circumstances I assented to Bolger's demand and requested Colonel Kelly to hear what he had to say. I instructed the three Centres and their Sub-Centres to be present on the next night at a place indicated. This is the meeting to which Bolger refers in his account.

I had, however, previously arranged to organize a circle down in the Black Country on that night, and as, if I failed to keep my appointment, the proposed new members might not come together again, it was absolutely necessary to fulfil that engagement. The three Centres and the other officers met with Colonel Kelly and Captain Deasy, who accompanied him.

Bolger's complaint was listened to. Melvin told of the instructions I had given him, proving that no slight was intended, and at the close of the meeting Kelly and Deasy went to a house in Shudehill where I had previously lodged, and where communications were still received, in order to get any of these that might have arrived. Soon after leaving the house – a little before midnight – they were arrested.

Thus did a silly display of wounded vanity lead to the arrest of the head of the organisation and his friend, and the death or incarceration of as brave men as ever pledged their devotion to the cause of Irish liberty.

As will become clear, Condon probably had every reason to be outraged by some of O'Bolger's statements regarding his (Condon's) part in the rescue, but for Condon to attempt to blame the arrest of the Fenian leaders on O'Bolger's petulant action is quite incomprehensible. According to Condon's own account, Kelly and Deasy met the Manchester Fenians and dealt with the complaint, before proceeding to the house in Shudehill. After spending some time there they were arrested as they left the premises. As there is no suggestion that they were followed from one meeting place to the other it is clear that the two events were completely unrelated.

The facts are that Kelly and Deasy, after leaving O'Bolger, Melvin and the others, made their way past the darkened buildings and stalls of Shudehill Market to Oak Street, where Henry Wilson, a dealer in second-hand clothes, had his premises.

Until a few years ago Oak Street was quite a busy thorough-fare, the hub of the city's wholesale greengrocery trade. Though parts of it still stand, the fruit and vegetable merchants are long gone. At the north end of Oak Street, at its junction with Swan Street, is the Band on the Wall public house, famous for its music. Oak Street runs south for a short distance before being cut in half by a new block of flats, just below which is the Wheatsheaf pub, which stands on the corner of Whittle Street.

Arriving at Wilson's, a house and shop combined, in a block known as Corporation Buildings, the Americans did not notice the patrolling police constable standing in the shadows across the street. Deasy tapped twice on the door, then, receiving a similar signal from within, turned to his companion and said,

'It's alright'.

He pushed open the door and entered the building. Kelly, though, did not follow immediately, but looked up and down the street several times. He walked to the corner of Whittle Street [still there in 2001], and looked around once more before returning to the shop.

The constable's suspicions were now thoroughly aroused, and after retiring some distance he blew his whistle to summon assistance. Kelly, apparently only slightly perturbed on hearing it, or possibly assuming that it was being blown in connection with some other incident not far away, now entered Wilson's shop, but came to the door two or three times to check that all was well.

Inside, the visitors found Wilson nursing a sick child. They did not stay long, leaving just before midnight, and on emerging were accompanied by two other men, one of whom came out into the street in advance of his companions, to make sure the coast was clear. He was observed by several policemen who had arrived at the scene. All seemed quiet enough and the other three men now came out of the shop. They did not disperse immediately, but stood in the street conversing in low tones.

The order to move in was given by the policeman in charge, Sergeant Brears, who led his men in a quick swoop on the strangers, whom he took to be burglars.

As Sergeant Brears approached him, Deasy drew a revolver, capped and loaded, which was quickly wrested from him. Kelly also carried a revolver, but was pounced upon before he could produce it. Their two companions proved much sharper than the Americans. They bolted at once and managed to get clean away, probably because they knew the area.

The two Fenian officers were handcuffed and conveyed to the nearest police station, where they gave their names as Wright* and Williams, demanding to know why they had been arrested and explaining that they were in the habit of carrying firearms for personal protection. This statement was viewed with the utmost suspicion, as was the fact that the prisoners spoke with pronounced Irish-American accents, although at this point the police had no idea of the importance of the arrests.

On the following morning the two 'prowlers' were brought up at the city police court and immediately insisted on being set at liberty,

* Reported in some newspapers as White.

84

claiming that they were American citizens and were being held unlawfully. Mr. Joule, the magistrate, ignoring this, asked Deasy his occupation.

'I'm a hatter.'

'Where do you live?'

'At Four Railway Street.'

'How long have you lived there?'

'Four or five weeks.'

'And before that – where?'

'I lived across the Atlantic – the great big pond.'

'What have you been doing in this country?'

'Nothing.'

'How have you lived?'

'I brought money with me.'

'What brought you to England?'

'Pleasure.'

'Did you come to Liverpool?'

'No sir, to London.'

'What vessel did you sail on?'

Deasy hesitated, then replied, 'I sailed from New York, but I cannot give you the name of the vessel.'

'You can't remember the name of the ship you sailed on?'

'No, sir.'

'What was the name of the Captain?'

'Oh, I was a steerage passenger. I had little to do with the Captain.'

Obviously not satisfied with the answers, Mr. Joule turned his attention to Kelly.

'Where are you living?'

'Nowhere.'

'Where did you come from?'

'London.'

'When?'

'Within the last week.'

'Where did you live in London?'

'In Rupert Street.'

'For how long?'

'About two months.'

'Where did you live before that?'

'In America.'

'Whom did you live with in America?'

'With a woman.'

'What woman?'

'A lodging-house keeper.'

'Do you remember the vessel you came over in?'

'No, I don't know the name.'

'What is your occupation?'

'I'm a bookbinder.'

'Did you bind any books in London?'

'No, sir.'

The prisoners answered and behaved very confidently while in court, occasionally glancing around and surveying the faces of the spectators, as though looking to see if any friends were present. Kelly, a strongly-built man of medium height and very determined aspect, might easily have been taken for the bookbinder he claimed to be. Deasy, on the other hand, had more of the look of an army officer about him, being tall, of commanding appearance and well dressed.

Mr. Joule, who had managed to elicit very little information from the two men, directed the Chief Constable, Captain Palin, to make further enquiries, and remanded them for a week.

'Remanded for a week!' exclaimed Deasy. 'I suppose there's no chance of getting bail?'

'None whatsoever', was Mr. Joule's curt reply.

Several Irishmen were, in fact, in court. After a whispered consultation they left quickly.

That morning Condon returned to Manchester and was given the shock news. He realised immediately that the great danger was that the prisoners' true identities might be discovered. Condon's first move therefore, was to call a meeting of the three Centres, Nolan, Neary and Lavery, to be held that evening at the home of one of them. Condon told the gathering that because of his recent sighting of Corydon he feared the worst.

Whether or not Corydon was still in Manchester was not known, but Condon was adamant that no effort should be spared to get Kelly and Deasy out of the hands of the law as rapidly as possible.

Any attempt to break into the city gaol would be doomed to failure. In this case there would be no help from inside. However, as the two Fenian leaders had been remanded for a week, they would have to be returned to court when the case was resumed, and Condon believed that a rescue bid while the prisoners were in transit might have a fair chance of succeeding.

At this point, Nolan urged Condon to recruit men from other areas to carry out the mission, but his advice was ignored, Condon feeling that to ask outsiders to do the job would be a slight on the Manchester Fenians. In fact, Nolan's idea was sound, and as later events were to prove, Condon made a grave error of judgement in failing to heed his advice.

On enquiring what resources were available, Condon was told that one pound, held by Nolan, was the sum total of the Manchester Fenian funds. They had no firearms whatsoever, so if weapons were to be carried in the rescue attempt they would have to be bought. Condon, who was holding a small sum of Fenian money, made it clear that more would have to be raised, and quickly.

The following day, Condon sent one of his men, William Darragh, to Birmingham, where most of the Brotherhood's arms had been purchased previously, to buy ten revolvers, with money collected from circles in and around Manchester. Condon himself visited the chambers of Mr. Ernest Jones, the well-known local barrister and Chartist leader, who advised him that the first step was to engage a solicitor, and recommended a Mr. Nuttall. At Condon's request, Nuttall went to see the prisoners and agreed to represent them. In the meantime, Condon made arrangements to have them served with regular meals by an outside caterer, a common practice in those days.

As the real identities of Kelly and Deasy had not yet been discovered, it was clear that Corydon was no longer in Manchester, but Condon knew that the prisoners' American accents alone would be enough to prompt the police to bring him back to the city. Over the next few days, men were detailed to keep a watch on the railway station. Condon also sent word to Colonel O'Sullivan Burke in London and Captain Murphy in Scotland, informing them of the situation and requesting their urgent presence in Manchester, his coded wire reading: *'Uncle dying, come immediately.'* As it happened, Murphy was away from Glasgow on an organising tour and did not receive the telegram until it was too late, but Colonel Burke arrived on the day prior to the prisoners' second appearance in court and met Condon to discuss the proposed rescue attempt.

On the same evening of 17 September, William Darragh returned from Birmingham with the revolvers, which he handed over to Condon. Accompanied by Colonel Burke and Captain Michael O'Brien, Condon met the Manchester Fenians and distributed the arms according to the recommendations of the three Centres.

'Nolan, Neary and Lavery', he wrote later, *'knew more about the quality of their men than I, a stranger, could possibly know.'*

All the same, it is unlikely that all those entrusted with the revolvers, which were brand new, had experience of handling firearms.

Certainly the Irish-Americans had, but they accounted for only a very small proportion of the party.

There has been much controversy regarding the names of those who actually took part in the rescue. Though only ten revolvers were given out, more than thirty Fenians were ultimately involved in the rescue. Because of conflicting accounts it is not easy to compile a list of the men who attended the meeting at which the arms were distributed, but those present almost certainly included Condon, Burke, O'Brien, Peter Ryan, John Stoneham, William Philip Allen, Michael Larkin, James Bellew, James Cahill, Joseph Keely, Michael Clooney, John Brennan, John Francis Nugent, Peter Hoey, Peter Rice, Henry Wilson, Timothy Featherstone, Daniel Reddin, William Martin, John Carroll, Charles Moorhouse, Thomas Scalley, William Murphy, William Brophy, James O'Brennan Chambers, O'Bolger, Neary, Nolan and Lavery.

To underline the contempt with which he regarded O'Bolger's version of the rescue, Condon wrote in his 1908 article:

Some of those named in Bolger's statement as having received arms from me were not even present at the meeting, and some of the names given belonged to those who took no part in the transaction, (the rescue) *while others actually present are omitted.*

John Neary, a mountain man, had been very deeply involved in the '48 rising, having been conspicuous in the guerrilla warfare that ensued. After the insurgents were finally defeated he had crossed with his family to England and settled among friends in Manchester, where he subsequently founded the St. Patrick's Brotherhood, which became an integral part of the Fenian Movement in the city.

During the course of the meeting Condon was approached by Peter Hoey, who asked to speak to him privately. Taking Condon to one side, Hoey told him that he (Hoey) was being watched by the police, who suspected him of being a Fenian. He asked Condon to provide him with money to get away from Manchester as quickly as possible, and received half a sovereign. Hoey immediately left the meeting and Condon was relieved to see him go, as he was in such a nervous state. O'Bolger named Hoey as having taken part in the rescue, which he did not.

As the men stood quiet and determined around the shabby, ill-lit room, Condon, with Colonel Burke at his elbow, slowly and painstakingly outlined his plan. Colonel Burke would attend the magisterial hearing on the following morning. If, as expected, the prisoners were retained in custody, they would be returned to Belle Vue Gaol, which

88

was situated on Hyde Road about two and a half miles from the city centre. O'Bolger was detailed to stand by outside the courthouse with a cab, for which Condon provided him with the necessary funds. As soon as he saw the prisoners being placed in the prison van he was to proceed to a point on Hyde Road where Condon and his men would be waiting, and notify them that the van was on its way. The idea was to waylay it and release the prisoners.

Condon explained that he had already made arrangements for Kelly and Deasy to be hidden by friends in the neighbouring town of Ashton-under-Lyne.

'In Ashton', Condon told the meeting, 'they will get a change of clothing and disguise themselves as far as possible. I will then travel with them to Newcastle or some other town on the North-East coast and arrange passage for them on a boat to the continent.'

As it would be vital to get them away from the scene as quickly as possible, Condon handed over money to John Brennan and told him to have another cab standing by at a certain position on the Ashton road [now known as Ashton Old Road], which runs roughly parallel with Hyde Road, the two, in 1867, being separated at that point by brick-fields and the railway yards.

The place chosen for the rescue attempt could not have been more ideal for the purpose. Close to the entrance of the Hyde Road Paper Mills and about half a mile from the gaol, was a bridge which carried the London and North-Western Railway across Hyde Road. It comprised three arches; the largest one over the main carriageway and two smaller passages, through which ran the footpaths, on either side. It was here that the rescuers would conceal themselves until the van had almost reached the bridge. Then, at a signal, they would run out into the road and force the driver to halt the horses before ordering the accompanying police officer or officers to open up the van and release the prisoners. It was not anticipated that the vehicle would carry more than the usual two 'bobbies".

Once the prisoners were out of the van they would be taken across the brickfields to the cab waiting in the Ashton road. Captain Michael O'Brien was to be the last man away from the scene, and it would be his responsibility to see that no one, either police or civilian, attempted to interfere with or follow the escaping Fenian officers.

After each man had been made fully aware of the part he would play, Condon, accompanied by Captain O'Brien and Colonel Burke, returned to his lodgings, where they settled down to wait for what would prove to be one of the most fateful days in Manchester's history – in Ireland's too for that matter.

89

On the following morning Condon and O'Brien met the rescue party at a house in Oldham Road, Colonel Burke having already left for the Police Court. Condon did not know it then, but he would not set eyes on Burke again until they met in New York more than eleven years later.

Condon insists in his account that he picked only ten men for the job, yet many more than this number took part in the rescue, most of the 'extras' being armed with various implements. This very fact certainly helps to refute O'Bolger's claim that Condon failed to provide tools with which to prise open the van.

Before the party left for Hyde Road, Condon distributed money among the men, telling them to keep off the streets and avoid drawing attention to themselves. There were several beerhouses near the bridge, he told them, into which they could go while awaiting the call to action. This would appear to have been a foolish suggestion on Condon's part, but he was obviously more concerned with keeping them out of sight than with keeping them sober.

After the men left for Hyde Road, Condon went to see Mr. Nuttall, who would attend court without Mr. Ernest Jones, the Manchester barrister having gone to Edinburgh to take part in a public discussion, a previously arranged engagement which he had been unable or unwilling to cancel.

The courtroom was densely packed, especially the public gallery, where the majority of spectators were obviously Irish. They took a keen interest in the proceedings, listening very carefully to all the evidence. In addition to those in court, an unusually large number of strangers crowded the corridors and open rooms below.

When the prisoners were placed in the dock, Superintendent Maybury of the Manchester Detective Force announced to the magistrates that Inspector Williams of the London police had an important piece of information to place before the bench. The Inspector was called and informed the magistrates that he carried instructions from Scotland Yard to apply for a further remand, as he had reason to suppose that the prisoners Wright and Williams were in fact Colonel Thomas J. Kelly and Captain Timothy Deasy, both Fenian leaders. He produced the warrants which had been out for them since the March rising in Ireland, and the prisoners were removed to the cells by Sergeant Brett, who was to become, perhaps, the most tragic figure in the whole affair. It was Brett's duty to convey prisoners to and from the courts in the police van, a job he had done efficiently and humanely for more than ten years.

Charles Brett was born at Sutton, near Macclesfield, Cheshire, on the 23 December, 1815, one of four brothers, all of whom became public servants. One was killed in the Indian Mutiny, another died in Canada after serving ten years in the army, while the third retired on a pension, having been a soldier for twenty-three years.

In 1846, Charles Brett entered the Manchester Police Force, being promoted to Sergeant in 1852. Four years later he was transferred to 'E' Division, which was composed of officers employed in duties connected with the courts. A modest, unassuming man, Brett was not overly ambitious, and quite content with the duty entrusted to him, that of escorting prisoners to and from the courts, bringing them up before the magistrates and transferring those convicted to the city gaol at Belle Vue.

For his courtesy and diligence he had gained the respect of his superiors. To the prisoners he attended he was known affectionately as 'Charlie' and was considered to be exceptionally fair-minded and good natured, though he was a strong-willed character who would never hesitate to give wayward young offenders a good dressing down if he felt it necessary to do so. This, however, was usually accompanied by sound advice, from which the recipients had been known to benefit. It was even said that the fatherly Sergeant Brett had gone so far as to share his morning meal with a hungry prisoner on more than one occasion.

A married man with three grown-up children, Brett, who also supported his seventy-eight year old father, lived in a terraced house in Wilson Street, off Oldham Road. He was fifty-one, and had been in the Force for more than twenty years.

On Kelly and Deasy being removed to the cells, most of the spectators left the courtroom and joined the crowd assembled downstairs in the corridors. By one o'clock, when the court's business finished for the day, most of them had left the building, but still continued to hang about in the narrow street outside. At three o'clock, when the van arrived to take the prisoners to Belle Vue, they were still there, and though the majority were well-behaved, there were some present who appeared openly hostile. A considerable force of police was detailed to clear a way so that the prisoners could be brought out.

Before this could be done, however, the attention of the officer in charge, Superintendent Gee, was drawn to the behaviour of two men who had been lounging about since early morning. Though well aware that they were being closely observed, they continued to act in an aggressive and impudent manner, glaring brazenly across at the Superintendent while humming Fenian airs. At one point they strutted arrogantly down the street, passing close to Superintendent Gee and staring him squarely in the face, humming loudly and grinning defiantly. They went off down the street, but re-appeared soon afterwards, still making a nuisance of themselves.

Fearing that the two might incite a riot if allowed to go unchecked, Gee ordered their arrest, and two policemen, Inspector Garner and Constable Shaw, approached them. Immediately, one of the trouble-makers ran off. The other, a tall, powerfully-built fellow, made no attempt to escape, but simply stood there eyeing the officers contemptuously and daring them to lay a hand on him. The police were not aware of it then, but the big, bold Irishman confronting them was in fact the firebrand lecturer, John Francis McAuliffe, who, it will be recalled, had been arrested in Chester the previous February and later released.

McAuliffe, who by all accounts feared no one, had not the slightest intention of being taken into custody again. With the law closing in rapidly he suddenly drew from his breast pocket a formidable-looking spring dagger. As the blade shot forward and the spring clicked, Inspector Garner seized McAuliffe by the wrist and attempted to wrench the weapon from his grasp. McAuliffe naturally resisted, and as Constable Shaw moved in to help his superior the big Irishman struck out with his free hand. Garner, however, evaded the punch, which caught P.C. Shaw full in the eye, causing him to stagger back. At least half-a-dozen constables now rushed in to complete the arrest, and after a fierce battle, in the course of which several of them felt the weight of McAuliffe's fists, the pugnacious preacher was handcuffed and dragged off to the cells below the court, still kicking and struggling.

Many Irishmen in the crowd witnessed McAuliffe's performance with disgust, including, no doubt, Colonel Ricard O'Sullivan Burke. Had the circumstances been different there is little doubt that he would have received their assistance, but to those who were aware of the planned rescue attempt it must have been only too clear that such an outrageous display of belligerence could only serve to place the authorities more on their guard. Nevertheless, further trouble might easily have broken out had it not been for the appearance a few minutes later of Kelly and Deasy. Along with several other prisoners, they were marched out of the court building flanked by a double line of constables. Though a murmur ran through the crowd as the two Fenian leaders, in handcuffs, were escorted to the van, there was no further violence, and with the outburst apparently quelled, the police obviously felt that the situation was now completely under control. What they could not know was that the McAuliffe episode, which might easily have wrecked the whole scheme, and which was over within a matter of minutes, was no more than a curtain raiser to the dramatic events that would follow.

The inside of the prison van was divided up into a series of small compartments, with a passage running down the centre. Kelly and Deasy were placed in separate boxes, facing each other, on either side of the passage at the far end. Among the prisoners in the van were two boys, Joseph Partington, aged twelve, who was charged with stealing a shilling from his employer, a Dr. Bowman, for whom he worked as an errand boy, and James Henry Baxter, charged with vagrancy. The two, who were being taken to the Ardwick Industrial School*, were also separated and placed in compartments next to the two occupied by Kelly and Deasy, each however, sharing his box with an adult male prisoner. The remaining compartments contained various other prisoners, while three women, Emma Halliday and Ellen Cooper, both charged with stealing, and Frances Armstrong, arrested for drunkenness, stood in the passage.

When the van cells had been locked up Sergeant Brett turned to a constable named Knox and said,

'As there's more of us than usual, I'll ride inside Matt. You lock up and then pass me the keys.'

Knox did so, handing the keys through a grille in the rear door of the van, to Brett, who remained in the passage with the female prisoners. Knox, along with another constable named Connell, rode on the footboard at the rear, while Constables Yarwood, Bromley, Taylor and Shaw – no doubt nursing a swollen and painful eye, were stationed on top of the vehicle with the driver, Charles Pollitt.

There were three keys on Brett's ring. Two fitted the locks in the outer door, while the third opened the interior compartments.

Before the prisoners left the building it had been suggested by one of the magistrates that the police escort ought to be issued with firearms. This was not, however, implemented, the only precaution being to place four policemen in a cab driven by James Worthington, a civilian, which would follow the van to Belle Vue Gaol.

*Presumably to be deposited there on the journey back, for the van made no stop as it came through Ardwick. This was probably a precaution in view of the importance of the Fenian prisoners.

It was revealed later that a telegram had been sent from the Earl of Mayo in Ireland, and another from the Home Office, advising that extra precautions should be taken in guarding the Fenian prisoners, as secret information had been received which suggested that an attempt might be made to rescue them. It was claimed that neither communication arrived until too late, but subsequent investigation was to show that the telegram from Ireland had been received in the morning. It had passed through several pairs of hands before ending up on someone's desk, where it remained all that day.

The prison van set off on its fateful journey at 3-30pm. Despite the feeling that there was little danger from the Irish community, the police, for safety's sake, had provided what they must have believed was a more than adequate security guard. Had they even suspected what awaited them two miles up the Hyde road, they would no doubt have called in a large and heavily-armed military escort.

CHAPTER 14

The fatal shot

A number of conflicting accounts have been written over the years regarding what actually took place at the Hyde Road Bridge on the afternoon of 18 September, 1867, and it is unfortunate that some historians have found it necessary to try to shift the blame for the ensuing tragedy from the man ultimately found guilty of firing the fatal shot to another member of the rescue party, Peter Rice, who was never apprehended. Their conclusions are, in the main, based on the second-hand accounts of such people as John Devoy, who was not present at the scene and whose memoirs were written many years afterwards. These writers appear to have ignored completely the evidence of the many eye-witnesses who were almost unanimous in stating that the man responsible was William Philip Allen.

O'Meagher Condon's account, written forty years after the event, also named Peter Rice as the killer. Condon, who was presumably in the thick of things himself at the time and not standing by as an observer, could have been mistaken – or he might have been attempting to show that the authorities were guilty of executing an innocent man. On the other hand, the passage of such a lengthy period of time could have made his memory somewhat hazy. Although much of what Condon later recalled had the ring of truth about it and fitted in with the proven facts, there were also several obvious inconsistencies, as will become clear.

Apart from the Allen/Rice controversy, it would seem that the main area of disagreement surrounds the question of intent. Did the rioters come prepared to take life if necessary, or did they merely fire to frighten into submission the custodians of Kelly and Deasy? The evidence would appear to indicate that no killing was ever intended. However, this makes little difference as far as the law is concerned.

It is a pity that certain writers have seen fit to come down on one side or the other instead of reporting the facts as contained in the evidence given at the trial. Of course, to get to the unbiased truth it is obviously best to study the case from as many angles as possible. The stories passed down in the folklore of Manchester and of Ireland certainly lack detail and substance. Of the greatest value is the sworn testimony of those people who witnessed the attack on the van and

95

who could be considered at least more impartial than the Fenians them-selves. Condon's account must, of course, be given careful consideration and may be helpful in filling in any gaps in the account of events.

Beneath one of the arches on Hyde Road stood a tavern, the Halfway House, the back door of which faced the Hyde Road Paper Mills. About mid-day on the 18 September, Hannah Pennington, wife of the landlord, was working in the bar when several men walked in and ordered drinks. They were mostly roughly-attired and were described by Mrs. Pennington later as being of the 'lowest class of Irish'.

The strangers remained until early afternoon, when they were joined by another large group. While serving them the landlady asked if there was a day trip on 'or something', but received no positive reply. Among the strangers was a lame man who came up to the bar, propped his crutch against it, and said with a laugh,

'I'll just set me horse to one side, eh?'

He asked for a pack of cards and started to play with some of the others.

Another, whom Mrs. Pennington particularly noticed, was a tall, pale-faced young man in a pepper and salt coat and a brown 'pot hat'. He seemed edgy, and kept glancing out of the window. This was William Philip Allen, an intense and fiercely patriotic County Cork man, who was destined to play the most prominent part of all in the attack on the van.

During the same period, from mid-day until mid-afternoon, a number of strangers had congregated at the bar of the Railway Inn, also close to the arch, on the Manchester side.

At about a quarter past three, George Pickup, a brickmaker who lived in West Gorton, was standing on a brow close to Heywood's Works when he noticed a number of men hanging about on some low hillocks not far off. Several were lying on the grass, some standing around, while others idly lobbed stones about. Pickup's first thought was that a fight was in the offing, for it was quite common in those days to see a couple of men punching and kicking each other while a bloodthirsty mob roared them on. These confrontations more often than not took place on spare ground close to a beerhouse, which is why Pickup came to such a conclusion.

The brickmaker observed the men for about twenty minutes, and when no fight ensued he began to wonder at the reason for their presence in such numbers. Shortly after three-thirty Pickup left the brickcroft and went to the hairdresser's shop owned by his friend John Griffiths, which was situated on Hyde Road quite close to the railway bridge, on the Manchester side.

After Pickup had told the barber of the odd goings-on nearby, the two men went outside. Looking through the arch in the direction of Belle Vue they could see a man on the far side, leaning against one of the pillars on the left hand side of the road. They noticed that he was holding what appeared to be a pistol. As they watched, the stranger came to the Manchester side of the arch and looked down the road towards the city centre. Pickup and Griffiths then saw a number of men come to the top of the grass-banking behind the man with the gun.

Within a short time the two puzzled observers had been joined by an acquaintance named Sprosson and several women. A boy named George Mulholland, who was playing on the banking a short distance away, also saw the men as they left the beerhouses and gathered at the bridge.

Around this time Edward O'Meagher Condon arrived on the scene and was dismayed to find that the first part of his plan had not gone as smoothly as he had hoped. Far from remaining as inconspicuous as possible, the rescue party had somehow contrived to attract a great deal of attention to themselves. Such a crowd was now gathering as could only have been expected had the event been advertised in the press. As well as Pickup's group, which stood eyeing the Fenians suspiciously from the opposite side of the road, Condon saw that three or four more women had arrived and were chattering away not many yards from where his men stood.

According to Condon's account, Captain O'Brien moved these women out of the way by inviting them into an eating-house some distance up the road, but this claim was never substantiated by any of the witnesses. No women came forward subsequently to testify that one of the Irishmen had invited them to go to an eating-house and Captain O'Brien does not appear to have left the scene. In fact, as a key figure in the rescue plan, it was hardly likely that he would. In addition, it is attested that quite a number of women were present when the van eventually arrived.

Condon also stated later that Neary, one of the most prominent Manchester Fenians, approached him and said that he felt ill and could not go through with it. His revolver was passed on to another member of the party. It is possible that the spare revolver was taken by Allen, who is known to have carried a gun in each hand during most of the fracas.

William Hulley, landlord of the Railway Inn, was in the back yard of his premises when he was called inside by his wife. As he entered he saw a large group of men just leaving. In the bar at the time were two of his regulars, Richard Bromley and James Kennedy. Hulley returned to the back yard, and looking over the wall, saw the men who had just left his pub gathered near the arch and looking towards Manchester. As he watched, a small man ran up to the group and spoke to them. Next, Hulley heard a whistle and saw what he later estimated to be more than thirty roughly-dressed men come from the top of the banking and go down to the others.

As the landlord looked on he saw a cab draw up and stop close to the bridge. Three men climbed out. One of them was obviously O'Bolger, but the identities of the other two are not known. O'Bolger informed Condon that the prison van was not far behind. He then paid the driver, and, according to Condon's account, allowed him to proceed on his way. Condon claimed that he was annoyed at this and said later that O'Bolger ought to have had enough sense to detain the cab, in case the driver, having seen the large crowd and possibly the revolvers, should hurry to the gaol and raise the alarm. Again Condon's memory appears faulty, as will soon become clear.

The moment of reckoning was now close at hand. What Condon had not bargained for was an audience. Yet after the initial shock of finding such a crowd gathered he had not panicked. There was no question of a discreet withdrawal. The van carrying the two leaders was only minutes away and Condon knew there would be no second chance.

It would very soon be seen just where the sympathies of the ordinary man in the street really lay. It had been a long-held Fenian belief that the common bond of poverty that existed between the oppressed Irish and the equally downtrodden English working classes would never allow either to side with the authorities against the other. Because of the unexpectedly large public turnout at the Hyde Road bridge this theory was about to be put to the test.

As the Irishmen waited by the arch, the pale-faced young man remained at Condon's side. If he was nervous he did not show it, but looked grimly determined. His friend Michael Larkin, however, seemed very edgy indeed. A skinny, undersized man of thirty-two, he had been quite ill during the preceding week, and, having a large family to support, including – according to Condon's account – '*a feeble old mother just arrived from Ireland*', he should never have been asked to take part in the rescue at all.

According to what Condon wrote later he had noticed that Larkin, though ready to join the rescue party, was far from well. He therefore sent him back into the tavern to rest and wait. Condon stated that as far as he knew, Larkin was unarmed at the time.

It is difficult to reconcile this part of Condon's statement, however, with the facts as supplied by eye-witnesses, for Larkin not only played a prominent part in what followed, but was one of the first men to step out in front of the van when it reached the bridge. It is a fact, though, that Larkin, a tailor, was in poor health, and must have summoned up all his courage to fling himself into the fray when in no fit state to do so.

At last the prison van came into view. From a speck on the skyline it quickly grew until it was almost upon them. Though the official rescue party was now concealed behind the pillars of the arch, the crowd of spectators was by this time quite considerable, and as the van approached the bridge the policemen riding on top must have seen that something was very much amiss. If so they did not stop to investigate, but attempted to drive straight on through.

As the vehicle passed under the bridge two men ran into the road on the far side of the archway. The first was Captain Michael O'Brien, the other Larkin. Both carried revolvers. Calling for the driver to pull up, they leapt in front of the horses, Larkin grabbing one of them by its bridle. At the same moment O'Brien fired at the other horse, the bullet striking it in the neck.

Police-Constable Yarwood, sitting up front, shouted, 'Drive on!' But Pollitt yelled back, 'I can't. My horses are shot.'

Only one horse, however, appeared to be badly injured. The other, which had been shot in the nostril, reared up and attempted to start off again, but only succeeded in dragging its companion and the van across the centre of the roadway.

A scene of almost indescribable chaos now followed. Larkin fired wildly in the general direction of those on top of the van. Whether he actually took aim or fired above their heads merely to frighten them will never be known for certain, but as a result of his volley the whole pack of them scuttled off the roof of the vehicle without bothering to make use of the steps. One bobby, P.C. Taylor, was struck by a brick before he could jump down.

P.C. Yarwood hit the cobblestones and scrambled quickly to his feet, only to find himself confronted by Larkin, who by this time was in a highly excited state. Fearing for his life, Yarwood picked up a stone and managed to knock the pistol up, a ball from it going high above his head. At that moment Yarwood was aware of what seemed to him a great number of men closing in on the van and later claimed that he was again fired on by Larkin and was extremely lucky to avoid being hit. Dodging and ducking, he ran off in the direction of Belle Vue. Not many yards beyond the bridge was a toll-bar* near which stood a cab. The shaken policeman jumped into it and ordered the driver to take him to the gaol as quickly as possible. It would seem likely that the cab was the one in which O'Bolger had travelled from Manchester, and which he had then arranged would wait a little way up the road, for no other reason was ever put forward as to why it was standing there at that time.

The sight of between thirty and forty wild Irishmen bearing down on them, armed with revolvers, hammers, hatchets and pick-axes was too much for the remaining policemen, who scattered in utter confusion. Along with those who had now arrived in the following vehicle, they made a quick dash to the opposite side of the road. Having no weapons with which to retaliate, they could do little more than hurl a few stones at their attackers, who were now setting about the van with a vengeance. A swarm of fiercely determined Fenians smashed and hacked at the sides of the vehicle, while two climbed up on top and attempted to batter a way in through the roof with a huge stone, handed up by their colleagues.

Vital questions were about to be answered. Would the crowd, witnessing this outrage being perpetrated in their midst, remain neutral, or would they take sides, and if so, which side? The answers were not long in coming. The startled on-lookers, at first too shocked to react at all, quickly gathered their wits. Seeing the hopeless position in which the police now found themselves, many spectators began to shout abuse at the Fenians and joined the bobbies in bombarding them with bricks and anything else they could lay their hands on.

But the rescuers were in no mood to be driven off. While the terrified horses shied and squealed pitifully and the beleaguered vehicle rocked and swayed crazily under the savage battering it was receiving, several of the attackers, led by Allen, discharged their pistols in the general direction of the police and the crowd, while a number of unarmed Irishmen returned the hail of masonry.

Most of the witnesses later agreed that Allen was the most prominent man there. Menacing the crowd while urging on those attacking the van, he waved his pair of pistols about wildly and threatened any spectators who ventured too close.

* Close to the present Toll Bar Street.

A section of the crowd, which had grown to quite a size in the space of a few minutes, now joined up with the police and attempted to rush the Irishmen, but were driven back by more shots fired above their heads. Again it was Allen who led the counter-charge, shouting, 'I'll shoot any man who comes near!'

One of the locals, Sprosson, bolder than the rest, made it clear that he had no intention of being intimidated, and would not budge when Allen yelled,

'Stand back!'

The young Fenian promptly put paid to his bravado by shooting him in the foot. Sprosson was helped back to the pavement by some of his neighbours, none of whom showed any inclination to replace him in the front line. A policeman named Seth Bromley was wounded in the thigh, while another officer had a narrow escape when a bullet took away a piece of his greatcoat.

Inside the van confusion and terror reigned. Clinging desperately to each other, the frightened women prisoners wept, prayed aloud, and screamed hysterically, while the male occupants were buffeted about in their tiny, box-like cells. Their fear could well be appreciated, for apart from the hammering on the van's sides, lead balls were flying thick and fast outside and the roof seemed likely to cave in at any moment.

At least one person inside the vehicle remained cool, despite the great danger. As events were to prove, Sergeant Charles Brett was a very brave man indeed. Amidst all the chaos he alone refused to panic, although he was in the most desperate and vulnerable position of all.

Locked in their compartments at the far end of the passage, Kelly and Deasy waited, tense and expectant. They must have known what was happening immediately the shooting began, and also realised that their rescue depended very much upon the time factor. For if the Fenians could not free them quickly, so leaving enough time to get them clear, more police would surely arrive and the great gamble would have failed.

During the course of the journey from the courthouse the grille in the van's rear door, which worked on a swivel, had been in the open position. At the onset of the attack, Brett peered through it, then, seeing the attackers approaching, slammed it shut and tried to calm the women, who were screeching and shouting,

'It's them Fenians. We'll all be killed.'

A voice on the outside yelled, 'Open the door. Let the prisoners out.' Then, on receiving no reply, 'Where are the keys? Come on, turn them up.' Brett answered that he would not give up his keys.

'Come on now, pass them out', called a thickly Irish-accented voice.

Again Brett refused, and was told that if he would give them up he would not be harmed. His answer came loud and clear through the grille,

'No, I'll stick to my post to the last.'

At this point the pounding on the roof became more fierce. It seemed to be immediately above Brett's head. As the roof began to give way the women seized hold of the police-sergeant by his arms and tried to pull him away from the rear of the van. Brett, though, would not be moved. The grille was still shut and he was doing his best to see that it remained so. However, possibly due to the interference of the women, the ventilator was forced open from the outside and a stone wedged firmly between the bars, so that it could not be closed again. Almost simultaneously the muzzle of a pistol was thrust inside. Still Brett refused to give up the keys and would not even move away from the door. One of the women, Emma Halliday, pleaded with him.

'Oh, Charlie, come away please or you'll be shot!'

She grabbed his coat and tried to drag him back. At that moment the gun went off and Brett fell against the door and slid to the floor. One of the women screamed,

'He's killed. Charlie's killed.'

Another cried out, 'God help us.'

A man on the outside again called for the keys, and after a short delay and further threats, they were passed through the grille, one of the women having taken them from the stricken policeman's belt. The van door was quickly opened and Sergeant Brett rolled onto the running board before falling heavily into the roadway. The rioters surged forward into the van, pushing the terrified women out of the way as they went.

The prisoners in the boxes had heard all that was going on but could see nothing, for although there was a wooden grating in each door Brett and the women were out of their line of vision. Also, there was very little light within the vehicle until the door burst open. When this happened, James Henry Baxter, one of the juvenile prisoners, peered through the grating, saw a man come up the passage carrying a bunch of keys, and heard him call out,

'Where's Pat Kelly?'

A voice at the far end of the van answered, 'I'm here.'

The man with the keys attempted to open Baxter's door, but Kelly shouted to him, 'No, I'm here.'

The man crossed to the end box on the other side of the passage, but tried two wrong keys before finally unlocking the door. After Kelly had been freed the box opposite was opened up and Deasy came out. Both men were handcuffed. The prisoner sharing Baxter's compartment, seeking to take advantage of the situation, called out,

'Here, open this door as well.'

Ignoring him, the rescuers hustled the two Fenian leaders out of the van. Allen was heard to say to Kelly as they emerged,

'Didn't I say I'd die for you before I'd give you up?'

Meanwhile, the women prisoners, shaking with terror and fearing for their lives, had scrambled down the steps of the van and were huddled together in the road, close to where Sergeant Brett lay dying. He had been shot in the head and must have presented an horrific sight to the onlookers, who at that moment were unable to go to his aid for fear of being shot themselves.

The main body of Fenians now crowded around the two manacled men and hustled them off up the banking and set off in the direction of the Ashton Old Road. Just a handful of Irishmen, acting under the direction of Captain Michael O'Brien, remained behind to prevent anyone from giving chase. Several policemen, along with some civilians, did in fact attempt to follow, but were forced back by another volley from O'Brien and his men.

By now help was on its way, for Constable Yarwood had lost no time in raising the alarm at Belle Vue Gaol. Within minutes of leaving the toll-bar he was on his way back in the cab, accompanied by several warders. They arrived just in time to see the last of the fleeing Fenians, about twenty in number, crossing the Manchester to Sheffield railway lines and running across the brickfields. The warders jumped from the cab and ran after them.

Michael Larkin was now in dire trouble. Already weak and sick, he had been unable to keep up with the rest and was helped over part of the distance by his friends Allen and O'Brien, who might well have got clear had they not chosen to turn back for him.

Many civilians, seeing the Fenians on the run, now gave chase along with the warders and police, and very quickly began to close the gap on the stragglers. To the forefront were John Hayes, Thomas Mulholland, Thomas Patterson, who had witnessed the rescue while working on the brickcroft, and a young man named Robert Hunter.

As Larkin was pounced upon, Allen and O'Brien again turned to help him, but on seeing several prison warders come up, they realised it was hopeless and ran on.

103

The mob then proceeded to lay into Larkin, punching and kicking him viciously until restrained by Warder Joseph Howard, who ordered them to 'let him alone.'

They took no notice and continued to assault the prisoner, who by now had been rendered almost senseless. Howard forced his way through the crowd and dragged Larkin clear, afterwards placing him in the custody of a policeman.

Allen and O'Brien were by this time on the far side of the Midland railway yard, having almost reached the Ashton Old Road, but their pursuers were closing in fast, and a brick, hurled by Mark Baxter, another turnkey, struck O'Brien on the back of the head, knocking him to the ground. He was quickly overpowered and placed under arrest. Allen, who had fired several rounds at those chasing him, was eventually overtaken. On Parkin's Croft, only a few yards short of Ashton Old Road, he was caught by Robert Hunter, who jumped on his back, and then wrestled the gun from his grasp. There was one bullet left in the chamber. John Hayes searched the prisoner and took a book, a clay pipe and several cartridges from his pocket, which he handed over to the police.

Of the escaped men there was no sign, but several other Fenians were quickly rounded up. O'Meagher Condon was one of the unlucky ones. His plan to convey Kelly and Deasy personally to their secret destination had misfired. According to Condon's account, John Brennan did not correctly carry out his part of the plan. Apparently, having arranged for a cab to be waiting on the Ashton Road for Condon, Kelly and Deasy, he handed over the money to the cab driver, but did not accompany him to the spot, the result being that the cab failed to appear on time.

Kelly and Deasy, then apparently crossed Ashton Road, for they were later spotted in the Bradford district, which is located between the Ashton and Oldham roads.

Condon's version of what happened, from the time the rescued prisoners emerged from the van to the time he himself was apprehended, once again appears to be at variance with the proven facts, but is nevertheless worth recounting.

The prisoners were both handcuffed when released. On seeing this I ran into a house and got some knives, with which, using a brick for a hammer, I attempted to cut the links of Deasy's handcuffs. They were too strong however, and I then told him and Kelly to start off, saying that we would keep the crowd back until they were at a safe distance.

Condon goes on to claim that he and a man named Miles Brennan, (not to be confused with John Brennan) held off the crowd until Kelly and Deasy were well clear. Brennan is alleged to have led Condon to the house of a friend, where the latter exchanged his coat and hat and cut off his moustache.

In the next paragraph this Miles Brennan has disappeared without any explanation and John Francis Nugent is mentioned. Condon says that Nugent took him to a livery stable to hire a cab so that he might follow Kelly and Deasy to Ashton-under-Lyne.

We found, however, that news of the rescue had spread all over the town, and when I asked the fare to Ashton those at the stable regarded us with suspicion and became so inquisitive that I felt sure we would be followed if we hired a conveyance there. Then, affecting to regard the fare demanded as too high, and stating that any other day would do as well for the journey, I left with my companion.

There is no eye-witness evidence to corroborate Condon's claim to have held back the crowd while Kelly and Deasy escaped. Allen, Larkin and O'Brien carried out that task, and it was this as much as Larkin's weakness which resulted in their capture.

If we disregard the sudden switch in travelling companions from Miles Brennan to Nugent, however, the rest of this part of Condon's account does stand up to scrutiny.

After leaving the livery stable they were seen on Oldham Road by a crowd of people which included an off-duty policeman named Joseph Hirst. For this Condon blamed Nugent, saying,

He frequently turned round to see if we were being followed. His movements attracted the attention of a detective and some others when we were crossing Oldham Road.

It was probably more than Nugent's manner, however, which caused the crowd to trail them, for news of the attack had travelled fast and the two men hurrying along looked dishevelled and had clay on their boots. Condon states that now there was nothing for it but to run, but says that on turning again he found that Nugent was no longer with him, apparently disappearing as suddenly as he had materialised.

Knowing nothing of the locality, I rushed up what appeared to be a street, but proved to be only a blind alley with no outlet. When I started back to make my way out the crowd gave way, but a detective struck me on the head with a heavy club, which he wielded with both hands, and this brought me to my knees for an instant. Rising, however, I again pushed on, tearing myself loose from those who tried to grab me until I came to a narrow bridge crossing a canal*. Here, among others, there were planted in my path two big half-drunken

* The Rochdale Canal.

105

women, who flung themselves on me, locking their arms around my neck as if I were their long-lost brother. I had never tackled a proposition of this kind before and no time was allowed me to consider how to deal with it.

The detectives [sic] and mob closed in, and after being badly battered on the head I was seized and overpowered. Some human beings among the horde of brutes ventured to expostulate at my treatment, and one man called out "Don't murder him." But this unfortunate party was quickly hammered into silence and fastened to me with a handcuff. Then I was dragged to a police station in the vicinity and thrown into a cell.

The *Manchester Evening News* of 2 November, 1867 reporting later on the trial, stated that;

Shore was apprehended in Richmond Street, off Prussia Street, on the afternoon of September 18, by Police-Constable Joseph Hirst of the Manchester Force, who was then in plain clothes. The prisoner was first seen in the company of another man in Oldham Road. Their shoes were bedaubed with clay and they had billycocks on.

The above more or less agrees with Condon's account, apart from the fact that there is no mention of any large, half-drunken women. Nor was there a bridge on or near Richmond Street, the nearest one being at the bottom end of Prussia Street. [There was a Prussia Street arm of the Rochdale Canal, which ran parallel to Prussia Street and all the way up to Portugal Street at its top end, close to Oldham Road. There was no footbridge over it]. These two streets are no longer in existence, though it is possible to pin-point just where they were located. Richmond Street, which ran parallel to Portugal Street (still there), was close to Oldham Road. So it could well have been that after being followed by a crowd of people, Condon attempted to escape their attentions by leaving the main road and running down a side street.

If he was clubbed about the head by P.C. Joseph Hirst, and managed to tear himself loose and run on, only to be grabbed by two large, drunken women on a canal bridge, then it would seem more than likely that the clubbing took place in Richmond Street and the arrest was completed on the footbridge at the bottom of Prussia Street, which crosses the Rochdale Canal*.

At the police station, the prisoner, bleeding from a head wound, was found to have a percussion cap and eight pounds, five shillings and tuppence half-penny in his pockets. Though Nugent had

* This bridge, though much altered, is still there today.

got clean away he had been clearly seen by several of the mob, some of whom apparently knew him by sight.

Shortly, afterwards Allen, Larkin and O'Brien were brought in, along with a number of other Irishmen. During the night many more were to join them, until they were, as Condon states, 'packed in as closely as were those in that other English prison known as the "Black Hole of Calcutta".'

Condon says he was surprised and shocked to see Larkin there. Larkin claimed that he had not wanted to join in the rescue, but had been goaded into it by O'Bolger, who told him that he must take part, and when Larkin pleaded that he was sick and had a large family to care for, O'Bolger declared that if he failed to be present he would be disgraced and regarded as a coward forever.

'I thought', the poor fellow added, according to Condon, 'that it was your orders, otherwise I would never have gone.'

Back at the scene of the outrage, Constable Knox attended to Sergeant Brett and did all he could for him until help arrived. Brett was lifted into a cab and taken to the Infirmary. He was a pitiful sight, for the bullet had struck him in the temple, forcing an eyeball from its socket. The rest of the wounded and injured were also attended to, but were found to be in no danger.

Though great efforts were made to save Sergeant Brett's life, they were all to no avail. He died at five-thirty the following morning without regaining consciousness.

The van continued on its way to Belle Vue, none of the other prisoners having been lost in the excitement. On being let out they were questioned and statements taken from the women and the two boys, one of whom, Joseph Partington, picked up a bullet from the floor of the van and handed it to Constable Knox, who passed it on to Inspector Shandley. It was the bullet which had killed Sergeant Brett.

In the vicinity of the bridge, police officers were busy taking statements from those who had witnessed the outrage, while others scoured the neighbouring terrain for evidence. A revolver, brand new, was found in a cellar in Clyde Street, where it had apparently been hastily thrown after the rescue, while several hammers and hatchets were picked up and handed to the police.

Later the same evening a police notice was issued, which read:

CITY OF MANCHESTER
POLICE NOTICE

Rescued from a police van, while being conveyed to gaol at 4pm
on the 18th inst., 2 Fenians.
COLONEL KELLY, 35 years of age,
5 ft. 6 ins. high, hazel eyes, brown hair, brown bushy whiskers,
small scar running across right arm, scar over right temple, one
tooth missing from upper jaw on right side. A native of Ireland.
Weighs about 160lbs.
CAPTAIN DEASY, 29 years of age,
5 ft. 10 ins. high, swarthy complexion, hazel eyes, dark brown
hair, brown moustache, whiskers shaved off, proportionate make.
Scar on left cheek near to ear.
About thirty men attacked the van with loaded revolvers.
A sergeant of the police shot dead, another through the thigh,
and a civilian in the foot.

Information to Captain Palin, Chief Constable,
Town Hall, King St. Manchester.

As well as a reward of £200 offered by the city magistrates for the apprehension of any other persons known to have attacked the van, £300 was also offered by Her Majesty's Government for the recapture of Kelly and Deasy.

News of the rescue travelled like wildfire among the Irish population, even reaching Ireland itself within a very short space of time. On the hills around Cork city bonfires were lit for two nights running and there was great rejoicing, with bands playing and yelling, cavorting mobs marching up and down the roads.

It is a remarkable fact that news of the attack reached certain Fenian ears in Liverpool almost as soon as it was relayed to the authorities. Hurried meetings were convened on street corners and in beerhouses, and the city's considerable Irish population was thrown into a state of great excitement at the sensational tidings, which arrived in the form of several telegrams received by people with known Fenian connections.

Both the escaped leaders were well known in Liverpool. Before the rising in Ireland, Deasy had put up at a hotel in Lord Nelson Street. Allen too had lived in the city. On receiving news of the outrage, the Liverpool police dispatched a number of men to various quarters for

108

which it was thought the escaped Fenians might make should they manage to get as far as the west coast seaport.

The morning following the rescue there were many rumours abroad in Manchester concerning Fenian activities, one of the most persistent being that an important meeting was to be held in Ancoats, a district heavily populated by Irish families. A gathering did, in fact, take place, and though matters of a political character were discussed, no mention was made of Fenianism and no disturbance took place. The police, of course, were obliged to be in attendance and kept a very close watch on the meeting, which is undoubtedly why it was held – to divert attention and manpower from pursuit of the fugitives.

CHAPTER 15

The big round-up

The net was now spreading rapidly throughout the northern part of Manchester. Aided by information from the public, the police soon began making further arrests. During the next few days thirty men were taken into custody. The two escaped Fenian leaders, however, were not among them. They appeared to have vanished completely, and speculation was rife as to whether they had got clear or were still in the vicinity of the city.

Four of the prisoners were immediately charged with murder. They gave their names as William O'Meara Allen, Michael Larkin, William Martin and William Gould. [Gould was, in fact, Captain Michael O'Brien]. The rest were charged with having caused a riot and with being concerned in Brett's death.

On apprehension, the prisoners were lodged in Belle Vue Gaol, and later removed to various lock-ups in and around the city to wait until witnesses were brought along to make official identification. During transit they were guarded, ironically, by troops of the 8th (The King's Royal Irish) Hussars, and, on being identified, were taken to Albert Street Police Station, the guard on them being strengthened by the arrival, from Salford Barracks, of a detachment of the 57th Foot, an additional precaution in case a further rescue bid should be made.

That night there was great excitement in the city as the daring escape and the killing of Sergeant Brett were discussed by crowds of people who congregated in the streets surrounding the Town Hall.

Police officers were still combing the Irish neighbourhoods. As well as searching for further suspects – for it was clear that not all the rioters were in custody – they were hoping to pick up some scrap of information which might lead them to the two fugitive Fenian leaders. Meanwhile, the Mayor and other top officials held an emergency meeting to discuss what action to take in the event of further outrages. Several magistrates went to see the prisoners at Albert Street, and were present when the charges were read out.

The names and descriptions of the men held in custody up to that time were given as follows:

William O'Meara Allen, 101, Sudell Street, Rochdale Road, joiner, aged 20, imperfectly educated, out of work, Irish.

Michael Larkin, 12, Eliza Street, Hulme, tailor, aged 32, of no education, Irish.

William Gould, (refused to give address), 32, well educated, out of work, Irish.

William Martin, Varley Street, Newton Heath, clerk, 35, well educated, out of work, Irish.

Louis Moore, Worth Street, joiner, 56, imperfectly educated, in employ, Irish.

Patrick Hogan, Garrett Street, Labourer, 26, of no education, in employ, Irish.

Charles Moorhouse, Menai Street, Mill Street, 22, well educated, out of work, Irish.

John Carroll, Bradley's Buildings, labourer, 23, of no education, in employ, Irish.

John Gleeson, Garrett Street, labourer, 42, imperfectly educated, in employ, Irish.

Patrick Barrigan, William Street, labourer, 49, imperfectly educated, in employ, Irish.

Henry Wilson, Oak Street, Smithfield Market, clothes dealer, 28, imperfectly educated, Irish.

Michael Joseph Boylan, Syndall Street, Ardwick, schoolmaster, 37, in employ, Irish.

William Wells, William Street, 29, of no education, out of work, Irish.

Michael Corcoran, Garrett Street, labourer, 29, of no education, in employ, Irish.

Edward Shore, [in reality Edward O'Meagher Condon], Clapton street, traveller, 26, imperfectly educated, out of work, Irish.

John Butler, Andrews Court, weaver, 54, imperfectly educated, in employ, Irish.

Patrick Clooney, William Street, sweeper, 69, in employ, Irish.

Patrick Kelly, Bengal Street, labourer, 35, of no education, in employ, Irish.

Michael Maguire, Corporation Buildings, Smithfield Market, clothier, 32, of no education, in employ, Irish.

William Luther, Garrett Street, striker, 19, of no education, in employ, Irish.

John Brennan, No. 2 Court, Cable Street, clothes dealer, 41, of no education, Irish.

Robert McWilliam, of no fixed address, Liverpool, joiner, imperfectly educated, out of work, Scotch.

Thomas Maguire, of the Royal Marines, on furlough.

Being wanted in connection with the rising in Ireland, O'Meagher Condon and Captain Michael O'Brien had obviously deemed it prudent to give false names. As well as those mentioned above, who were variously charged with murder, riot and rescuing prisoners, the names Thomas Kelly, Michael Morris, John Wemms and Thomas Ryan were also included in the list, though no further details were issued regarding these men.

John Francis McAuliffe, no address, lecturer, aged 26, well educated, Irish, was charged with being in possession of an offensive weapon for an unlawful purpose.

Information had now reached the police which revealed that Kelly and Deasy had been seen in the Bradford district of Manchester within an hour of the outrage. At around four-thirty that afternoon three strangers had appeared in Taylor Street. One of them, whose description fitted Kelly perfectly, went into a shop and bought half an ounce of tobacco. Another of the men knocked at the door of a nearby house, then went inside, asking the occupant, Daniel Rider, if he might bring a friend in. Receiving an affirmative answer, he went back and motioned the third man, who also entered, followed by the man who had bought the tobacco.

Although an attempt was made to conceal the fact, Rider's wife noticed that one of the men was handcuffed. The man thought to be Kelly asked if he might borrow a hammer, as his friend had some nails sticking up in his boots. Fearing that something was amiss, the woman left the house, but returned soon afterwards and heard banging coming from her kitchen. When the three men emerged from the kitchen there was no sign of the handcuffs. Leaving almost immediately, they split up and went off in different directions, but were seen to meet up again some distance further on.

The man whose handcuffs were removed was undoubtedly Deasy, according to the description given, and it was believed that Kelly's cuffs had been smashed with a stone on the brickcroft after the rescue.

Police officers from Manchester were being sent to various parts of the country as greater efforts were made to pick up the trail of the escaped Fenian leaders. As soon as news reached surrounding towns, local police forces received descriptions of the fugitives and were warned to be on the alert. A meeting of magistrates was held that night in nearby Ashton-under-Lyne, and arrangements made to intensify the guard kept on the volunteer arms.

At about six-thirty that evening police constables Harrop and Eaton observed two men in the street whose appearance at once aroused their suspicions. Their shoes were covered in clay, which led the Ashton bobbies to suppose that they had been walking through the fields.

113

The suspects, realising they were being watched, became very ill-at-ease and seemed at a loss as to which direction to take. One of them suddenly entered a plumbers' and glaziers' shop, where he asked for a ha'pennyworth of putty. However, as he had no money with which to pay for it, he emerged empty-handed. The second man, on seeing the constables approaching, ran off and was not seen again, but his companion was arrested as he left the shop.

Giving his name as James Woods, he claimed that he had walked all the way from Pendleton, Salford, where he had slept the previous night, but could furnish no exact address. Nor was he able to give a satisfactory account of his movements over the previous week, although he insisted that he had been living in Leeds. Woods, a 22-year-old Irishman, of no education and out of work, was taken to Manchester and subsequently identified as one of the men who had narrowly escaped arrest outside Henry Wilson's shop in Shudehill on the night Kelly and Deasy were taken into custody.

News that the Fenian prisoners would appear at the police court soon after their apprehension spread very quickly among the general public of Manchester. Several hours before the court opened, a large crowd had assembled in Bridge Street to await the arrival of the prison van from Albert Street Police Station, where an even bigger crowd had gathered. All were anxious to have a good view of the Fenians and many paid for the privilege of being allowed to climb up onto passing carts which had been brought to a standstill. Some spectators were even to be seen perched precariously on neighbouring rooftops.

The prisoners had been well guarded during the night. Now, at about 10am, a relief guard of 48 men, under the command of Captain Clark, arrived to take over for the day. As they entered the street a great cheer went up from the crowd. The gates of the yard were thrown open and the new guard, with fixed bayonets, marched inside amid more cheering.

About half-a-dozen prisoners charged with minor offences such as drunkenness were removed to the court in advance of the Fenians, and the crowd paid little attention to them as they left Albert Street, escorted by the retiring night guard.

The sightseers were in for a very long wait, for the business of identification still had to be dealt with before the accused could be taken to court. The prisoners were ordered out of their cells and told to stand in the passage while witnesses passed along the line and were asked to identify any man they had seen take part in the rescue.

114

Some of the prisoners were described at the time as 'hang-dog looking fellows, who presented such a villainous appearance as to make walking down the passage so close to them a rather daunting prospect'. This, of course, was absolute nonsense, although several of the witnesses did appear somewhat apprehensive and had to be urged by the police to pass along the line and back again.

One of the prisoners, James Woods, stood on the cold stone floor of the corridor as he had spent the night – without boots. After his arrest in Ashton-under-Lyne they had been taken away from him so as to preserve the evidence of the clay adhering to them.

Another prisoner, Robert McWilliam, strongly protested his innocence, saying he was in no way concerned in the Fenian attack, and that he was under suspicion because he had no settled address, owing to the fact that he had only a few days previously arrived in England from Australia. He was eventually released. The *Oldham Standard* reported:

The demeanour of these fellows towards each other is most familiar, and the courteous manner in which a jug of water, provided for their common use, was passed around, suggested a strong fraternal feeling.

One man who drew much attention to himself was Robert McWilliam. Very erect and self-possessed, he looked like a soldier in undress. With few exceptions the other men appear to be of the lowest class of Irish and of the most unprepossessing appearance. Allen, with wounds on his left cheek and with the top of his head plastered, paced up and down in a restless manner and was again the most prominent figure amongst the prisoners.

At 1-30pm the prisoners were taken from Albert Street to the court, but to the great disappointment of those patiently waiting in the street to catch a glimpse of the notorious 'Fenian desperadoes', they were loaded into the vans inside the yard before being driven through the crowded street under armed guard. The prisoners were briefly seen as they were taken from the vans and marched in by the back door of the courthouse in Somerset Street.

The accused men were lined up in the courtroom, where they faced a full bench of magistrates under the Stipendiary, Mr. Robinson Fowler. In reply to his initial questions, all the prisoners except two stated that they wished to call witnesses.

Mr. Fowler addressed the crowded court,

'Before entering into this case I wish to say a word regarding the great loss sustained by all connected with this court in the death of

Sergeant Brett. For many years as an officer of this dock he performed the most difficult duties with admirable firmness, good temper and credit to himself, and carries with him to his last resting place the universal respect of all with whom he has been associated'.

Superintendent Gee said he was confident that all the prisoners could be satisfactorily identified as having been involved in the Hyde Road Bridge incident. However, as there were still others not yet apprehended he would have to ask for a remand. McAuliffe interrupted him, saying that he was not represented by counsel and that he wished to be accorded the privilege of questioning, himself, any witness brought against him. He was told by Mr. Fowler that he would be afforded every convenience the court could allow. The magistrate, however, was unwilling to go into McAuliffe's case further at this stage, as he wished to deal with the main item on the agenda first.

Several of the prisoners engaged the services of two solicitors, named Roberts and Bennett, both of whom happened to be in court at the time on other business.

Police-Constable Yarwood said he believed that Michael Larkin had deliberately tried to shoot him. Apart from Larkin, Yarwood identified Allen, Henry Wilson and Michael Joseph Boylan. Constable Shaw also named Larkin.

'He had a revolver, which I think I saw him use.'

He had seen William Martin throwing stones and believed he also carried a revolver. Asked by Mr. Fowler about the shooting of Sergeant Brett, Shaw pointed out Allen.

'I saw him put a pistol to the van and fire. He seemed to shoot through the keyhole, to burst the lock. I heard someone inside the van cry out, "he's killed".'

He was asked by the defending solicitor Mr. Roberts, roughly how many shots he thought had been fired altogether, and replied that there must have been forty at least.

'And where did they go to?'

'I believe most of them went against the railway arch. There were a good many marks there. They missed me anyway and I'm thankful for that.'

'And well you may be', added Mr. Fowler.

'Were the shots fired at random?, suggested Roberts.

'Well, I don't think the men were much experienced at shooting, or we should not be here to tell the tale.'

After a revolver had been produced, which, it was stated, could be directly linked with one of the prisoners, Mr. Fowler said he did not propose to take any further evidence if Superintendent Gee believed that he could bring the charge home to all prisoners in the dock. He was assured by Gee that there was no doubt about it. Mr. Fowler then informed the prisoners that he had heard sufficient evidence to justify their being remanded for a week, and added that they would be given every opportunity to produce witnesses and engage professional counsel.

One of the prisoners, Michael Maguire, protested that he had not been involved in the affair, having been at his work on the day in question from 5-30am until 8-30pm. Several of the others joined him in proclaiming their innocence. All were quickly removed from the court.

The case of John Francis McAuliffe was then proceeded with. The charge against the big Irishman had now been amended to 'being a suspected person,' having been observed loitering about on the corner of Bridge Street and Water Street and adopting a defiant attitude towards the police.

McAuliffe told the court that he was a public lecturer and had obtained his livelihood in that capacity for a good many years. He was to have lectured at Runcorn in Cheshire on the evening of his arrest, but, of course, had been prevented from doing so.

Superintendent Gee pointed out that the prisoner had been involved in the Chester Castle affair, but Mr. Fowler replied that this was of no concern to him.

'Yes', chipped in McAuliffe, 'it's perfectly true that I was at Chester, but I proved my innocence and was set at liberty. A lot of per-jurers of the blackest kind, men capable of anything, tried to swear my life away on that occasion, and I have no doubt that Superintendent Gee will be prepared to do the same if he can get anybody to help him.'

Mr. Fowler said that if the prisoner could give respectable references, state who he was and where he came from, he would be happy to let him go, provided he was satisfied that he had not been loitering about the streets for some dishonest purpose.

In view of the fact that McAuliffe had used a knife in attempting to resist arrest, this would seem to have been an extremely lenient attitude on the magistrate's part.

McAuliffe, however, was unable to fulfil the necessary conditions.

'I am a public lecturer', he repeated. 'I came to Manchester to meet a lady, a first cousin of mine, who is going to America shortly'.

'Give me her address', said the magistrate.

'I don't know where she lives at present. I was to meet her at the Albert Road bridge, at three o'clock that afternoon. She -'

'That will do'. Mr. Fowler cut him short. 'Have you any other references?'

'No'.

'Then you must be remanded for a week.'

McAuliffe was led from the court, protesting, and locked up along with the other prisoners. Later that afternoon they were all transported to Belle Vue Gaol under an escort of infantry, plus three troops of the 8th Hussars.

From the courthouse all the way up Deansgate there was a dense mass of people, a great number of whom were Irish. Some openly expressed sympathy for the prisoners, and one experienced police officer remarked that the number of Fenians in the crowd was greater than had ever assembled in Manchester before.

The troops in attendance carried loaded carbines, while the Hussars rode with drawn sabres. The procession, moving at a steady pace, went along Bridge Street, Princess Street, Mosley Street, Piccadilly, London Road and on to Hyde Road, the pavements being crowded along the entire distance. At various points along the route the troops were cheered by the spectators. After the prisoners had been delivered safely to the gaol a large detachment of troops remained to stand guard over them.

On Friday morning 20 September, two days after the outrage, an inquest on Sergeant Brett was held at the City Coroner's Court, St. John Street.

After the jurors had been sworn in they were informed by the Coroner that it was his intention to hold no more than a preliminary inquiry, in view of the fact that the case itself was in the process of being examined by another court.

'I must first have one witness who will identify the body.'

This was done by Superintendent Anderton. Edward Brett was called, and told the court,

'The deceased was my brother. He would have been 52 years of age in December, and lived at 7 Wilson Street, off Oldham Road. He has left a widow and three children, all grown up.'

Constable George Shaw then took the witness stand and repeated the evidence he had given before the magistrates on the previous day, swearing that William O'Meara Allen was the man who killed Sergeant Brett.

John R. Woodcock, house surgeon at the Manchester Royal Infirmary, said in evidence,

118

'I saw the deceased shortly after his admission at about 4-30pm on September 18th. He was unconscious and in a dying state. He died next morning at 5-25am, without regaining consciousness. I have since made a post mortem examination by the Coroner's order, and found a fracture in the roof of the right orbit where a ball entered the cavity of the skull. There was a second fracture on the right side of the crown of the head where a ball had passed out again. There was extensive laceration of the brain caused by the passage of the ball. The other half of the brain and all the internal organs were perfectly healthy'.

Mr. Woodcock also mentioned that the deceased was a tall man and was asked by the Coroner:

'Supposing he was standing upright when the ball entered his head. What direction would it have taken do you think?'

'It must have passed upwards I would say at an angle of about 45 degrees.'

The inquest was adjourned, pending completion of the magisterial hearing.

CHAPTER 16

Further arrests

It was becoming clear that the authorities had been extremely lax in allowing the two Fenian leaders to slip through their fingers. On Wednesday 25 September, just one week after their escape, the Lord Mayor of Manchester, Mr. Robert Neill, placed a report before the City Council explaining some of the circumstances. In it he stated:

The first information I received of the attack on the police van was a message from Superintendent Gee, in consequence of which I at once proceeded to the Town Hall. Up to that time I was quite unaware that the custody of these prisoners was attended by any unusual risk, or that any attempted rescue was to be apprehended.

A telegram from the Home Office reached me at ten minutes past five pm containing suggestions for the safe custody of the prisoners. Had this message reached me in sufficient time, effective measures and precautions would, I feel sure, have been adopted. A telegram to a like effect from the authorities in Dublin was also received at the Town Hall about three hours after the outrage.

This last statement was not entirely accurate. In fact, although the Home Office communication addressed to the Mayor did not arrive at the Town Hall until almost two hours after the rescue had taken place, the telegram from Dublin had been received as early as midday, leaving ample time for the necessary precautions to have been taken. Unfortunately, it was addressed to Mr. Maybury, Acting Chief Constable, who was out on duty at the time.

According to a later explanation given by the Mayor, he had happened to go into the detective office between six and seven o'clock that evening and noticed the telegram on Mr. Maybury's desk. On asking what it was, he was told by Maybury,

'It's a telegram. I've only just received it.'

It had, in fact, been received by a clerk earlier in the day and passed through several pairs of hands before arriving on the Acting Chief Constable's desk, where it had lain unopened until Maybury came in that evening.

Although no further breach of the peace was anticipated, the authority of the Home Office was sought and obtained for the

121

Manchester police to be issued with firearms when dealing with any disturbance of a potentially dangerous nature. Colt revolvers were placed at their disposal should they be needed.

Four more Fenians were rounded up and appeared before the magistrates. They were Hugh Foley (arrested in Preston), Patrick Coffey, Michael Kennedy and Patrick Toole. Because the evidence against the last-named appeared flimsy, he was discharged, the others being remanded for a week. They were removed to Belle Vue by a troop of Hussars. One of the three had been arrested whilst attempting to make his escape down Barnes Street. He was cornered in the yard of the Clarence Hotel by police and a soldier of the 57th Foot, and put up a fierce struggle before being overpowered and handcuffed.

After a Gorton man had found a revolver on the railway lines, two London detectives, Clarke and Campbell, visited the spot. While they were there, the canvas covering of a goods wagon was removed by two railwaymen in the course of their duties, and a second revolver fell to the ground at Clarke's feet. It was partly loaded and bore the name of the maker – Mortimer, London. It had obviously been hidden under the canvas by one of the escaping Fenians.

The city was being turned inside out for Fenian suspects. In the early hours of a grey, drizzly Saturday morning, police officers entered a house at 68, Buckley Street, Rochdale Road, and arrested two brothers, James and Joseph Sherry. Neither of them, however, proved to be the man whom the police had expected to find there, for information had been received that an Irishman, described as one of the ringleaders, was in the house.

Before leaving the premises, however, the officers decided to search an outbuilding. Hiding inside they found a third man, a powerful fellow of six feet, two inches, who refused to surrender to them. The fugitive's only weapon was a rusty old handsaw, with which he proceeded to defend himself, keeping the officers at bay for a good fifteen minutes. At last, after a determined rush by P.C. Goode, the Irishman was overpowered and handcuffed. Along with the Sherry brothers, the big man was taken to Livesey Street police station. On him was found a letter identifying the prisoner as John Francis Nugent, and congratulating him on his 'many daring escapes from the bluecoats'. The letter appeared to indicate that Nugent had been implicated in the Fenian troubles in Ireland earlier in the year, a fact that would be bourne out later. His appearance tallied closely with a sketch drawn by the police with the assistance of a member of the public.

The three Irishmen were taken to Albert Road Police Station, along with two others arrested in Deansgate, also in the early hours of

Saturday morning. Nugent was quickly identified by two policemen and three civilians as having been one of the most conspicuous of the Hyde Road bridge rioters.

A number of communications regarding the whereabouts of the escaped Fenian leaders were received by the Manchester police, following the outrage. All led nowhere, and as the days passed without any reliable intelligence coming in, hopes that they would be recaptured grew fainter. Police in neighbouring towns were on constant alert and a strict watch was being kept on all seaports.

As it had been positively established that Kelly and Deasy had been seen in the Bradford district of Manchester , roughly an hour after the rescue, it was clear that they had either managed to obtain some form of secret transport, or were being hidden by friends somewhere in the city.

A letter was received at the detective office during the weekend, informing the police that a body of Fenians would meet outside the Royal Infirmary and carry out a plan for the destruction of several public buildings. It was claimed that the head of the fire brigade would be assassinated in order to prevent him from organising his men to render assistance. No heed was paid to this warning and no disturbance took place.

Though a very large proportion of the anonymous correspondence arriving on Superintendent Maybury's desk was worthless, and a constant source of time wasting, each communication had to be read and evaluated before most were consigned to the waste paper basket. One letter gave such detailed information regarding the alleged hiding place of Colonel Kelly that the Superintendent felt obliged to follow it up. The unknown writer stated quite positively that the fugitive was concealed in a house in Every Street, Ancoats, a predominantly Irish district of the city.

Four officers, under Detective Drabble, were sent to the house. They banged on the door and demanded admittance. When this was refused Drabble left his men on guard outside and sought out a magistrate, returning eventually with a search warrant and a further squad of policemen, armed with revolvers and commanded by Inspector Garner.

Even when they were informed that a warrant had been obtained, the occupants still refused to open up, leaving the police with no alternative but to break down the door. Inside they found a young man and two women, whom they placed under arrest and conducted to Fairfield Street police station. Of Kelly there was no sign.

The house, which was rented at £24 per annum, contained scarcely any furniture. There were clear signs, however, that it had recently been used as a Fenian meeting place. On a wall in one room hung a portrait of James Stephens, bearing the caption 'Fenian Head Centre for Ireland'. In another room were discovered several men's hats of various sizes, along with a number of rather cryptic, but apparently incriminating, letters. One of these was signed F.B. (which the officers took to stand for Fenian Brotherhood). Beneath the signature were the words, 'Longing for the Irish Republic'.

A large crowd had gathered around the house, but the police managed to leave unmolested with their prisoners. These were, however, released within a matter of days, as they could not be directly connected either with the attack on the van or with the escaped Fenians.

That weekend nineteen people were arrested and paraded in front of witnesses, after which the number was whittled down to nine. These were charged on the Monday and gave their names as:

John Martin, Varley Street, aged 34, (whose brother William had been arrested during the first swoop);

Patrick Kelly, (not to be confused with the Patrick Kelly already in custody), no fixed address, aged 25;

Michael Bryan, 42, Riga Street, aged 21;

Peter Lynn, aged 38, Bedale Street, (stated to be a former member of the Irish Constabulary);

Matthew Boulger, 3, Byrom Place, aged 18;

James Sherry, 68, Buckley Street, aged 21;

Joseph Sherry, 3, Hyde Street, Hulme, aged 37;

John Bacon, 29, Cable Street, aged 40;

John Francis Nugent, also of Buckley Street, aged 24.

All were remanded until the following Thursday, when they would be brought up with the others. The prisoner Martin objected to a remand in his own case, insisting he could prove he was at work when the attack on the van took place.

He was told by Mr. Fowler,

'As I have already said to the other prisoners, it is quite possible that some individual cases of hardship may occur. But I have the sworn evidence of Superintendent Gee that he has every reason to suppose he can bring this charge home to all of you. Therefore, I must remand you in custody.'

'I want to write letters to my friends,' said Martin.

'I believe every opportunity will be afforded to the prisoners to communicate with their solicitors in order that they may be able to prepare a defence,' he was told.

'But what is done, sir, when people do not have the means to employ a solicitor and wish to get the witnesses themselves?'

'In such a case,' replied the magistrate, 'if the prisoner will give me the names of those witnesses he wishes to call on his behalf, I will take care that they are sent for.'

Patrick Kelly then spoke up, saying he could provide an alibi 'at once', as also did Peter Lynn. Both were advised to reserve their defence. The prisoners were led out under armed guard, but although there was again a large crowd in Bridge Street, no demonstration took place.

One aftermath of the arrests, however, concerned a married couple, James and Mary Foley, who were brought up at the police court on the following day, charged with intimidating a witness named Ellis. Upon learning that his brother Hugh had been arrested on the evidence of Ellis, James Foley, accompanied by his wife, had gone to Ellis's house and threatened him, Mary Foley swearing that they would be revenged on him even if she had to 'swing for it'. Her husband also threatened Ellis with physical violence.

Mr. W.P. Roberts, appearing on behalf of the accused, appealed to the magistrate, again Mr. Fowler, not to take the charge too seriously. Mr. Fowler, however, felt that the case should certainly not be taken lightly, particularly in view of the fact that the victim had been threatened in his own home.

Ellis told the court that he now went in fear of his life, but Mr. Roberts contended that this was not a case of malicious intent, rather one of hasty words, and he asked that the Foleys might be discharged. Mr. Fowler could not be prevailed upon to agree, telling him,

'This is a serious offence. For these people, by their conduct, have identified themselves with a movement which must be put down with a strong hand.'

'But the hand', replied Mr. Roberts, 'need not be vindictive, even if strong.'

'That is not the question. The question is how to deal with the case before me, and it is my opinion that the prisoners should be remanded, although bail will be accepted.'

'For mercy's sake sir, please consider carefully just what you are doing. What offence have my clients committed? Let me know and I will address the Home Secretary on it this very night.'

Mr. Fowler repeated the charge, adding that the witness in a case of felony now went in fear of his life.

'There is a legal remedy for that', replied Mr. Roberts. 'You can bind my clients over to keep the peace. For God's sake sir, don't commit yourself, or you will stand alone among the magistracy of this country.'

'I am in no doubt Mr. Roberts, that I at present occupy a position that no man would envy. I have, however, to the best of my ability, performed my duties with fairness – and, I hope, with firmness also.'

The prisoners were subsequently allowed bail.

That week further arrests were made in Manchester and Salford, several of those taken into custody being domestic employees in large houses. It seemed that almost every Irishman the police could lay hands on was being apprehended.

Still there was no trace at all of Kelly and Deasy. Some alarm was caused at Dover by the arrival of a number of Irish-Americans, and it was rumoured that their intention was to smuggle the fugitives to the continent should they manage to get as far as Dover. The authorities redoubled their efforts, vigorously searching every steamer leaving the port, but without result.

Another story, which apparently originated in Liverpool, was that Kelly and Deasy had arrived there on foot and embarked on the steamer *Hibernia* for Quebec. Though this rumour was discredited by the Liverpool police, who had remained on constant alert from the moment news of the rescue reached them, a telegram was sent off, nevertheless, to ensure that all passengers leaving the boat on the Canadian side were thoroughly scrutinised before being allowed to proceed on their way.

It was considered highly probable, however, that the two fugitives were still in the north of England, and it was there that the efforts of the police were still concentrated. From all parts of the country reports were coming in of possible 'sightings', and more than one innocent person was inconvenienced as a result. On Monday 23 September, a young man, apparently answering closely to the description of Captain Deasy, was seen to arrive at Leicester on a north-bound train. When he purchased a ticket to Liverpool the police were immediately informed. The unfortunate young man was quickly arrested on suspicion of being the wanted Fenian. Although there appeared to be a definite facial resemblance and also an American accent, it was clear that there were also certain discrepancies. The appearance of the traveller, in fact, seemed to correspond with that of the fugitive in every detail but two. For his features were pitted with smallpox marks, while Deasy was said to have a clear skin. Neither was there a scar on the man's cheek, though Deasy had such a disfigurement just below one of his ears.

The young man protested his innocence, but despite the discrepancies in appearance he was marched off to the local police

126

station, where he told his interrogators that he had lived in America for ten years and was returning there following a visit to his brother, who was landlord of the Railway Inn at Sharnbrook, near Bedford. He had left there that morning to return to the United States. The brother was summoned by telegraph, arrived at Leicester later that day, and immediately identified the prisoner. Still this was not considered sufficient grounds to warrant his release. Then, at his own suggestion, the young man was taken back to the railway station, where his trunk was opened and the contents examined. Nothing was revealed to implicate the owner in any Fenian activities, although much fuss was made over a pair of American knuckledusters found among his belongings.

Finally the Station Master at Sharnbrook was contacted, and assured the police that the man they were holding was well known in the district and had been seen frequently by him during the previous fortnight, when he was known to have been staying at his brother's inn.

The unfortunate traveller was at last set free. He had by this time missed his connection, but proceeded to Liverpool on the following morning, no doubt extremely relieved.

The funeral of Sergeant Brett took place on Sunday 29 September at Harpurhey Cemetery. Because the deceased had been such a well-known and greatly respected figure locally, and also because of the circumstances surrounding his death, the funeral attracted vast crowds of sympathisers, among them many Irish people who were genuinely saddened by such a tragic and unnecessary loss of life.

Almost the entire route, from Brett's modest cottage in Wilson Street to the cemetery, was lined with spectators. As the cortége passed by, hats were removed and blinds drawn. The Mayor, with a group of Aldermen, headed the procession, which also included a large body of policemen led by the Chief Constable, Captain Palin. All those officers from the City Police Court, who had worked closely with Sergeant Brett, wore black hatbands. It was estimated that, including spectators along the route, upwards of 15,000 people witnessed the funeral.

At the cemetery, policemen lined the path from the gates to the chapel, to which the mourners were conveyed in their carriages. Apart from friends and other relatives, the principal mourners were the Sergeant's wife, three grown-up children, his father and his brother.

After the ceremony in the chapel the mourners went outside for the burial. As the coffin was lowered into the ground a respectful silence fell upon the vast crowd, the whole scene being at once sad and profoundly impressive.

127

CHAPTER 17

Manacled

T he Fenian prisoners were brought up at the Police Court on Thursday 3 October, under armed escort. Mr. Higgin, Deputy Recorder of Manchester, acted as prosecutor, while Robinson Fowler again presided, with a large number of City Justices also present on the bench.

Higgin stated at once that he did not intend to include all the prisoners in his initial charge – that of the murder of Sergeant Brett. As soon as that charge was disposed of he would be in a position to state the course he wished to take in respect of the others in custody.

The first batch of prisoners was therefore placed in the dock, their legal representatives having been engaged by the subscribers to a defence fund.

Defended by Mr. Roberts, solicitor, were: John Carroll, John Gleeson, Michael Kennedy, John Morris, Hugh Foley, Patrick Kelly (from Leitrim), Patrick Coffey, Thomas Kelly and Thomas Scalley.

Defended by Mr. Ernest Jones, barrister, were: William O'Meara Allen, Edward Shore, Henry Wilson and William Gould.

Mr. J. Cottingham, barrister, appeared for Michael Larkin, Patrick Kelly (Galway), John Brennan, John Bacon, William Martin and Charles Moorhouse.

Mr. Ward, solicitor, defended Robert McWilliam, and Mr. Bennett appeared on behalf of Michael Maguire, Michael Morris, Thomas Maguire, Michael Bryan, Michael Corcoran, Thomas Ryan and Patrick Daley.

Of these, John Morris and Thomas Scalley must have been arrested later, as their names were not on any previous list of prisoners.

Before the proceedings began Mr. Ernest Jones informed the magistrates that he had a very serious matter to put before them.

'The prisoners have been brought into this court for preliminary examination with handcuffs on them. Now I know that this is a most unusual case, but such a thing is unheard of. It appears to me to be discreditable to the administration of justice, that men whom the law presumes to be innocent until found guilty should be brought into court handcuffed together like pairs of hounds.'

Mr. Jones suggested that the magistrate should immediately order that the handcuffs be removed. Mr. Cottingham, in making a

129

similar application, remarked that he had witnessed a case of the turnkeys being ordered to remove handcuffs from a prisoner when they had proceeded to manacle him after sentence of death had been passed.

'There is sufficient force to guard them in court', he said. 'While they are being examined the irons should be removed.'

'I don't believe it is a matter for me at all', replied Mr. Fowler. 'We as magistrates are here to inquire into this case. But the police are the ones answerable for the prisoners' safety while in court. The prisoners are their charges and the responsibility rests with them, not with me.'

'You are the superior authority in this court', Mr. Jones insisted.

'Not so. The police assure me that with the force at their disposal in this court, they find it necessary to keep the prisoners handcuffed.'

'But there is both a police and a military force present. Surely that is sufficient?'

'To use your own words, Mr. Jones, it is a most unusual case we are dealing with. I shall not interfere.'

Mr. Higgin, opening for the prosecution, said it was his duty to prefer a charge of murder against the men in the dock, or those of them who should be proved to the satisfaction of the bench to have taken part in the outrage.

'That Manchester has been startled from its propriety by the knowledge that a police vehicle has been attacked in one of the most frequented streets of this city by an armed mob, and a rescue effected at the expense of a man's life in the exercise of his duty, is highly discreditable, and calculated to arouse alarm and apprehension in the minds of all peaceable citizens', he told the court.

Mr. Higgin then related the events of the previous Wednesday. Describing how the accused prisoners had stopped the van, he stated:

'From their demeanour, and the way in which they conducted themselves, there can be no room left in a reasonable man's mind that they were assembled for the express purpose of violence, by extreme force if necessary, to effect their deliberate objective – that of stopping the van and by force removing some of the prisoners therein.

'Whether one or more shots were fired through the ventilator there might be some doubt, but it is certain that one shot was fired with deliberate aim, and it took effect upon the head of Brett, entering the skull on the right hand side and coming out of the other. There can be no doubt whatsoever that Sergeant Brett was murdered. The bench have no doubt with respect to Allen and also to Larkin, that they each played a prominent part in the outrage'.

130

Higgin was asked by Mr. Fowler if he did not think it desirable to have the van inspected, as it was so close to the court. Higgin agreed that it was, and the magistrates, accompanied by all counsel involved in the case, left the courtroom, returning after a short interval, when proceedings were resumed.

Higgin said he had decided that in the case of John Morris he would withdraw the charge.

'If there is no evidence against him', said Mr. Fowler, 'let him be removed.'

After this had been done the depositions of the witnesses were read out. Constable Yarwood, who had previously sworn he could identify five of the prisoners, was now asked if he could name any others. He picked out Thomas Maguire and John Bacon, who was lame.

On hearing this, Maguire interposed, 'I beg your pardon sir. He did not see me there at all.'

When it was realised that police witnesses other than Yarwood were in court, proceedings were suspended until they had filed out.

Constable George Shaw was called, and after giving his evidence, was cross-examined by Mr. Ernest Jones, who asked if he had heard any of the evidence given by the previous witness.

'Yes sir, I heard part of it. But I left the court immediately the other witnesses were ordered out.'

Shaw admitted that there had been several people between himself and Allen during the skirmish, but insisted that he had clearly seen Allen put a pistol to the ventilator and fire. He was equally certain that Allen was also the man who shot Sprosson in the foot.

At the conclusion of P.C. Shaw's evidence there was an adjournment of half an hour, when the court re-assembled, but before the case could be continued Mr. Jones announced:

'I must repeat my application with regard to the handcuffs on these men. In the first place they are too small. Allen and Gould have shown me their wrists, and they are very badly swollen. They tell me that the pain and inconvenience caused, and the indignity, prevent them giving their full attention to the evidence, and therefore they are unable to make any observations or suggestions to counsel.

'In the interests of justice I request that these manacles be taken off. Another thing, if I might be permitted to say it. As an officer of the court – which every member of the Bar is – and as a citizen of Manchester, it is most unseemly, in my view, that a part of the military force should be on the bench where the magistrates are sitting'.

Following this statement, Mr. Roberts asked:

131

'Is it likely – is it possible, that men suffering under the imprisonment, the assault and the torture that these men are, can have the same mental capacity and bodily strength that they would have if they were brought into court in the ordinary way?'

He asked that his clients be placed, as far as possible, in the same position of liberty and freedom as those who charged them and gave evidence against them.

Mr. Cottingham said that Michael Larkin had complained to him of the extreme pain and inconvenience he had suffered for several hours owing to the pressure of the handcuffs and submitted to Mr. Fowler that he had complete power to deal with the situation, saying that the gentlemen around him were merely spectators of the scene.

'Not so', replied Fowler. 'I am Chairman of a Bench of Magistrates.'

'According to the statute under which you are acting sir,' said Mr. Cottingham, 'you have the power to try the case yourself.'

'No, I am only one here, bound by the majority.'

'You are in the position of a judge at Assizes, and as such you have the power to direct that the prisoners be relieved from the pressure of these manacles. When a man is on trial for a capital offence in an Assize court he is not permitted to be brought into the dock manacled and chained, as it is regarded as an insult to the court and an opprobrium to English justice. I am therefore at a loss to know why this court should arrogate to itself a power which the law does not give to a judge of the Assizes. Why not put them in leg irons as well? It is quite unprecedented. You have not the precedent of the senior courts. You have a competent force in this court to subdue anything like an attempt at rescue or escape. I just cannot see any valid reason for all this. Except perhaps to impress on the public mind that they are desperate men.

'And that we are a set of cowards', added the other defence attorney, Mr. Bennett. 'And contemptible cowards too.'

Mr. Fowler was unimpressed, and replied, 'With regard to Mr. Jones's observations about the officers, I must say that I am exceedingly sorry he made them. The military have been called upon by the magistrates of Manchester to perform certain duties. Not all of the military present in court are on duty in fact. Some of the officers happened to come here as private friends of my own and are sitting with me on the bench. They are here mainly as spectators.'

'If they are friends of yours', replied Mr. Jones, pointing to the gallery, 'there is the place for them. Private friends of mine are up there, and that is where your friends should be.'

132

'I shall take no further notice of that remark', rejoined Robinson Fowler. 'With regard to the manacles, the police have been called upon to protect the interests of justice and this court, and if they feel that handcuffing the prisoners is necessary then I cannot take it upon myself to interfere. But if I find that a prisoner is suffering because his manacles are too small then I will see to it that he shall have other handcuffs put upon him which will not hurt.'

'Then', said Mr. Jones, 'as a member of the English Bar, I decline to sit in any court where the police over-ride the magistrates. I will not lend myself to any such violation of the ordinary course of justice.'

Then, turning to his instructing solicitor, 'There is your brief Mr. Roberts. I'm sorry to return it, but I cannot disgrace the Bar by proceeding with the defence in these circumstances.'

At this there were loud hisses from the gallery. Mr. Jones handed another brief to the solicitor, Mr. Nuttall, gathered up his papers and umbrella, and strode out of the courtroom.

After a short pause Robinson Fowler gathered himself and addressed Mr. Jones's abandoned clients,

'Allen, Shore, Gould and Wilson, I regret that you have been deprived of the services of Mr. Jones. I will at once, if you request it, adjourn the case until you can acquire further legal assistance.'

Replying from the dock, Gould told him,

'We have more confidence in Mr. Jones than in any other legal gentleman.'

'There is no necessity for handcuffing them,' interposed Mr. Bennett. 'It is an act of sheer cowardice.'

'They are as quiet as sheep in a pen', added Mr. Cottingham. 'While they are being brought here or removed back to prison it may be all very well, but to have them handcuffed during the inquiry is monstrous.'

'Before we go any further', said Fowler, 'I will ask the magistrates to retire with me and we will consult with Captain Palin. And I might tell you that no one is more unhappy than I am, to see men standing before me in shackles.'

The magistrates and the Police Chief then retired, and Mr. Roberts sent a clerk after Mr. Ernest Jones, asking him to remain in the court building until the result of the consultation was made known. Mr. Jones, however, declined to return and left for his chambers. About fifteen minutes later the magistrates filed in and Fowler asked if Mr. Jones was present in the court.

'No', replied Mr. Roberts. 'He has sent word that he will not return until the manacles have been taken off.'

133

'All I have to say is this', Mr. Fowler said. 'We are unanimous in our opinion. Much as we regret having to place the prisoners under restraint, yet from information which has been given to us we cannot undertake to order the removal of those restraints which the authorities have thought necessary to place on the prisoners.'

This announcement brought loud cheers from the gallery, and Mr. Fowler added,

'The court will be cleared if there is any further expression of approbation or dissent during this inquiry.

'Any prisoner who complains that he is suffering will be examined by a medical man, and every proper means shall be taken to relieve him. Allen, Shore, Gould and Wilson, you still have your solicitor Mr. Roberts. Do you wish to engage any further legal assistance'?

'They have instructed me', replied Roberts, 'that they wish to be defended by no one but Mr. Jones, and in his absence they will not be defended at all.'

'We have placed our liberty and our lives in the hands of Mr. Jones', said Gould. 'If this court wishes to take them away by foul means, let it do so. In the first place, after my arrest I was chained by the legs and so was another man there, evidently for the purpose of drawing the attention of those who had come to identify us. If this is fair – if this is English justice – then I am done with it.'

'You decline to be defended?' Mr. Fowler asked him. 'That is all I wish to know.'

'Unless Mr. Jones defends us.'

'Or until the handcuffs are taken off', added Roberts.

'You must not advise the prisoners in open court', the magistrate told him.

'I have a perfect right to advise them. I am their solicitor.'

'Allen', said Mr. Fowler. 'Do you wish someone else to defend you?'

'No one but Mr. Jones.' replied Allen.

'And not until the handcuffs are taken off', said Roberts again.

'And not until the handcuffs are taken off', repeated Allen, parrot fashion.

The prisoner Shore then addressed the bench, 'Sir, I respectfully beg that these handcuffs be taken off. If they were not oppressively painful I would not object. I do not know about English courts of justice. I do not know if it is the custom to manacle prisoners, but I do know that these 'cuffs are very painful. I decline to be defended by anyone but Mr. Jones, unless the handcuffs are removed.'

Henry Wilson, the Shudehill second-hand clothes dealer, replied similarly to Mr. Fowler's question, and the prisoners were informed that they themselves would be allowed to cross-examine any witnesses brought against them, but Gould, shaking his head, interrupted the magistrate.

'No, I decline to take any further part in this transaction. If it is going to be a farce, I'll have nothing at all to do with it.'

'I don't really think this inquiry should be continued', said Mr. Cottingham, 'until the medical man you mentioned has examined the prisoners. I've seen for myself the painful way in which the handcuffs are pressing on their wrists.'

However, it did not appear that all the prisoners were suffering, for Mr. Fowler remarked, 'It is absurd to say that a man who can laugh and talk the way Larkin does is in pain.'

Larkin claimed that he had sores on the wrist to which the handcuffs were fastened. They were taken off and he was manacled to his companion, Shore, by the other hand. When the handcuffs of several of the other prisoners had been transferred, Mr. Cottingham said that if what was now being done proved to be satisfactory, he himself would have nothing further to say.

The proceedings were at last continued. The evidence of each identifying witness would be vital, for a man had lost his life. If the charge against his killer were proven, then not only he, but all who had aided and abetted, in other words, all those involved in the rescue, could be deemed equally guilty of murder. The law was quite clear on that point, therefore the witnesses' statements regarding identification were extremely important at this – the magisterial hearing.

The first witness called was Thomas Patterson of West Gorton, who described himself as a puddler*, employed at Mr. Ashworth's forge in Openshaw. On the afternoon in question he had been about 400 yards from the bridge in Hyde Road, when he heard a banging noise and crossed the brick-field to investigate. Climbing up onto 'Heywood's Wall' he found himself only about ten yards from the bridge, on the Manchester side. Through the arch he could see the prison van, which had been stopped. Between thirty and forty men surrounded it. They were firing pistols, throwing stones and attempting to smash the back of the van. One man was on top trying to batter a way in through the roof with a massive stone, which had been handed up to him.

'This man was Allen', said Patterson, pointing him out in court. Also, [and this would cause much controversy later] the witness swore that it was Thomas Maguire who handed up the stone.

Patterson next stated that Allen had climbed down, and while others continued to hammer at the van, he ran about with two revolvers,

* A foundry worker.

135

threatening to shoot anyone who might approach him. Another man dressed in a 'slop', or full-length workcoat, cord breeches and waistcoat, whom he could not see in court, was also prominent. This man, according to the witness, shouted 'Kill the – – – – – – – ! He's inside.'

Allen ran to the back of the van and placed both revolvers in the ventilator. He fired, and there was a woman's scream from inside the van. The witness said he heard the report of one gun only, however.

After the van door had been opened and Sergeant Brett fell into the roadway, the witness had seen three women alight from the vehicle. They were shortly followed by the two Fenian prisoners and their rescuers. He had heard Allen say to one of the handcuffed men, 'Arrah Kelly, I'll die for you before I'll deliver you up.'

After the prisoners had reached the brickcroft Allen also prepared to leave the scene. Before he went he shouted that he would shoot any man who attempted to follow. With Gould and Larkin he stayed behind until Kelly and Deasy had gone a long way across the brick-field. The three of them ran off towards the Sheffield line, the same direction the others had taken.

Asked if he could identify any others, Patterson named William Martin, whom he had seen throwing stones, and Patrick Kelly (Galway), whom he had seen throwing stones at the van and also at a policeman. He had not seen Gould do anything.

Patterson told the court that during all the commotion he had remained on the wall, but after the last of the Fenians ran off he climbed down and went to look at Sergeant Brett. After that he had joined in the chase and had been among those who caught up with Larkin. He had also assisted in capturing Allen and Gould, after Allen had turned and fired at a man named Thomas Mulholland.

Patterson was cross-examined thoroughly by Mr. Cottingham. Explaining why he had not been at his work on the 18th, Patterson said that the forge was stopped, and for that day he had been employed on the brickcroft owned by John Hayes.

'Did you go back to your own work on the following day?', Mr. Cottingham asked.

'No'.

'Why not?'

'Because the police came and got me out of bed to go and identify some prisoners.'

'Have you been to your work at all since then?'

'No'.

'You have spent a good deal of your time, I believe, at the Albert Road Police Station.'

136

'Yes'.

'Have you been there all the time? Have you slept there?'

'No, I've slept at home'.

Questioned further, the witness agreed that initially he had been taken to the gaol, but denied that he had, at that time, been unable to identify some of the men he had identified since. He said he received only a meal of some bread and cheese at the police station. When Mr. Cottingham pointed out that he had earned no money the previous week he said he had been to the forge and received some money from his master which was owing to him. He did not expect any money from the court, apart from his expenses as a witness.

Questioned by Mr. Cottingham regarding the distance between Heywood's Wall and the van, he eventually admitted that it was more like 30 yards, and that he could not actually see the back of the van from where he had been perched.

Pressed again on the subject of money, Patterson said he expected to be paid the sum of 4/6d per day as a witness, which was about what he would have earned at his work. 'But I'd rather be working ten times over than be here.'

At this there was loud applause from the gallery, which was quickly suppressed by Mr. Fowler, who did not, however, carry out his earlier threat to clear the court.

'You're a great man for being taken backwards and forwards aren't you?', said Mr. Roberts.

'Who is?'

'You travel in the prison van, don't you?'

'No, I walk.'

Asked if they wished to question the witness, Allen, Shore, Gould and Wilson declined. Questioned again by Mr. Roberts, Patterson stated that he had been to the police station at Albert Road six times, and once to Belle Vue Gaol. He had made his identification on the day after the rescue, when the prisoners were lined up in a lobby.

'You were told to do so and you did', suggested Mr. Roberts.

'No I was not. There were about thirty men in the lobby and I picked out those I've picked out today.'

George Pickup, brickmaker, also of West Gorton, was the next witness, and said that the rioters had come from a field and out of several beer-houses just before the van arrived at the bridge. He saw about a dozen pistols among them and noticed a man in a cap, white slop, and greasy trousers standing close to the abutment. This man fired one shot at the officers riding on the back of the van. The witness also saw a man in a light suit climb on top of the vehicle, but had not seem him since. He saw another man striking the door of the van with a hammer. That man was Larkin. Next he saw Allen brandishing a pair of pistols. After he had fired and hit Sprosson in the foot he went to the ventilator at the back of the van and fired half a dozen shots into it.

Pickup stated that when Allen brought Colonel Kelly out of the van he said to him, 'Kelly, did I say I would die for you, and lose the last drop of blood I have for you?'

'I tried to follow them', Pickup told the court. 'Allen turned round and said if I did not go back he would shoot me.'

Asked if he could identify any others, Pickup pointed out Patrick Coffey and said he had seen him throwing stones.

'I've never been there!', shouted Coffey.

The witness also identified John Gleeson as another of the stone-throwers. Cross-examined by Mr. Cottingham, Pickup said,

"I am as certain of Coffey and Gleeson as I am about Allen and Larkin. I am certain about them all. There were three of us going up with stones to chuck at them. I saw the whole thing from the left hand side of the road going towards Manchester.'

'Is it not true that you passed by Gleeson three or four times before you finally identified him?'

'No it is not true. I identified him the first day I went down to the police station.'

Pressed further, Pickup added, 'I think I picked him out the first day. I told the policeman then that I owned* him, but I was most certain of him the next time I saw him.'

Regarding Coffey, Pickup testified, 'I went into a public house and I recognised him in a minute. I sent for a policeman.'

The prisoners declined to ask the witness any questions, and Gould shouted, 'I'll have no part in it.'

Mr. Higgin then informed the magistrates that as the last witness was the only person he could call to identify John Gleeson, he felt it would not be right on his part to press the bench to commit this prisoner on the unsupported evidence of one witness. Therefore, when the hearing was over, he would be prepared to say what course he intended to take with him.

'If you're saying that there is no evidence beyond what you already have against Gleeson', said Mr. Fowler, 'then I feel it is only right that you should withdraw so far as he is concerned. We shall be obliged to discharge him. He must be discharged today.'

* A colloquial expression meaning he recognised him.

138

Gleeson then gave Mr. Fowler a military salute. 'Thank you your Lordship.'

The Court was now adjourned until the following morning. Shore, before being taken away, told the magistrates that the police had removed his chest from his lodgings.

'I have money in the savings bank, and I would like to have the key of the chest delivered to my friends in order that they might draw money for my defence.'

'You must consult your lawyer', replied Fowler.

The prisoners came up in court next day, still manacled, and with the exception of Mr. Ernest Jones, the same legal representatives appeared.

John Francis McAuliffe was also present, but Mr. Fowler again decided that it would be impossible to hear his case that day. He would therefore be remanded for a further week.

'Might I speak a word sir?', interposed McAuliffe.

'No, Mr. Roberts defends you', he was told. The police returned him to the cells.

John Griffiths, the barber, identified John Francis Nugent as the man he and his friend Pickup had seen standing at the end of the arch, armed with a pistol. Shortly afterwards, when the van had been stopped, he saw a man in a light suit and a brown 'pot' hat fire his pistol at police constables Shaw and Trueman. This was Allen.

'One of the shots he aimed at Shaw hit a civilian named Sprosson in the foot. 'After that, he said, 'Allen fired again at the van's lock', the witness thought. Griffiths admitted, however, that he was 40 or 50 yards from the scene at the time.

Griffiths also identified Michael Bryan and William Martin, each of whom, he claimed, had a pistol, and Thomas Maguire, whom he had seen standing by the van. Griffiths added that he had not, however, seen Maguire do anything. Under cross-examination, the witness admitted that he had had a slight acquaintance with some of the prisoners prior to the attack.

The witness told Mr. Cottingham that on the evening of the 18th, he had been tapped on the shoulder, and found himself face to face with Clent, the Gorton bobby, who took him to a nearby beer-house, where police officers Shandley and Henderson were questioning people. When he saw them, he said, he had wanted to get away.

'Why?', he was asked.

'Because I didn't want to get mixed up in this business.'

However, he had remained with the officers for about ten minutes, and had given them descriptions of Allen and Nugent. Later that night, at the police station, and on the following morning, he had made further identifications.

The evidence of twelve-year-old George Mulholland conflicted in several details with that of the other witnesses. From the top of the bank near the arch where he had been playing, the boy, whose father worked locally as a brickmaker, had seen the van stopped. Allen, he stated, had rushed from the banking into the road and fired at the horses, at the same time yelling to the driver,

'Stop or I'll blow your brains out.'

The boy named Thomas Maguire as the one he had seen on top of the van,

'Smashing in the roof with a big stone.' This, he said, had been handed up by Michael Larkin. He had also seen Larkin fire through the ventilator in the front end of the van, and seen Allen snatch a hammer from a man who was trying to break in at the rear of the vehicle. Allen had then used the hammer, 'which was a hatchet at one side', himself. Another man, 'a very big one', who carried a saw, had shouted, 'Kill the – – – – – – – !' also, Allen had tried to smash in the ventilator, then fired through it. The boy said he saw Larkin holding two revolvers, and thought he was the one who wounded Sprosson in the foot.

He also remembered seeing, among the crowd, John Brennan, William Martin and Thomas Scalley. Scalley had a pistol, which he fired just as a woman was getting out of the van. The shot had grazed a policeman. Brennan had also carried large stones to break into the van, while William Martin was throwing stones at the police.

As events at the trial proper would prove, young Mulholland was not the most reliable of witnesses.

After several other witnesses had given evidence, proceedings were adjourned for the day and the prisoners removed to Albert Street Police Station under a strong military guard. It was reported that threats had been issued and information received that Fenian sympathisers in Manchester and neighbouring towns were exhibiting a restless and aggressive spirit and it was feared that further outbreaks of violence would ensue. Fenians as far away as Sunderland, in the North-East, were said to be holding meetings and threatening drastic action if the Manchester Irishmen were found guilty.

At the close of the day's proceedings a singular incident occurred in the courtroom, when several Irishmen, who were there for the purpose of giving evidence on behalf of some of the prisoners, were recognised by several of the prosecution witnesses as having taken part in the riot themselves. They were seized by the police and locked up along with those they had hoped to help free.

An even stranger incident took place during the same week at a factory in Barnsley, Yorkshire, which clearly showed just how strong were the feelings of the English working classes on the question of Fenianism. A young man in the employ of T. Taylor & Sons declared himself to be a Fenian, and told his workmates he was very much in sympathy with those held in custody in Manchester.

The other men immediately took exception to this statement and several of them decided to teach him a lesson. A 'jury' was empanelled and the young man subjected to a mock trial. What obviously started out as a joke turned into a nightmare for the principal in the affair, and could quite easily have ended tragically. For no sooner had the prisoner been found 'guilty', than a rope was produced, slung over a beam, and a noose placed around the 'offender's' neck. Not content with that, the self-appointed 'executioners' proceeded to draw up the rope until the young man's feet were off the floor. The loose end was then made fast and the victim left suspended in mid-air. Within a very short space of time he began to lose consciousness. Fortunately, commonsense prevailed, the victim being quickly cut down. He had gone blue in the face, and the mark of the rope was starkly imprinted on his neck.

Luckily for all concerned, the young man, a Roman Catholic, made a complete recovery. His assailants were dealt with by the management, being severely reprimanded and fined ten shillings each, the money going into the workers' accident insurance fund.

On the following morning, when proceedings were to recommence, Mr. Roberts addressed the magistrates:

'I wish to make an application. The prisoners have asked if they may be allowed to change their places in the dock. They believe that the witnesses have come here knowing the order in which those they are asked to identify have been placed – 1, 2, 3, 4 and 5, as the case may be'.

The magistrates nodded agreement and the prisoners reshuffled themselves, then settled again to listen to the evidence.

It was now the turn of the three women prisoners to give evidence, Emma Halliday being the first called. She stated that after

141

peering through the grille to see what was happening Sergeant Brett had slammed it shut, 'but had not fastened it'.

The banging on the roof of the van was immediately above Brett's head. The roof began to cave in. Soon a hole appeared and a stone dropped through it. Brett stepped back to avoid it. As he did so the ventilator was forced open from the outside and a stone wedged between the grille bars.

'A man came to the door and asked for the keys. He said, 'If you give us the keys we'll let the two men out and do you no harm.'

'Charlie told him no. He would stick to his post till the last. Charlie was looking through the upper part of the ventilator. I saw a pistol placed through the opening and I caught hold of Sergeant Brett and told him, "Oh, Charlie, do come away."

'I pulled him back and his head came on a level with the pistol, which was discharged, and Charlie fell. The man who fired the shot was Allen'.

The witness also pointed out Michael Maguire. 'Him there. The man in the grey coat. He was there.'

After giving a full account of all that she had seen taking place, she was questioned by Mr. Cottingham, and admitted that she had been sent to gaol for stealing, and that it was not for the first time. In fact, she had only come out in July, after serving three months for stealing a watch. She was also questioned by Roberts and Bennett on various details of her story, but could not be shaken on any point.

Ellen Cooper, who had taken the keys from Sergeant Brett's pocket, identified Allen, 'The one in the light coat.' He had pointed a pistol at her and said he would shoot her if she did not give him the keys. Cooper also identified Michael Maguire as being one of those who broke into the van.

The first question the witness was asked in cross-examination was,

'What is your trade or profession?'

The question was put by Mr. Bennett, on whom Cooper now turned angrily.

'It is of no significance to you. It is written down.'

'You are a convicted thief are you not? Mr. Fowler asked her.

'Yes,'

'And, in fact, have often been defended by Mr. Bennett.'

'Yes,'

'I cannot help that', said Bennett, somewhat embarrassed.

Before leaving the stand, Cooper admitted that she was in custody for robbing a man in the street.

The third woman, Frances Armstrong, corroborated the evidence of her fellow prisoners. She was 'almost sure that the one in blue' (Allen) was the man who had called for the keys. She could also identify John Brennan as having been there. Michael Corcoran she had seen standing by the van.

The first thing Mr. Cottingham did in cross-examining the witness was to dredge up her rather sordid past. She was a married woman living apart from her husband, had been to prison once for stealing and several times for drunkenness. But apart from showing her up as a thoroughly unsavoury character, he could do little to discredit her testimony.

The Belle Vue warders and the boy Joseph Partington gave evidence, Partington admitting to Mr. Roberts that he had already made public his version of what happened at the bridge, by giving the whole story to 'a gentleman from the newspapers.'

Next to appear was Constable Knox, a retired soldier formerly of the 10th Regiment, North Lincoln, who said that at the start of the attack he had approached a man with a revolver, who was standing at the horses' heads surrounded by others. Knox testified that he had said to them, 'Men, do not be foolish.' On receiving no response he had stamped his foot firmly on the ground, and striking his breast, had told them, 'Fire then you cowardly rascals, and be damned to you!' At this there was laughter in the court.

Under cross-examination Knox stated that he had spoken in the way described because 'the old military blood was up.' (More laughter)

John Accomb, a little boy, testified to having seen William Martin with a revolver, threatening the onlookers; and Thomas Sperry, a railway worker, gave details of Larkin's capture and also identified Gould as having helped Larkin as the rioters were pursued over the brick-field.

That day, five men were discharged for lack of evidence. They were John and Michael Morris, James Sherry, Patrick Daley and Michael Bryan.

Mr. Bennett also requested the release of Michael Maguire, but Higgin would not agree, and Mr. Fowler remarked that the evidence of the women who identified him could not be disregarded simply because they were criminals or did not live with their husbands.

When proceedings were resumed on the Monday, Mr. Cottingham again asked for the manacles to be removed, but Mr. Fowler told him,

'I shall only repeat what I have already said. That no one regrets this more than I. But at the same time, for reasons which I have already expressed, I feel I cannot interfere.'

143

Elizabeth Robinson told the court that she had been coming up Hyde Road on the afternoon of the 18th and had witnessed the affray. 'I saw that man there – the one with the curly hair.' She pointed out Allen. 'He had a revolver in each hand, but I didn't see him doing anything.'

The same applied to Patrick Kelly (Galway). She had seen him among the crowd of Fenians. John Carroll she had seen throwing stones, while Michael Kennedy had fired a revolver, the ball striking the arch. She had noticed Gould standing near the right-hand horse, holding a gun.

Henry Slack, cab proprietor, said he had seen a man with a large stone on top of the van. When asked to point him out, the witness, after a lengthy pause, indicated Thomas Maguire.

'I have no doubt that it was him', said Slack, 'although he was dressed differently then. He had a loose slop on.'

Josiah Munn, a cab driver employed by Slack, said he had driven up Hyde Road soon after the van, and saw Allen, Nugent, William Martin and Thomas Maguire at the scene of the outrage.

Another witness, George Partridge, identified Allen and Larkin, adding that he had been present in court on the day Kelly and Deasy were remanded, and had noticed Larkin among the spectators in the gallery. Larkin, he said, had left rather hurriedly on hearing the result. Noting that the witness had only one eye, Mr. Cottingham asked him, pointing to a clock high on the wall,

'What o'clock is it?'

'Twenty-one minutes past two', answered Partridge smartly.

'A very fair way of testing the fact', observed Mr. Fowler.

Allen, William Martin and John Carroll were identified by another witness, William Carrington. Then, after an application by Mr. Roberts, the prosecution withdrew its case against Patrick Kelly (Leitrim) for lack of evidence.

Witness Edwin Walton claimed to have seen Larkin on top of the van with a stone handed up to him by another man. Also on the roof was Carroll. Walton said he had seen Allen brandishing his brace of pistols. Nugent was another Fenian he identified.

During the questioning of the witness there was hissing from the gallery, which was silenced when Mr. Fowler again threatened to clear the court. Those responsible were referred to by Mr. Roberts as the 'swell mob.' On hearing a disparaging remark made about him, Allen angrily took up a fighting attitude.

Walton's evidence seemed to cause some commotion amongst the prisoners, who whispered together in an agitated manner while he was in the witness box.

In answer to Mr. Cottingham's question, Walton admitted that he had carried a loaded gun into court with him.

'I carried it at the suggestion of the police, and I will use it if necessary for my own protection.'

Asked if he had ever expressed an opinion concerning his feelings towards Fenianism, the witness declined to answer.

'Since you knew rewards were being offered, I suppose you have been very active in identifying prisoners?' suggested Mr. Cottingham.

'As an Englishman I have tried to do my best in pointing out all who were concerned in the riot that I know of', replied Walton, who denied having said, while he was at the police station, that he would personally like to hang every last one of the prisoners.

At this there was hissing from some of those in the dock. Walton then admitted that after Larkin was captured, he had said to him,

'I have never seen a man hanged, but if you are I'll see you.'

'And I have no doubt that you would carry out your promise', said Mr. Roberts.

'Yes, I intend to do so', replied the witness, quite brazenly.

'Good God! What wretches do live. Have you a family?'

'Yes', replied the witness. 'A wife I respect and a mother and a sister whom I support.'

'And have you taken tickets for reserved seats for them all to see the exhibition?'

'No sir.'

Allen then shouted from the dock, 'It will require a better man than you are to hang me!'

This only brought derisive laughter from the majority of the spectators.

On the following morning the first witness to be called was Robert Hunter, the young man who had jumped on Allen's back in the railway yard. He immediately identified not only Allen, but Larkin, Martin and Michael Maguire.

'Do you mean me?' asked Maguire.

'Yes', replied Hunter.

The witness then denied having expressed the sentiment that all the captured Fenians ought to be hanged.

'What I said was – I could hang Allen for what I saw him do.'

'You are a bad one', Mr. Roberts told him.

145

'Don't say that Mr. Roberts', interrupted the magistrate. 'He has given his evidence very fairly.'

'He has expressed his opinion', snapped Roberts, 'and I shall express mine.'

Joseph Smith, who told the court that he worked in Beyer, Peacock's boiler shop and lived near the Hyde Road bridge, said he had been at home on the day the van was stopped and had gone to his window when he heard what sounded like a pistol shot. He had seen two men with guns standing by the arch. These he identified as Allen and Nugent.

A witness named Charles Thomas, when asked if he knew anything about Fenianism, replied,

'Yes, I have read a deal about it. I believe they are a lot who want to upset the country and murder anyone who resists them. They proved themselves to be so on the 18th of September.'

John Taylor, a police officer, stated that he had seen the prisoner Hugh Foley standing on the bank with a revolver in his hand. He had also noticed a man with a crutch, but could not swear that it was John Bacon. However, as Taylor's evidence was uncorroborated, Foley was released at the end of the day's proceedings.

Next day several new prisoners were brought into court. They were the would-be defence witnesses who had themselves been placed under arrest, and gave their names as: Robert Nugent (father of the prisoner John F. Nugent), William Murphy, Thomas Johnson, Timothy Featherstone and Daniel Lynch. Mr. Cottingham defended the last two. Mr. Ambler appeared for Murphy, Mr. Ward for Nugent and Mr. Roberts for Johnson.

'Before my friend opens the case for the prosecution', said Mr. Cottingham, 'I have an application to make. It is that the prisoners be remanded for a week, this also to include the men against whom the prosecution has closed.'

'I am instructed to make the same application', said Mr. Roberts. 'We are not yet prepared to go into a proper defence. I have a list of twenty witnesses, some in Ashton-under-Lyne, and I have not seen one of them yet.'

'You say you are unable to do justice to them?' asked Mr. Fowler.

'I have not got my proofs', replied Mr. Cottingham. 'I do not know what my witnesses are going to say.'

146

'That is the fault of the gentlemen who instruct you.'

The magistrate eventually agreed to allow the defence one day's grace only, but added that although evidence for the defence need not be heard that day, he still intended to hear from the prosecution with regard to the new prisoners, and witnesses were called to swear to their presence at the scene of the attack.

In identifying Murphy, James Kennedy, a mechanic, said he remembered him clearly because just prior to the van being stopped he had been in the Railway Inn, and Murphy had held out his mug of beer and invited him to 'sup'. The prisoner was subsequently identified by other witnesses as one of those who had hurled stones at the police and at the side of the van, as also were the other accused.

Next day, Mr. Cottingham, before calling evidence for the defence, mentioned that the court had witnessed the humiliating spectacle of men in irons, against whom not a particle of evidence existed, and the dismissal of several such prisoners proved this.

'There have never been irons on them', said Mr. Fowler. 'They were handcuffed.'

'I am at a loss to see the distinction', replied Mr. Cottingham. 'I must say, since I have been interrupted by the bench, that it is the first time in civilised English history that we have seen British subjects brought up for their trial in irons or handcuffs and tried beneath the bayonets of the military.'

'That is not so', said Mr. Fowler. 'The Liverpool pirates were tried in irons in the Queen's Bench.'

'That sir, was an exceptional case.'

'So is this', snapped Fowler.

'They were Americans I believe', said Mr. Cottingham. 'But I am glad sir that you have found a precedent. A precedent, but not a justification. I can only repeat that you were forced to dismiss some of these men whom you had in handcuffs. And sir, I should have been glad if you had accompanied their dismissal with some expression of regret for the injury they had suffered!'

Now it was the turn of the defence. The first witness called was William McConnell, chairmaker, who stated that he was not even an acquaintance, let alone a friend, of the prisoner John Brennan. McConnell then swore to having seen Brennan in Cable Street on the afternoon of the 18th of September. Later that day he had seen him again in Swan Street, Shudehill, at around 4pm.

The employer of Thomas Johnson stated that the prisoner had been working for him as a pavior in Gorton on the 18th, and had not been out of his sight from six o'clock in the morning until six-thirty that night. [A statement which gives some idea of the harshness of the life of a working man in those days.] This testimony was corroborated by another pavior named Jeffreys, who claimed that Johnson had not moved more than ten yards away from him all day.

Mary Burn, jack tenter, said that she had seen Brennan, a clothes dealer, at twenty minutes to four, and again ten minutes later in Oak Street, Shudehill, on the day referred to. Three further witnesses gave evidence on Brennan's behalf.

William Hadfield, potato salesman, and Patrick Featherstone, a porter at the Oldham Road potato market, stood witness for Patrick Kelly (Galway), Featherstone raising a laugh among the spectators when he told the court that the prisoner had helped him bag potatoes from 3–45 until 4–15pm, during which time Kelly was 'putting in the toppers'. Asked to explain, he said that the term 'topping' referred to placing the best potatoes at the top of each sack. Michael Monaghan, Edward Sweeney and Patrick Ryan, all market men, also gave evidence to show that Kelly had been at the Oldham Road potato market all day on 18 September.

During the remainder of that week further witnesses were produced by the defence, several more prisoners subsequently being dismissed.

William Gould, who had doggedly refused either to defend himself or to be defended by anyone other than Ernest Jones, did, however, lodge a complaint regarding the manner in which he had been identified by witnesses at the police station, where, he claimed, he had been paraded before them in handcuffs and leg irons.

'Give me the names of any witness you wish to call to support this claim', said Mr. Fowler.

'You expect a prisoner to give names of officers of the police?' Receiving no reply to this, Gould said,

'Very well, I wish to call the policeman who locked me up in the cell and the officer in charge of the station. I cannot give their names. I don't suppose justice is intended here, but I'll give you the chance of showing it.'

A police constable was placed on the witness stand, but little or nothing could be elicited from him to substantiate the prisoner's claim. Then Gould lost his temper. 'This is not a court of justice. It's enough to make a man wild. How can I cross-examine with another man chained to me?'

Mr. Fowler said that all the remaining prisoners had been sworn to by the witnesses so as to establish a *prima facie* case against them. He then formally committed them to stand trial for 'Wilful Murder'.

148

At the Coroner's Court on the following Monday, the adjourned inquiry into the death of Sergeant Brett was resumed, and a verdict of 'Wilful Murder' returned against William O'Meara Allen and others unknown.

James and Mary Foley, the Irish couple on remand charged with threatening a witness, were brought up in court again, when their solicitor, Mr. Roberts, repeated his request that they be discharged.

The victim, Ellis, seemed very much changed in appearance, and claimed that the whole affair had had an adverse effect on his health. The fact that he lived in Hyde Road, surrounded by Irish neighbours, had not helped, and he told the court that he still feared for his life. The decline in his health had been accompanied not only by a loss of appetite, but also a loss of memory, for his subsequent refusal to testify against Hugh Foley had resulted in the latter's discharge. Ellis was one of several witnesses whom the police complained had not the courage to repeat in the witness box what they had been only too eager to say when identifying the prisoners.

In applying for compensation, Ellis pointed out that he had been unfit to work since the Foleys had threatened him. He was informed by the Clerk of the Court that this was not the proper place to make such an application.

The pugnacious Irish pair were told they would have to find sureties of £50 each, and also enter into their own cognizance for £100 to keep the peace for six months.

The decision of the magistrates to take no action regarding the manacles may have seemed inhuman to some, but the discovery of a number of half-bricks and other missiles, left behind in the public gallery of the court, caused many to change their views. Strong rumour had it that some of the most desperate Fenians were still at large.

In nearby Stockport, speculation was rife regarding the supposed designs of members of the Brotherhood in that town. In consequence, a day and night guard was posted on the armoury. After a large body of Irishmen had congregated in a public house, a Fenian meeting of over 300 men was held just outside Middlesbrough. It was eventually broken up by a handful of policemen without any breach of the peace occurring.

The attack on the van had been most untimely, as far as some Fenians were concerned, for it was now revealed that the Government

149

had actually been in the process of arranging to remit the unexpired terms of the sentences passed on some of the less notorious Fenians then in English gaols. In return, the released prisoners were required to emigrate to New Zealand and remain there permanently, since there could be no question of their ever being allowed to return to Ireland.

It was not just a rumour, for some of the convicts to whom it applied had already been in touch with their families and friends on the subject. The outrage at Manchester, however, caused the plan to be postponed indefinitely, and also served to bring home clearly to the Government that Fenianism, far from fizzling out, was still a danger to the peace of the country.

One Fenian who would most certainly not have been considered for parole was Jeremiah O'Donovan Rossa, who was still giving trouble to his gaolers at Millbank, and being flogged repeatedly for his pains.

1. A portrait of Theobald Wolfe Tone.

2. The surrender of French General Humbert to General Lake at Ballinamuck, on 8 September, 1798.

3. The executioner holds Robert Emmet's head aloft, after it had been severed from his still-warm body, following his hanging.

4. Destitution in Ireland – the failure of the potato crop in 1846.

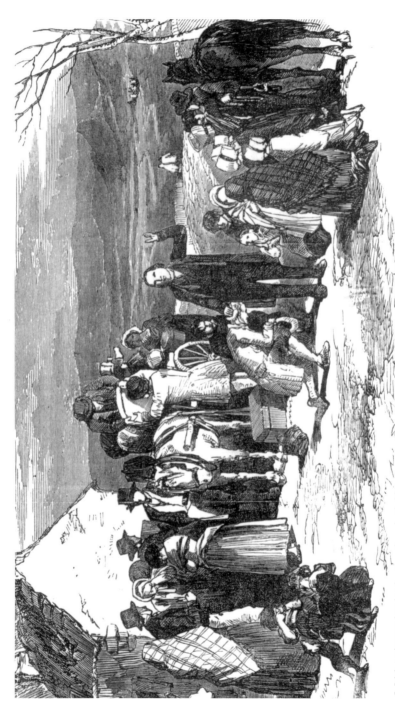

5. Irish emigrants leaving home – the priest's blessing.

6. The departure of the *Nimrod* and *Athlone* steamers, with emigrants on board, bound for Liverpool.

7. Irish emigrants preparing to leave Queenstown Harbour for the voyage to America.

8. The quarter-deck of an emigrant ship just before departure – the roll call.

9. Dancing between decks – a perfect example of the unquenchable Irish spirit – happy to be escaping the death, disease and poverty caused by the potato famine, with hope for the future.

10. Above: William Smith O'Brien.

11. Below: James Stephens – the Father of Fenianism.

12. John Mitchel, from a photograph taken in the last year of life.

13. Jeremiah O'Donovan Rossa.

14. John Devoy

15. Thomas Clarke Luby.

16. John O'Leary.

17. Colonel John O'Mahoney.

18. Michael Doheny.

19. Charles Kickham.

20. The Richmond Bridewell, from where James Stephens made his escape.

21. The Fenian insurrection: The Police barracks at Kilmallock, County Limerick.

22. The Fenian Insurrection: A fire-fight with the police at Tallaght, Dublin.

23. A scene in the courtyard of Dublin Castle. Bringing in the Fenian prisoners on the day after the uprising.

24. The American Fenian ship *"Erin's Hope"* saluting the raising of the green flag.

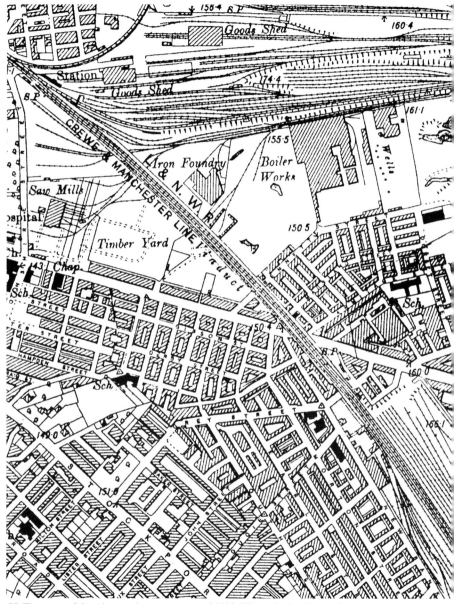

25. The scene of the crime as shown on a map of 1893. Where the London to Manchester Railway line abo crosses Hyde Road is where the ambush of the police van took place on 18 September, 1867. The short dis from the Belle Vue Prison can be judged. Although there had been much new building north of Hyde Road the 26 years since the outrage, a brick field can still be seen towards Ashton Road – now called Ashton Ol

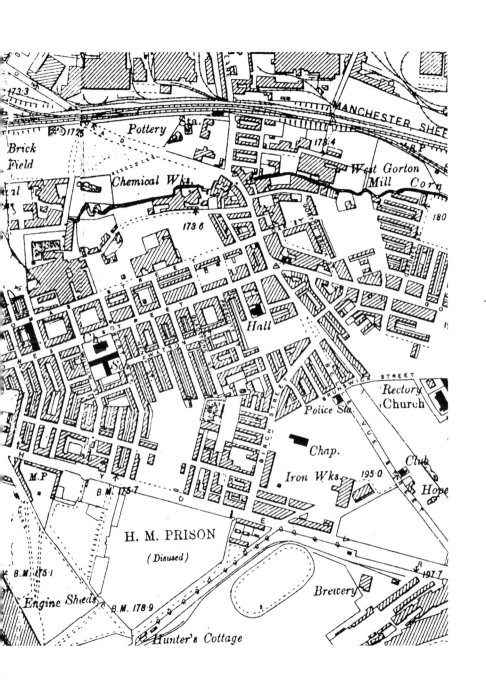

26. Outrage on the streets of Manchester – gunsmoke fills the air, bullets and stones fly, women scream and
terrified horses rear up as the desperadoes attack the police van. The dramatic rescue of two high-ranking F
officers, which resulted in the death of a very brave police officer, is captured on a steel engraving of the tin

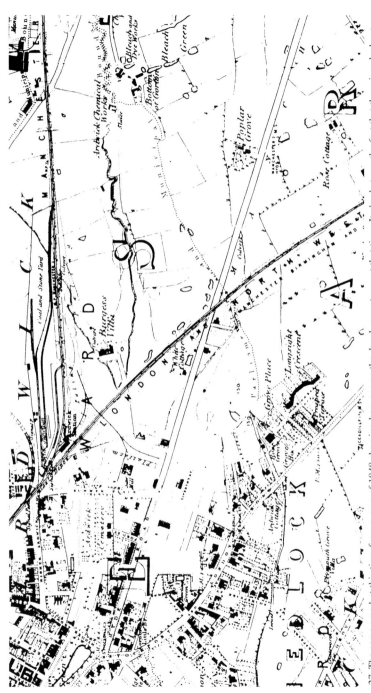

27. The same area but this time from a map of 1848 showing how sparse the development was at that time. It also betrays the fact that the prison had not then been built, the area being almost completely rural in nature. A far cry from its later, but dubious claim to fame as the most densely populated area in the world. The closely-packed two-up, two-down cottages housed a greater density of people per square mile – rivalled only by Shanghai in China.

28. Sergeant Charles Brett, who was shot on the 18th September, 1867.
(From a photograph by J. Eastham, Manchester.)

29. The funeral of Sergeant Brett, with sympathetic crowds lining the streets of Manchester.

In
Affectionate
Remembrance of
SERGEANT
CHARLES BRETT
OF THE MANCHESTER POLICE FORCE
WHO DIED IN THE DISCHARGE
OF HIS DUTY AT HYDE ROAD
SEPT 18TH 1867
IN THE 52ND YEAR OF HIS AGE
I DARE NOT I MUST DO MY DUTY
ALSO MARY,
RELICT OF THE ABOVE,
WHO DIED DEC 5TH 1893,
AGED 80 YEARS.

ALSO WILLIAM BRETT,
FATHER OF THE ABOVE,

ALSO ANNIE ATKIN,

30. "I dare not – I must do my duty." The inscription on the headstone of Police Sergeant Charles Brett in Harpurhey Cemetery, North Manchester.

31. The pub on Oak Street, Shudehill, Manchester – as it is today – close to where Kelly and Deasy were apprehended. *(Photograph by Jack Ireland).*

32. The site where Condon was obstructed by two large women and captured by a mob. The original footbridge, over the Ashton Canal, was replaced many years ago. *(Photo by G. Turner).*

33. A bridge over the Rochdale Canal, Manchester in 2001 showing the construction of a typical canal bridge, as it would have been at the time of Condon's capture. *(Photographs by Jack Ireland).*

34. A view over the canal bridge showing the narrowness of the footpath.

35. The courtroom at Manchester Assizes during the Fenian trials.

36. Monsignor Gadd, who ministered diligently to the condemned men.

37. An artist's impression of some of the main characters in the Fenian tragedy that was the Manchester Outrage on 18th September, 1867. This representation of them, together with an account of the events of that fateful day, written by Condon, was published in *The Irish World and American Industrial Liberator* in 1908.

38. The horrific scene of death and destruction two hours after the Clerkenwell expolsion.

39. A recent memorial placed close to the Hyde Road bridge.

40. The monument to the Manchester Martyrs, Moston Cemetery, Manchester.

CHAPTER 18

Further troubles –
the search for Colonel Kelly

O n the day the Fenian prisoners were committed for trial, a further outrage occurred, this time in London, which, rightly or wrongly, was also attributed to the Fenian Brotherhood.

In the early hours of the morning, three bandsmen belonging to a guards regiment were walking along a Bloomsbury street after leaving Weston's Music Hall, when they encountered a group of Irishmen who had apparently just left a public house in High Street, Holborn, a suspected Fenian haunt kept by a widow named Brown.

The bandsmen were not in uniform, and the Irishmen, possibly believing them to be plain clothes detectives, judging by their height and bearing, allegedly attacked them in the street. Though the fight was fought mainly with fists, someone produced a revolver, and unfortunately one of the bandsmen was shot. The Irishmen ran off and the wounded man was conveyed to University College Hospital. His name was Edwin McDonnell, and after appearing to recover somewhat, the bandsman suffered a sudden relapse and died a few days later.

A reward was immediately offered and a description put out as follows:

**THE MURDERER IS SUPPOSED TO BE TALL,
WITH SHORT LIGHT-COLOURED HAIR AND
IS RESPECTABLY DRESSED.**

An Irishman named John Groves was soon picked up and taken to Bow Street under heavy guard, mounted police with cutlasses accompanying the prison van.

Great excitement prevailed in the beerhouses around Bloomsbury all that week, and a man believed to be a police informer was set upon and brutally beaten at almost the exact spot where Bandsman McDonnell had been shot.

When Groves was brought up for examination prior to his possible committal, it was stated that the character of a woman named Jenman, who had given evidence at the inquest, was now very much in question. Without her the case against the prisoner would be extremely flimsy. It was therefore found necessary, reluctantly to discharge him.

151

Though no proof could be found to show that the soldier's death had been caused by a Fenian bullet, the incident had the effect of causing a measure of panic, and the rumours began to fly thick and fast again. One of the most persistent was that information had been received by the police 'from a reliable source' of an intended Fenian swoop on the volunteer arms being kept at various storehouses in London. Immediate precautions were taken, the authorities bringing in large detachments of troops to stand guard until the arms could be removed to the Tower.

In Liverpool it was rumoured that the Fenians had drawn up an elaborate plan not only to plunder the armoury and gunmakers' establishments, but also to attack the local gasworks with a view to plunging the city into darkness, a move supposedly calculated to assist them in their evil designs.

The appearance of a detachment of the 8th Hussars in Rochdale, Lancashire, was the cause of many stories of Fenian outrages in that area, with a strong rumour going round that several policemen had been shot. The soldiers, it turned out, were merely passing through the town on their way from Manchester to Burnley, and the claims of policemen being shot were totally false. The police, in fact, were at that time engaging in a little target practice of their own – with Colt revolvers issued by the Government for use in an emergency.

Stories intended to show the Fenians in as bad a light as possible continued to appear in some newspapers – a notable one concerned an Irishman named Ryan, who was serving a sentence in Longford Gaol for attempting to seduce soldiers from their allegiance to the Crown. He reportedly asked a turnkey to read to him a newspaper account of the Manchester rescue. Allegedly, Ryan then repaid this kindness by reporting the incident to the Governor of the prison, with the result that the warder was ultimately dismissed from his position.

In the Yorkshire town of Halifax, a very well attended meeting of Irishmen was held, not for any illegal purpose, but to discuss the uneasy situation and to reassure the public that not all Irish residents of Halifax were in sympathy with Fenianism. Several speeches to this effect were delivered, and Fenian activities in general and the Manchester killing in particular were thoroughly condemned. Quite a number of English people were present and testified to the warm feeling existing between the two nationalities in the town.

However, it could hardly be said that the situation was as serene in other towns as it was at Halifax. Because of the possibility of further Fenian activity in the North of England, the 70th (The East Surrey

152

Regiment), stationed at Aldershot and commanded by Lieutenant-Colonel William Cooper, was placed under orders to leave for Carlisle, Bury and Ashton-under-Lyne. There were strong indications of Fenian unrest in those towns and the surrounding areas. Other regiments put on stand-by were the 54th (The Dorset Regiment), the 56th (The Essex Regiment), the 86th (The Royal Ulster Rifles) and the 72nd (The Seaforth Highlanders).

However, apart from a minor explosion of Greek fire on the roof of the Police Court at Chester, following which the neck of a three-ounce bottle smelling strongly of sulphur was discovered, almost nothing of an 'outrageous' nature was reported.

The Lancashire mill town of Oldham, seven miles from Manchester and close to the Yorkshire border, was certainly not without its Fenian element. Following the Manchester rescue many rumours were abroad as to the intentions of local Fenians, after reports of men drilling in fields and the usual speculation regarding the volunteer arms began to circulate. A particularly prevalent rumour was that the Market Hall would be set on fire and the railway lines torn up. All this, of course, was wild supposition.

The fears of the locals, however, were not entirely without foundation, for on a Wednesday in early October, a member of the public called at the Oldham police station and reported having seen a number of men, in groups of 5 or 6, and numbering altogether about 50, going up Ripponden Road in the direction of Watersheddings, between 11 and midnight on the previous evening. Seeing their faces under a gas-lamp the informant was quite sure that all appeared to be Irish. It struck him as very strange that so many men should be going the same way at one time and so late at night, especially as they were heading for an isolated part of the town.

On receiving this information, the Chief Constable issued instructions to all policemen out on the beat to report anything of a suspicious nature at once. The following day at around one o'clock in the morning, P.C. Reeve, working out of the Townfield police station, was on duty at the top of Greenacres Moor, when he heard a voice shout out the words 'fix bayonets', then, 'charge bayonets'. Going down a steep hill in the direction of the shouting, Reeve reached a spot known as Millbottom, then, concealing himself behind a hedge, he was able to peer into a field where a number of men, some with rifles, others with revolvers, were drilling under the command of a man giving military instructions. The constable crept along behind the hedge until he reached a gate leading into the field, where he remained for some

153

time observing the drilling. At this point he was about 50 yards away and could not distinguish any faces.

When the command 'charge' was given again P.C. Reeve realised that the men were rushing in his direction, and concluded very wisely that the time had come to make a strategic withdrawal. Fifteen minutes later he arrived, breathless, at the Townfield station situated at the bottom of the moor, and blurted out his story. From there Reeve was driven by police wagon to the Town Hall. The Chief Constable soon arrived there too, having been 'knocked up'. He quickly issued orders for the immediate summoning of all available men from other divisions in the area.

As soon as they were mustered, more than forty policemen, armed with cutlasses and revolvers, set off for Millbottom and on arrival surrounded the field. But valuable time had been lost. There was no sign of any Fenians, and though the police divided themselves into smaller groups and thoroughly searched all adjoining roads and fields, no trace of the phantom drillers could be found. At dawn the 'bobbies' made their weary way back over the moor.

News of P.C. Reeves' discovery quickly spread, causing great excitement, and resulted in several awkward incidents. Any gathering of men was instantly viewed with the greatest scepticism. One typical case concerned a group of keen dog fanciers, up at the crack of dawn to exercise their animals for a coming event. In keeping them under surveillance, the police spent some considerable time dodging behind trees and bushes before finally realising that the objects of their suspicions were no more than a bunch of enthusiastic sportsmen.

Around this time, the authorities came across what they considered to be a positive lead to the whereabouts of Colonel Kelly. Again the town of Oldham was involved.

From information passed on to the police it was ascertained that for a period just prior to the outbreak of violence in Ireland earlier in the year [a time, incidentally, when Kelly's exact whereabouts were in some doubt] a large number of letters addressed to a person named Kelly were received at a local post office, where it was directed they should remain until called for. Mr. Andrews, the postmaster, clearly remembered the man who had collected them and immediately recognised the face when he saw it again on a 'wanted' poster following the Manchester rescue. If Kelly had, in fact, been in Oldham earlier in the year, he would obviously have been familiar with the area and might well have decided to head that way after Condon's plan to transport him to Ashton-under-Lyne had come unstuck.

An immediate search was mounted throughout the heavily-populated Irish districts of the town, but no trace of the Fenian leader was discovered. The searchers, however, were now convinced that Kelly had been resident in Oldham at one time, and information was elicited from some of those questioned that a group of Irishmen were lodged at a house near the Oldham Waterworks, a couple of miles out of town, near the Yorkshire border. Apparently, these men kept in close touch with their countrymen in Oldham, and it was conjectured that an isolated community on the edge of the moors might be the ideal spot to hide a couple of wanted men.

A detachment of the County Constabulary and Oldham Borough police formed the party which set out late on a Saturday night at the end of September, led by an officer who claimed to have a good knowledge of the area. The guide, however, soon became hopelessly lost, and contrived to fall headlong down an embankment after losing his footing in the dark. He was badly shaken, but otherwise uninjured.

Eventually, their destination was reached and the house surrounded. There were no lights burning, the occupants having retired for the night. They were knocked up and subjected to close scrutiny, but it soon became clear that none of the sleepy Irishmen answered the fugitive's descriptions, nor were the police able to obtain any helpful information from them, though they retained their suspicions. The owner of the house was an Englishman, but his wife was Irish, as were all of his lodgers, and it was firmly believed that the premises were, or had been, a harbour for wanted Fenians.

The police, disappointed and weary from their long hike, ended the night in a country pub, where they drowned their sorrows and tried to forget the lost reward money to which the capture of the notorious Colonel Kelly would have entitled them.

Near the end of October, just prior to the sitting of a special commission to hear the case against the Manchester Fenians, another strange story concerning Kelly began to circulate. On Sunday 27 October, the two appointed judges arrived in Manchester and attended a service at the Cathedral, being escorted from their lodgings by the High Sheriff, Mr. T. Dicconson.

On the return journey the carriage was passing through the area know as Strangeways when a well-dressed man stepped between the lance-bearing escorts and raised his hand. The window was lowered and the stranger handed to one of the occupants, Mr. Justice Mellor, a silver pocket watch, after which he quickly disappeared into the crowd, although he had been seen by two detectives accompanying the party. The watch was passed to the Under Sheriff, who gave it into the possession of the County Constabulary.

Foremost among the many rumours that followed this odd occurrence was one to the effect that the mysterious stranger had been none other than the escaped Fenian leader himself. It was believed that he had shown himself in public and stopped the High Sheriff's carriage to hand over his pocket watch to prove his identity and let the authorities know that he had remained in the city under their very noses.

Whatever the truth regarding the watch and its owner, it is doubtful that Kelly was the man who intercepted the carriage. Perhaps one of the occupants of the carriage had dropped his timepiece when leaving the Cathedral and a member of the public was merely returning it. As usual, however, the incident was embroidered into another fanciful tale guaranteed to perpetuate the growing legend of the ubiquitous Colonel Kelly.

CHAPTER 19

McAuliffe's letter

O f the missing Kelly and Deasy there was still not a trace, though rumours were rife. Several Irish newspapers published a letter, supposedly written by Colonel Kelly, in which the writer gloated over his escape from Manchester.

In *The Nation* it was reported that a committee was in the process of being formed in Manchester to receive subscriptions *'for the purpose of obtaining a fair trial for our unfortunate countrymen so ruthlessly treated by the white-livered police of that city.'*

Another paper, *The Irishman*, stated,

Small are the chances of mercy the men accused of partaking in the daring act that liberated Colonel Kelly will receive at the hands of the English law, or from the audience of an English court. The most unseemly and disgraceful scenes have already taken place amongst the mob who thronged that at Manchester during the week. If the advocates defending the prisoners dared to discharge their duty with zeal, earnestness and honesty, they were hissed and hooted.

Scratch a Russian, says the well-known proverb, and beneath the skin you will find a Tartar. Take the skin off an Anglo-Saxon of the lower type and a ruffian stands before you, if an Irishman is concerned. There are indeed Englishmen whose sympathies are more generous, whose feelings are more Catholic, but there are few of them to be found either as witnesses during this investigation or as attendants in court.

In the same newspaper was a letter headed, *"Man. City Gaol 29th Sept."*, and signed *"John Francis McAuliffe, Knight of St. Gregory."* No explanation was given as to how it had been smuggled from the prison and reached Ireland, but as a sample of the kind of fare being served up in the columns of a section of the Irish press at that time it is well worth reproducing. McAuliffe wrote:

On Tuesday night 17th of Sept., I came to Manchester to see a lady friend of mine who is about to leave the country. Soon after my arrival I met her, spent some time in her company, then parted and met her again at 10am next morning, when she agreed to meet me at 3pm in the lower part of Bridge Street, but – much to my astonishment – about five minutes before the appointed time, I happened to be passing the City Court when three policemen rushed on me and dragged me into the station like a dog.

157

After getting me inside one fellow cried out to me, 'Come now you ruffian, turn up that revolver.' A second cried, 'Hold his hands. He's a dangerous man', while the third one said, 'Strip and search him. He has documents on him.'

At all events, when the police saw that they were disappointed in not finding anything on my person that would assist them in procuring a conviction, either against myself or anyone else, they knocked me down, kicked and almost strangled me to death, from the effects of which I have spit an immense quantity of blood.

After all this inhuman work was over I was flung into a filthy cell, and after being about two hours in this beastly kennel my next visitor was a stalwart detective of the Royal Dublin Blues, who tried to get up my sleeve with the cunning of a fox. On entering my cell this 'peace officer' cried out: "Ah my poor McAuliffe, are you here? Indeed Mr McAuliffe, we might expect better things from you. They will hang you this time. But if you give me any information that will lead to the arrest and conviction of the parties who committed this outrageous deed I will set you at liberty and get you as much money as will place you in an independent position for the remainder of your life."

I assure you that such talk just astonished an innocent man like myself. So much so indeed that I said, "What deed do you mean sir?" – "Ah", he said, "you know all about it. And you had better tell us or you're done for this time."

I then turned away from the miscreant with a scornful look and told him I could not understand his insinuations.

"Well", he said. "Colonel Kelly and Captain Deasy are rescued, and a man and a horse shot. So if you give us any information on the subject you will be a happy man for the rest of your life." I asked him if he wanted a second Massey.

"Yes indeed", said he, "Mr Massey is a conscientious, honest man, and another like him at present would be very useful in bringing these murderous villains to justice." "Well", said I, "You must go to hell to find him, because you have not got one in me."

In any case, even if I'd wished to I could not have helped him, for I have never in all my life met one of those daring and invisible Fenians.

On the 19th, we were all paraded in the police station, guarded by cavalry and infantry soldiers, while all sorts of people, including prostitutes, were allowed to inspect us and point out those whom they saw amongst the crowd at the scene of action. As a matter of course some pointed myself out as having taken a leading part in breaking the

158

van, shooting horses etc. But naturally enough the police came to the conclusion that the fact of them identifying me, who had been in the lock-up an hour before the occurrence took place, would weaken the evidence of those witnesses against the other men. Consequently, they locked me up and never paraded me for examination again.

After all these preliminary matters were gone through, we were all, about 50 in number, chained together and escorted to the city gaol by a regiment of cavalry, three companies of foot soldiers, and about 500 police armed with revolvers.

After arriving at the gaol we were locked up in separate cells, deprived of all recreation, of going to Mass on Sundays, and of all privileges to which prison rules (now hanging in my cell), entitle the most degraded of human beings. Our friends would not be allowed to bring us food, clean linen, or any necessities which we badly required. In a word, from the 19th till the 27th they deprived us of everything but that which was beyond their reach – communicating with God by solemn prayer, which is the Catholic's only consolation when he is confined within the dungeon walls of his country's rulers.

After spending those eight days as above described they brought us forth from our dens on Thursday morning last, chained us together, and as usual escorted us with a heavy guard to the courthouse.

The chains were taken off when we got there, but we were then hand-cuffed together and taken before the bench in that manner – a thing never known before in any Christian country.

When that day's proceedings were over we were taken to the head police station and twelve of us put into each small cell, when we had to lie on the flags like so many pigs till morning. Then we were chained up again and escorted to the courthouse by [the] military and police as usual.

After I was remanded, through my case being different from the others, I have heard nothing of them, and to my grief they will probably leave here without my having the pleasure of seeing or speaking to them. Language could not explain to you or your readers the cruel indignities to which we are subjected since our arrest.

On 14 October four more prisoners were brought up at the police court on a charge of complicity in the murder of Sergeant Brett. They were Daniel Reddin, Francis Mc'Namara, William Joseph Brophy and James O'Brennan Chambers, the last two having been arrested in Liverpool on the previous Friday night. As no evidence was produced against Mc'Namara he was set free.

The prosecution in this instance was undertaken by Mr. W.H. Talbot, Assistant Town Clerk, Mr. W.P. Roberts defending the prisoners.

Coach proprietor Henry Wilson Slack testified to having seen Reddin on the banking beyond the arch.

'He was giving orders to the others in the manner of an army officer. Waving his arms around and shouting to the men who were attacking the rear of the van.'

The witness, however, had not been near enough to hear what Reddin called out.

The prisoner was also identified by John Knowles, grocer, of Hyde Road, who could not say what Reddin was doing 'because the confusion was so great.'

'The fact is', said Mr. Roberts, 'you saw him doing nothing that you can speak of.'

'I did not. I had enough to do to mind myself.'

'But you are quite certain that you saw Reddin among the men attacking the van?' Mr. Talbot asked the witness.

'Yes sir, I'm certain.'

It became fairly clear, however, that Knowles was not so certain in his identification as he claimed, for under further cross-examination he was forced to admit that he had been in some doubt when confronted by the prisoner in the cells a week before. On seeing him again, however, he had now come to the conclusion that Reddin was one of the rioters.

Emma Halliday, who at first stated that she could not identify any of the new prisoners, suddenly pointed to Reddin, and said,

'Oh yes, the third man there. I saw him throwing stones at people.'

Reddin was further identified by Thomas Sperry, who said he had seen him running through the Midland Railway yard with some others, in the direction of Ashton Road.

'I spoke to the men. One of them said there'd been a prize fight and they were running away from the law. I told Reddin he could get over the wall easier at a point lower down the yard.'

The witness could not remember what Reddin was wearing, except for his boots, which were made of a peculiar-coloured leather.

'Like those he has on now?' he was asked.

'Yes, similar. Those could be the ones.'

James O'Brennan Chambers was identified by George Pickup and also by P.C. Trueman, who claimed that the prisoner had thrown a stone which struck him on the back. He had also seen Chambers battering at the van door with big stones.

'I went to a public house in Liverpool last Friday night,' said

160

Trueman, 'and saw Chambers there. I recognised him at once. I then went outside and spoke to detectives, who went in and arrested him.'

Medwin Sheriff of Kay Street, West Gorton, stone carver and mason, said that on the 18th September he was in Hyde Road. Several men prevented him from going through the archway. Revolvers were presented and stones thrown at him. He also saw Chambers throwing stones at people who were attempting to assist the police.

Ellen Cooper and John Beck swore they had seen William Brophy at the scene. Detective-Sergeant Torr stated that he had taken Brophy and Chambers into custody at a beerhouse in Adlington Street, Liverpool. They were drinking together and offered no resistance. All three prisoners pleaded not guilty, Brophy claiming that he could bring witnesses to prove he had been at work in Liverpool at Messrs. Blanes and Sons, Brunswick Street, on the day of the attack.

'And what is the nature of your alibi?' Chambers was asked.

'I was out of work and in search of a job all that day.'

On behalf of Reddin, Mrs. McKane of 16, Great Newton Street, Manchester, stated that the prisoner had lodged with her for six or seven weeks.

'On the day the van was stopped he was never out of the house for more than half-an-hour at a time. He worked as a plasterer for Morgan and Molloy, but he'd been discharged from his job on the Saturday before, and he was spending what little money he'd saved. He was drunk the whole of the day and went to bed at half-past four in the afternoon.'

According to Mrs. Hannah Maria Wright, who also rented a room from Mrs. McKane, Reddin had been in and out of the house all day on the 18th, returning finally around 4pm with another man with whom he had been drinking. Reddin was clearly intoxicated and was put to bed soon afterwards.

After the landlady's sister, Mrs. Esther Williams, had given supporting evidence, Lawrence Molloy, a tailor, living in Willoughby's Court, came to the witness stand and stated that he had seen Reddin going into the lodging house at five minutes past four in the afternoon.

'I remember looking at my clock just as he went in.'

'Were you drinking with him that day?' asked the magistrate.

'I had a glass with him, yes.'

'At what time?'

'Just after he went into the house at half-past – no, five-past-four.'

The witness' hasty correction brought laughter from the audience, most of whom obviously believed that the Irish were intent on sticking together at all costs.

161

John Shannon, of Blossom Street, Ancoats, said he had a slight acquaintance with Reddin, who was a 'well-conducted young man.' He had seen him in Ancoats Lane at five-past-four on the afternoon of the 18th, but could not say whether he was drunk or sober. Cross-examined by Mr. Talbot, the witness admitted that Reddin had been in the habit of coming to his house to see a man known as J.S. O'Donnell, who lodged there, but who had now disappeared.

'Did O'Donnell leave you on the night of 18th September?'

'He left to go to Liverpool to see a friend there, but I can't say for sure on what date.'

'You swore you saw the prisoner at five-past-four on 18th September, and yet you can't say when the lodger left you?'

'No sir.'

'Will you undertake to swear that he did not leave on the night of the 18th.'

'I believe it was a week after. I'm not accustomed to taking lodgers.'

The case was then adjourned, coming up again on the following Wednesday.

Mr. Roberts said he had sent to Liverpool for witnesses named by the prisoners, but that none would come to testify on Brophy's behalf unless they were subpoenaed. For Chambers he had four witnesses, one of whom would also speak for Brophy.

One of these, Mrs. Esther Rossiter, said her husband was a beerhouse keeper in Adlington Street, Liverpool. She continued:

'Between two and three o'clock on the afternoon of 18th September Chambers was in there drinking. Between six and seven the same evening I served Brophy with a pint of beer. About an hour after that, I heard about the attack on the police van at Manchester.'

Three other witnesses corroborated her story, the last of whom, Lucy Gavin, of Clifton Street, Liverpool, stated that Chambers occasionally stayed with her and her brother. Under cross-examination, the witness admitted that some of the walls of her house were adorned with pictures of Fenian officers.

The prisoners were committed for trial charged with "Wilful Murder".

Before the court broke up, Mr. Fowler announced that he had received several small sums from the public for the widow of Sergeant Brett. The Reverend W. Richardson and Captain Palin had also collected money, and Captain Elgee, Chief-Constable of Liverpool, had sent word that the men of the County Force had collected the sum of £32 for the widow. To his letter Captain Elgee had added a footnote:

I should be glad if you would inform Mrs. Brett that she and her family have the sincere sympathy of our entire force in the heavy affliction which has befallen them, and how much we respect and admire the gallantry and determination shown by Sergeant Brett in the defence of his prisoners.

At their meeting that week the Manchester Watch Committee awarded Mrs. Brett an annuity of 7/6d per week, the full amount authorised by an Act of Parliament to cover such cases, and Captain Palin received £100 from a Mr. Robert Barnes for Sergeant Brett's family.

CHAPTER 20
'God Save Ireland!'

I t was announced that the Attorney-General, Sir John Kerslake, would lead the prosecution team, while the defence received something of a set-back when it was learned that Mr. Isaac Butt, Q.C. would not, after all, be available to represent the prisoners as had been hoped.

The defence, in fact, was in some difficulty, and nowhere near well enough prepared for the fight ahead. During the week ending 26 October a letter was forwarded to the Home Office requesting that the trials be postponed until after Christmas. One defence attorney, however, did not agree with this and refused to put his signature to the letter. He was Mr. W. Bennett, whose chambers were in Bridge Street, Manchester, and who, in a following letter, assured the Home Secretary that he was quite ready to defend those prisoners for whom he had been retained.

These men, he stated, *will, I believe, be given a fair and impartial trial. I will not believe that an Englishman, having taken his oath, would do otherwise. There is not a point of law which has arisen during the hearing of the case that the mind of Mr. Roberts, or any other attorney, has not had ample time to grapple with.*

Why should my clients, who are ready to take their trial, and for whom alibis of an honest stamp will be proved, lie in gaol until after Christmas to suit the convenience of Mr. Roberts or anyone else?

This seemed a convincing argument, but on closer examination of the facts it would appear that Mr. Bennett was mistaken in taking such a stand, for an earlier communication from the Home Secretary had been received at the office of Mr. Roberts at Gresham Chambers, 44 Princess Street, Manchester, informing him that in addition to the already formidable army of prosecution witnesses, a further 25 had been found who would give evidence before the Special Commission.

It is altogether impossible, wrote Mr. Roberts in reply, *that proper defence can be made without time for inquiry and proper consultation with the prisoners, no two of whom can be seen at the same time. The supposed evidence corresponding with what these new witnesses would have said at the magistrates' court should have been sent to me at least a fortnight ago, as indeed was promised when the case was before the magistrates.*

The Home Secretary's reply was not long in coming:

I cannot in any way interfere with the opening of the Commission. I am informed that it is not necessary, but common as a matter of fairness, to give the names of new witnesses who may possibly be called. This has been done as soon as was practicable.

Your application by letter that the Government should bear the expenses of the defence cannot be entertained.

This application did not perhaps, deserve to be entertained, but the request for a postponement would seem to have been reasonable. The killing of Sergeant Brett had occurred only five weeks or so before. The prosecution was ready, but a section of the defence clearly was not, yet the Crown was insisting that the trial be got under way without delay. Irishmen everywhere remained firmly convinced that this unseemly haste only reflected the Government's determination not to allow the flame of public anger to die down by granting a postponement.

At a special meeting of the justices, held before the opening of the Commission, a resolution was passed rendering all citizens whose names appeared on the city's electoral roll liable to be sworn in as special constables during the trials.

Proceedings opened on Saturday 2 November at 10am. Two hours earlier a squadron of the 8th Hussars and two companies of the 72nd (The Seaforth Highlanders) mustered at the New Bailey Prison, where the prisoners were now held, to escort them to the Assize Court.

The Fenians, looking haggard and dejected, were all herded into one van, drawn up in the prison yard. The vehicle then proceeded along New Bailey Street. As well as the troops – almost enough of them to start a war – the van was also accompanied by Mr. H.L. Trafford, stipendiary magistrate, who was there to issue the necessary authorisation for action to be taken in the event of any major disturbance.

In addition to the military, a considerable force of armed policemen under Captain Sylvester, Chief Constable of Salford, was on duty at the prison gates and lined the streets up to Salford Bridge. On the Manchester side of the river the streets crawled with constables of the City Police Force, armed with revolvers, while men of the County Constabulary guarded the Assize Courts. The entire route was lined with the most motley assortment of civilians, both well-dressed and ragged, but no incident of any significance occurred.

The court was packed when Justices Blackburn and Mellor took their seats on the bench, although the ladies' galleries were kept

166

empty, two small fire appliances, known as *L'Extincteur,* being placed there. All standing room in court was quickly taken up, admission to the seats being by ticket only. The front row seats were occupied by the legal representatives, while the second and third rows, reserved for the press, were well-filled by reporters representing newspapers all over the country. Outside, a large crowd had assembled and stood around for the greater part of the day, watched by the soldiers on duty at the main entrance.

After further dismissals, the number of men charged now stood at twenty-six. They were: William O'Meara Allen, William Gould [O'Brien], Edward Shore [Condon], Michael Larkin, Patrick Kelly (Galway), Charles Moorhouse, John Martin, Michael Maguire, Thomas Maguire, John Brennan, John Francis Nugent, William Martin, Michael Joseph Boylan, John Carroll, Michael Kennedy, John Bacon, Henry Wilson, Thomas Ryan, Patrick Coffey, Thomas Johnson, Timothy Featherstone, Thomas Scalley, William Murphy, Daniel Reddin, James O'Brennan Chambers and William Brophy.

Seats were provided for the prisoners in four rows, each with an upright wand bearing the name of the occupant.

The following high-ranking citizens were sworn in as the Grand Jury, which was then the practice in this country, as it still is in America:

Sir Robert Tolver Gerrard, Bart. of Bryan (foreman); The Hon. A.F. Egerton, M.P., Worsley Old Hall; William Ince Anderton; Henry Tootal Broadhurst; Henry George Brunslow; John Cheetham, M.P. Stalybridge; Sir William Henry Fielden, Bart., Peniscowles; Sir Gilbert Greenall, M.P., Walton Hall, Warrington; John Tomlinson Hibbert, M.P., Urmston Grange; Robert Henry Norreys, Davyhulme Hall; John Platt, M.P., Werneth Park, Oldham; Richard Milne Redhead, Springfield, Seedley; Charles Hilditch Richards, Seymour Grove, Old Trafford; Clement Molyneux Royds; Samuel Henry Thompson; Benjamin Whitworth, M.P., Irwell House, Prestwich; Richard Mayor Wilson; Thomas E. Withington; William Raynor Wood, Singleton Lodge; and Nathan Worthington, Hollinwood, Oldham.

In his opening address to these gentlemen, all of whom would appear to have been persons of considerable means and position, Mr. Justice Blackburn described the scene of the attack on the van as 'a place chosen with considerable skill for the purpose.' He also gave it as his opinion that:

'To a certain extent, the facts of this case are plain and undeniable. A variety of crimes have been committed, including an attempt to rescue

167

prisoners in lawful custody and assaults upon the police in the execution of their duty – two men have been wounded.

'But the great crime into which you will principally have to inquire is the causing of the death of Charles Brett, and though the man who fired the shot is actually the man who committed the crime, everyone who aided and abetted is equally guilty of murder. As to one of the prisoners, Allen, there is strong evidence that he actually fired the shot. Of him I will say nothing. Because if he did fire it he is obviously guilty of murder. But as to each of the other prisoners it is for you to consider whether or not he was aiding and abetting in the crime.

'I must explain to you that it is not essential, to constitute the crime of murder, that the main object should have been to kill the particular person who lost his life. Murder is killing by malice aforethought, but that does not necessarily imply that there was an intention to kill a particular man. Both in law and in common sense it has always been held that when violence dangerous to human life is used for the purpose of committing an unlawful act and death is the result, then the crime is murder. And what one man did is the act of all who, in that common design, were aiding and assisting. And each, if you are convinced that he was there, is as guilty of murder as if he had fired the shot.'

The Judge's remarks, though of course quite correct according to law, did not bode well for the men in the dock.

It was left to the prosecution to decide in what form the bills against the prisoners should be presented to the Grand Jury. The prisoners could all be listed in one bill, or in batches. And it would be the duty of the Grand Jury to decide, after hearing the prosecution's side of the case only, whether or not the prisoners should stand trial. In the event of an affirmative decision the trials would begin without further delay.

After Mr. Justice Blackburn had completed his charge, the Grand Jury members retired from the courtroom. Mr. Digby Seymour, Q.C., then addressed the judge on behalf of the defence,

'I have an application to put before the justices. It is that the court should adjourn the hearing of any indictment which may be brought by the Grand Jury till tomorrow morning.

'I make this application under very peculiar and exceptional circumstances. Every effort had been made by the gentlemen who instruct me to put us in a position to meet the case on behalf of the prisoners, but as yet the preparations are not sufficiently completed to enable us to feel that we are ready to undertake that onerous and responsible duty. My learnéd friends and I have had no opportunity of consulting together and considering various important questions which may arise as to the course it may be incumbent on us to take'.

Mr. Blackburn, after conferring with Mr. Justice Mellor, replied,

'Mr. Seymour, it is impossible for us to form any opinion, or come to any decision on the course you propose until some bills have been found, and the pleas taken.'

Around noon, the Grand Jury returned to their seats and handed in a true bill against William O'Meara Allen, William Gould [O'Brien], Michael Larkin, Edward Shore [Condon] and Thomas Maguire.

These men, now minus handcuffs, were placed in the dock. Each pleaded not guilty. Mr. Seymour stated that, with Mr. Ernest Jones, he appeared on behalf of Allen, Shore and Gould; Mr. Sergeant O'Brien, along with Mr. Cottingham, for Larkin and Maguire.

Digby Seymour's earlier application for an adjournment until the following morning was granted and proceedings closed for that day.

In the course of the next day the Grand Jury found true bills against all the prisoners: for murder, felony and misdemeanor. The members were thanked by Mr. Justice Blackburn and discharged.

The five prisoners first arraigned were then placed on trial. Each was given a printed copy of the whole of the depositions sworn against him, and all appeared to make full use of these in conferring with their respective lawyers.

Digby Seymour then caused a minor sensation by applying for the trials to be transferred to the Central Criminal Court in London.

'That is perfectly impossible', replied Mr. Justice Blackburn. 'We are sitting under a Special Commission sent by Her Majesty, on the recommendation of Her responsible advisers. To agree to your application would be to directly contradict what Her Majesty has thought it proper to direct.

'The words of the Statute 19 Vic. Chapter 16 are clear and absolute', Mr. Seymour told him. 'And, I would submit, override any Special Commission. I understand, your lordships, that if we can bring an affidavit which states circumstances calculated to show that a fair and impartial trial cannot be secured -'

'I would explain to you sir', Mr. Blackburn cut in, 'that nothing I have yet heard convinces me that this Special Commission is not a proper tribunal, but anything you may advance to show that there are grounds for your application will be readily heard.'

An affidavit, drawn up by Mr. Roberts, was read out. It expressed the view that, owing to a variety of circumstances, it would

169

be unrealistic to expect a fair and impartial trial. It pointed out that increasing excitement and alarm prevailed in the minds of the people of Manchester, caused by the most exaggerated fears and rumours of impending outbreaks of Fenian violence, and by extraordinary precautions being taken both in court and in the town.

After a short consultation, the judges ruled that there was no reason whatsoever to interfere with the proceedings, and Digby Seymour, having listened very carefully himself to the contents of Mr. Roberts' affidavit, had to agree with them.

The names of the jury to do duty in the trial proper were drawn by ballot, several of them being challenged by the defence. After making one such challenge, Mr. Roberts added,

'I am objecting for Allen now'. Whereupon Mr. Justice Blackburn told him, 'The defence counsel have elected to challenge jointly, and no attorney may interfere. I have not minded you making the objections, but I cannot hear anything else from you.'

'I object to all of those jurors living in the neighbourhood of Manchester', said Roberts.

'I have to explain to you Mr. Roberts that counsel only may be heard. If you speak once more, or interfere, I will order you into custody for contempt.'

At this there was great applause in the courtroom, which did not please Mr. Roberts at all.

'I take that observation as completely uncalled for my lord!' he told the judge, repeating twice in a very loud voice, 'completely uncalled for!'

The ballot continued, then Roberts, challenging again, said, 'I object on the part of Allen.'

'Take that man into custody and remove him', snapped a now very irate Justice Blackburn. 'I will not suffer the business of the court to be interrupted in this way.'

A policeman was about to remove Roberts when Mr. Digby Seymour stepped forward and appealed to the judge. After patiently hearing him out, Mr. Justice Blackburn finally agreed to let Mr. Roberts remain, but added,

'I will have him removed immediately if there is any further interference.'

The formation of the jury was then completed without further incident. Apart from one man, none was from the City of Manchester itself. The jurors were: James Ashworth, John Butterworth, James

170

Hollows, John King, Joseph Henry King, (all of Castleton, near Rochdale) Benjamin Wortham, (Reddish, Manchester) Henry Stephenson, John Robinson, John Jones, (all of Bolton) Cyrus Lees (Ashton-under-Lyne) Abraham Parker Halliday and John Wolstenholme (Bury).

P.C. Shaw told the court that after scrambling off the top of the van he had dashed across the road and taken refuge behind the embankment, from where he had watched as the rioters battered the van. Questioned by the defence, Shaw stated that he had stuck his head out to see what was going on, 'but not too far out'.

At this there was laughter, but Digby Seymour had at least got the witness to admit that he had not been in the ideal position to observe clearly all that had happened. This, unfortunately for the defence, had the effect of nullifying Shaw's next statement, which was that he had gained the impression that Allen had fired only to burst open the lock.

Thomas Patterson again insisted that Allen was the man who tried to batter the van's roof – with a stone handed up to him by Thomas Maguire, and added that his evidence could be borne out by a man named Jack Berger, who had been sitting on the wall with him.

There was much controversy surrounding the prisoner Thomas Maguire, a Marine on furlough, who strongly denied having been anywhere near the scene, although P.C. Yarwood was sure he had seen him, as also was witness John Griffiths, who was still positive about having seen Maguire standing by the van. 'I saw him. He wore a white hat and clothes of a tweed mixture.'

Twelve-year-old George Mulholland repeated his evidence, which conflicted sharply in detail with that of most of the other witnesses. He did not know it when he took the stand, but the boy was in for a very rough ride indeed, owing mainly to his own impudence.

Cross-examined by Digby Seymour, Mulholland stated,

'During the attack I stood near the footpath on the grass bank, about ten yards nearer the arch than Heywood's wall. I didn't want to be in the way of any shooting.'

'You weren't frightened were you?'

'Wasn't I?' (laughter from the spectators)

'You stood bravely looking on. Why didn't you go to the assistance of the police?'

'I'm nowt to a man or I might have.' (more laughter)

Mulholland was questioned next by Mr. Sergeant O'Brien, who clearly had no intention of allowing the youth of the witness to influence the cross-examination. The boy, unfortunately, encouraged by the spectators' response to his light-hearted remarks, attempted to take further liberties and quickly discovered he had picked on the wrong man.

When Sergeant O'Brien prefaced his first question with the observation,

'Now you're a sharp lad', Mulholland interrupted him.

'Yes, perhaps I'll be a lawyer some day.' Again there was laughter. Mr. O'Brien, however, was not amused. After repeating the question, O'Brien still did not get a clear answer.

'Will you answer the question please?', he said icily.

'I only saw one shot fired at the horses.'

'But didn't you previously say that as the van got through the archway a man who stood on the banking fired at the horses and shouted to the driver, "Stop or I'll blow your brains out. Allen is that man." Didn't you say that?'

'I might make a mistake as well as you!' replied the boy, smiling. Angry now, O'Brien told him, 'I wish you to answer my questions with a little more responsibility and not with such sharpness. Now, didn't you say, "Allen is that man". Aye or no?'

'I don't recollect.'

'What! You don't recollect what you swore on the 26th of September? I must have an answer. Did you not say, "Allen is that man?"'

'I don't recollect,' replied the boy doggedly.

'Oh yes you do.'

'No I don't.'

'Were not your depositions read over to you before you signed them?'

'I didn't sign them then.'

'Can't you write?'

'Yes, I put my name down on a piece of paper, but I didn't sign them then', replied Mulholland, making very little sense.

'Weren't they read over to you?'

'Yes, before that.'

'When?'

'As soon as I went into court.'

'Let me see the original depositions', cut in Justice Blackburn. After looking them over the judge addressed the witness.

'Your name is written here. Did you write it or not?'

'Yes.'

'Was the deposition first read over to you?'

'No' – then after a pause –'Yes it was.'

'Pray be attentive!', said Mr. O'Brien. 'Now be careful. It was read over to you?'

172

'Yes.'

'Didn't you observe that you were *made* to say "Allen is that man?"'

'I can't recollect. It might be right.'

'Read the whole passage', said the Attorney-General.

'The correct course', said the judge, 'is to read over the entire passage bearing on a particular statement, and then question the witness upon it.'

Sergeant O'Brien read over the witness's deposition.

'When you signed that', asked the judge, 'did you observe what was written down?'

'No, I didn't notice it.'

'Didn't notice it!' snapped O'Brien. 'But do you mean to say now that you did not say before the magistrates that a man fired at the horses before the attack began and that Allen was that man?'

'I can't say. You might be right and I might be wrong.'

'Didn't you say Allen was that man?'

'I can't remember.'

'Let me take you to another part of your deposition. "Allen went to the back of the van with a hammer and lent it to another man, and this man started breaking the door open. I didn't know this other man." Did you say that?'

'I said it then.'

'But you say now that Larkin was that other man?'

'Yes.'

'And you saw him, I suppose, in prison, before you were examined?'

'Yes, I saw Larkin there.'

'How often did you see him before you were examined?'

'Twice.'

'Then explain what you meant by saying. "I didn't know this other man."'

After a pause Mulholland replied, 'I may have thought it over since then.'

'Did you talk to anyone about it?'

'No, only to my father.'

'I am not speaking of your father. How would thinking it over help you?'

'Because I took notice of the clothes and then saw which man it was.'

The boy, under heavy fire from the defence, was eventually forced to admit that the statement he had made in the magistrates' court

173

about having seen Larkin hand up the large stone to the man on the van's roof was not entirely true. Mulholland now changed his story, saying that the man had been dressed in something like the style of Larkin, but he could not for certain identify him as Larkin. However, he still stuck to his statement that Thomas Maguire had been the man on the roof of the van.

The following witness, on the other hand, a railway clerk named John Beck, who stated he had seen the attack while walking along Hyde Road, insisted that Larkin had been the man on top of the van. The stone, he said, was handed up by William Brophy, another prisoner altogether.

As well as these two, the witness could also identify Gould, Allen and Thomas Maguire. 'I took the bullet out of Sprosson's foot', he added.

'Just how many men were on top of that van?', asked Digby Seymour.

'There was only one, Larkin.'

As it was now ten minutes to six, the court adjourned for the day. On resumption the following morning the question of who had been on the roof of the van was again taken up, and John Knowles, a grocer, added to the confusion by stating that it was not one of the men in the dock. He had, however, seen Allen wielding an axe, Larkin trying to open the van door, and Gould firing at the horses.

'Did you see Gould at the police station?', Digby Seymour asked him, 'chained to another man. One of the Martins?'

'No, I'm not aware that I did.'

'Are you sure?'

'Yes.'

'Is it possible', interrupted the judge helpfully, 'that the witness may make a distinction between chains and handcuffs? Ask the question so that it will not be misunderstood.'

'I will my lord. Were there not two men handcuffed together?'

'I didn't see them.'

'Did you see any chains?'

'Well... I saw a chain on the floor, but I thought Gould was playing with it.'

William Hughes, an engine fitter, swore that Maguire had handed stones up to Allen, who was on top of the van. He was as sure he said, as he had been in his identification of the Sherry brothers, which could not have impressed anyone, for both had been discharged for lack of corroborative evidence.

174

Another witness, Thomas Barlow, said he had been working about a mile away from the arch when he heard a commotion and saw men running from Hyde Road over the railway slope.

'I thought there'd been a pitch-in.'

Translated, this turned out to mean a collision of two railway carriages. Setting off over the brick-field, Barlow had met up with Allen and Gould who were running 'arm-in-arm'. He said to them,

'It's you two fellows yon chaps is after, isn't it?'

'If you come a step nearer', Allen told him, 'I'll blow your brains out.'

'"If I'd done nowt only stole summat, or had a row, I'd throw that thing away", I told him. The crowd were getting closer and one man shouted, "He's shot a policeman". Gould threw his revolver down and they ran off. I went up Pump Street and got a bobby. When I went back I saw they'd captured Allen. They were hitting him about the head with his own revolver. I said it was a shame and they turned round and punced me in the shins.'

'Did Allen fire his pistol in the brick-field?', Digby Seymour asked him.

'Yes, but on the ground. Not to hurt anybody.'

Police Constable Seth Bromley, still not fully recovered from injuries received in the attack, told the court,

'After the horses were shot I got down from the van as quickly as possible, but before I did I noticed Allen with a gun in his hand pointing straight at me. I raised my left hand just as he fired. I was shot in the thick part of the thigh, I was the last off the van as far as I know. I turned round, looked towards the van again and saw Allen on top. He started to strike at the roof with a large stone. After I got to the other side of the road I saw him hitting the van's handle with an axe-hammer. Constable Trueman ran towards the van and Gould pointed a pistol at him, then chased him to the other side of the arch. I was disabled and could give no assistance. Constable Trueman ducked down as Gould fired at him and the bullet just grazed his back. After that Gould ran back to the van. I got into a cab and drove to Fairfield Street police station, where I got together some more constables, then went back to the bridge, but by that time all the people had gone. I was taken to the Infirmary and kept in for over three weeks. I'm still not well'.

P.C. Trueman, who had travelled in the cab which followed the police van from the court building, said,

'We made several rushes at the van, but were driven back each time. I was grazed by a bullet below the left shoulder, which bruised my side and made a hole in my coat. I saw Deasy coming out of the van. Kelly by this time was on the embankment. We made another rush, but Allen and some others drove us back. I saw Shore a few times during the attack. He was throwing stones.'

The wounded civilian, Henry Sprosson, hobbled to the witness box and told the court that he had heard shots on the afternoon of the 18th and had gone to investigate.

'Some constables were there. They were asking people to give assistance against the men who were breaking into the prison van. I went straight away towards the arch and heard someone yell after me, "Come back you fool, come back." When I heard that I turned round. I then felt myself shot and limped back as fast as I could'.

William Hulley, painter and decorator, and also landlord of the Railway Inn, Hyde Road, said he and his wife had been fired at by Allen while standing near their premises.

'There is the mark of a bullet on the urinal at my house. Allen was at the abutment of the arch when he fired at us. I saw him fire at Sprosson after that.'

Another witness, William Batty, said he had been travelling along Hyde Road in a cab with his wife and family when he heard what he took to be a fog warning signal. After looking out and seeing what was going on he had stopped the cab and bundled his wife and three children into a bread shop for safety. He could identify Larkin, who was throwing stones, and Shore, who was in the act of lifting a large stone from the ground.

'At that moment another big stone fell off the top of the van and appeared to strike Shore a glancing blow on the side of the head.'

John Robertson Woodcock, house surgeon of the Manchester Royal Infirmary, said that the prisoner Shore had been brought to him on the 30th September.

'There was a wound on the side of his head, which he said had been caused by a blow from a policeman's staff.'

'In your opinion', he was asked by the defence, 'could that have been so?'

'Yes, it could have happened in that way.'

Digby Seymour then submitted that the detention of Kelly and Deasy was in the first place unlawful, both from an excess of jurisdiction on the part of the magistrate who committed them, and also because of an irregularity in the warrant. It therefore became a question of what degree of force the prisoners would have been justified in using in order to regain their liberty. The law, he claimed, gave very reasonable discretion in this respect. It gave power to a person to exert himself to the utmost to procure his escape from what amounted to illegal apprehension. And not only might a person so detained forcibly strive to effect his own release, but friends who assisted him might, in like manner, be excused.

Mr. Justice Blackburn said he was very much inclined to doubt that any person under restraint of liberty was entitled to kill.

Digby Seymour said he thought the phrase 'entitled to kill' was putting it rather strongly. He then came to the main point of his argument, saying that under the circumstances of the case the crime might in fact be considered manslaughter rather than murder. As to the irregularity in the warrant, Digby Seymour argued that there had not been sufficient evidence put before the magistrate to entitle him to remand Kelly and Deasy in the first place. Also, the remand warrant stated that they were charged with felony, when in fact they had only been apprehended on suspicion that they were about to commit a felony.

Justice Blackburn had a ready answer to this.

'But even supposing that their being held in custody was illegal, they would have had a perfect right to seek to have the matter rectified legally, before a judge, rather than for their friends to engage in an attack on the officers in charge of the police van, using dangerous weapons.'

Digby Seymour said that the defence intended to call only a few witnesses, and that he would reserve any further remarks until after they had been heard. Sergeant O'Brien said he would do likewise.

Mary Flanagan was the first to testify for the prisoners, stating that she worked as a governess at the home of Mr. Lecomb, merchant, of 264 Oxford Street, Manchester.

While taking a walk on the afternoon of September 18th she had seen Gould outside a pub near the city gaol at Belle Vue.

'I didn't know him before that day. I was standing talking to a man named Wilson. It would be about ten-to-four, and I saw Gould with some friends. I stood there for ten minutes or so and did not lose sight of him during that time.'

She was asked by the Attorney-General her present address, and admitted that she was staying with a Mrs. Wilson, wife of one of the prisoners.

'Did you know that the escaped men, Kelly and Deasy, frequently went in and out of the Wilson's premises?'

'No', was the reply. 'I didn't. Before I went to stay I was only there twice before. I've known Mrs. Wilson since about two months before the rescue, that's all.'

Mary O'Leary said she clearly remembered September 18th. 'I left Wilson's house in Shudehill market on that day, about three o'clock, with Mr. Wilson and his wife and child. We went in a Belle Vue omnibus and got off at the city gaol. I saw Gould, who I knew, at the door of the Justice Birch Inn, nearly opposite the gaol. That would be at a few minutes to four. He appeared to be just passing and we had a word. He stopped and spoke to the child. A cab passed at the time with a policeman in it. Gould was still with us after the cab had gone by.'

Under cross-examination, the witness admitted to being Wilson's sister-in-law. Asked why she and the Wilsons had decided to go to the Hyde Road on that particular afternoon she replied that Wilson had been drinking and wanted a day in the country to walk it off.

Mrs. O'Leary agreed that she was acquainted with one of the escaped prisoners, but added. 'I didn't know they called him Deasy until after he was arrested.'

She did not know Kelly, she said, but Deasy had lodged with her for about six or seven weeks. Yes, it was true that he had visited the Wilsons, but that was to buy clothes for himself. She also admitted that Gould had been to her house.

'But not to see Deasy. He called to see another lodger of mine. Gould was with me near the city gaol about ten minutes before the disturbance took place. We saw people running and two young men told us what had happened. This was before Gould left me. In fact it was all over before he went.'

The defence managed to elicit from Superintendent Gee of the Manchester police force that Gould had, after his arrest, been kept in the cells with irons on his hands and feet all night, and that when witnesses arrived on the following morning he was chained to another prisoner.

Isobella Fee, beerhouse keeper, and her son Joseph, testified that the prisoner Shore had been in their tavern at 227 Rochdale Road on the day of the raid at about a quarter-to-four.

Another witness, Francis Kelly, a tailor, of 201 Rochdale Road, had seen Shore 'sitting with a glass of beer in front of him.'

Elizabeth Perkins was called on behalf of Thomas Maguire. A widow, she was the prisoner's sister, and put him up at her house in Salford whenever he came home on leave from the Marines, in which he had served for thirteen years. He had stayed with her from 18th August, after travelling up from Plymouth.

'On the 18th September he stayed in bed till half-past-three in the afternoon. He didn't feel well that day, and it was about a quarter-to-seven in the evening before he went out.'

178

Mary Ingram of Greengate, Salford, said,

'The house I live in is next door to Mrs. Perkins'. I know Thomas Maguire. On the day the van was stopped he spoke to me from his bedroom window. It was half-past-three to be exact. He was in his shirt sleeves and had no braces on.'

Another woman, Martha Handcock, stated,

'I saw Thomas Maguire that afternoon. I was throwing slops out and saw him washing himself in the backyard. It would be about four o'clock.'

Louisa Carroll, of the same neighbourhood, also saw Maguire in the backyard that afternoon, as did Elizabeth Blackburn, Elizabeth Ingram and James Grant, a mason's labourer, who lived nearby.

A police officer named Beal stated that he knew Maguire and that the prisoner was a quiet man, not in the habit of keeping loose company, who spent most of his time at home with his sister.

On the following morning, Digby Seymour addressed the jury on behalf of the prisoners. He reminded them that the Attorney-General had quite rightly cautioned them not to let anything but the bare evidence fill their minds. The dying police officer, Sergeant Brett, had refused to give up his keys. He had sworn to do his duty no matter what the cost. If such a man were in the jury box he would not surrender to personal fear nor popular prejudice the keys that controlled his conscience.

'The outrage', he told them, 'has excited a panic throughout the country. Her Majesty's Government has thought it proper to send down a Special Commission. Moreover, the court and all corridors and other approaches are protected by forces of police and military – precautions which I hope none in this court will ever live to see repeated. The streets are filled with placards bearing the words *Trial of the Fenians*, and a political significance has been given to this case which the facts themselves do not warrant.

'I may be a countryman of the prisoners, but let it not be supposed for one instant that I have any sympathy at all for Fenianism. Of all the curses that ever befell an unhappy country, Fenianism is the blackest and the worst, and ought not to receive the sanction or encouragement of any man who has the welfare of Ireland at heart'.

Seymour then went on to say that he was most anxious that his clients should be tried, not as Fenians, but as men without the taint of revolutionaries upon them.

'For let the jury remember that if there are Fenians on trial, then British justice is also on trial.'

They ought not, he felt, to find any prisoner guilty, unless intent, which was the element of the charge, was proven.

He then proceeded to analyse the evidence of the prosecution and to point out the discrepancies in it, remarking on the fact that Sprosson had only been shot in the foot, when the man who fired might just as easily have aimed for his head. Also, Allen had, according to P.C. Shaw, discharged his pistol at the lock, and when chased, had not fired at his pursuers, but at the ground. Seymour contended that this evidence all went to show that there was no intent to commit murder. Only to effect a rescue.

He asked the jury to do the witness Mrs. Flanagan justice and not to treat her oath lightly. Either she had committed perjury or she had acquitted Gould of any complicity in the earlier part of the affray at least, for if she had, in fact, seen him near the gaol at the time stated, then he could not possibly have been at the bridge when the shots were fired.

Digby Seymour had occupied the stage for nearly three hours when he concluded with the words,

'Let me ask you, before I sit down, to think of these men apart from the agitations and fears which pervade the public mind. Do not exaggerate this abominable evil of Fenianism. Do not let it alarm you. It is but some fungus growth. A compound and cross between Irish discontent and Yankee rowdyism. It has no dwelling in the hearts of the loyal Protestants and Catholics of Ireland'.

Mr. Sergeant O'Brien, who followed, began by admitting to the jury that if a number of men combined in a common design for rescuing prisoners by means dangerous to human life and this resulted in a man's death, then this was in fact murder. But if the act of one was to be considered the act of all, then there must be a common agreement among the rescuers as to the means by which their objective was to be accomplished. The jury must be satisfied that the minds of his clients were in accord with those directly responsible for Brett's death. But there was an entire absence of any evidence to show that this was, in fact, the case.

Also it was strange that only one policeman should speak of Maguire – and then only to say that he had not seen him play any particular part in the outrage. He could not deny that Larkin had had a pistol in his possession, nor that he had fired it, but pointed out that this had obviously been done in a moment of reckless bravado. Even then he had discharged it well above the heads of the police officers, apparently just to frighten them.

'It is a very serious matter, yes, but does the jury consider that for doing such a thing he is deserving of death?'

180

O'Brien concluded by expressing every confidence that the jury members would discharge their duty faithfully and honestly.

Following a half-hour adjournment, the Attorney-General began his address for the prosecution, going painstakingly over the events of the case from the time of the arrests in Shudehill to the killing of Sergeant Brett.

He pointed out that all those who took part in the rescue must have known that dangerous weapons were to be used. Taking that fact into account it was very clear that everyone concerned knew perfectly well what was to be done, consented to it, and had made up his mind, not with malice to any particular individual, to kill anyone who opposed them.

Regarding the strong police and military turnout, he felt that this was no more than necessary in the circumstances. If nothing else was learned from the trials he trusted that they would at least show those foolish enough to believe that they could upset the constitution of the country, by setting up a movement called Fenianism, that they would never have a chance of doing so, for the public spirit of its people would always prevent such a thing happening. Also, the example which would be shown in the present case would have the effect of warning others, and showing them that the country's laws were strong enough to protect Her Majesty's subjects and society from such an outrage.

In his summing up, Mr. Justice Blackburn pointed out that,

'Murder, technically, is killing with malice aforethought. But in order to make out a case of murder in the eyes of the law it is not required that there should be the intention to kill any particular person. If a shot is fired with the purpose of disabling a man in order to effect a preconceived design, and the man is killed, it is murder.

'If the persons agreeing to rescue Kelly and Deasy had arranged as part of their plan that violence dangerous to human life should be used by any one of their confederates if necessary for their purpose, then they are all equally guilty parties'.

The judge now made a highly controversial, and, it would seem, unjustified observation, bearing in mind some of the testimony, when he added,

'There is very strong evidence that the shot which killed Brett was intended to kill.'

In concluding a summing-up which lasted nearly two hours, Mr. Justice Blackburn told the jury that they would have to decide whether Brett's death had been caused by a shot fired with the intention of killing – or of inflicting serious injury on the police sergeant. He did

181

not mention the third possibility – that Allen might have fired only to break the lock.

The judge indicated that should the jury entertain any doubt in their minds as to the complicity of any of the prisoners, they must give them the benefit of that doubt. But if the case was made out in every instance, then nothing should prevent them from doing their duty no matter how unpleasant it might be.

The jury retired to consider their verdict at a quarter-past-six, while the prisoners and their counsel held a whispered conference. Gould, who had maintained an off-handed, carefree air throughout, was heard to laugh aloud several times. When the prisoners were led back to the cells he vaulted cockily over a couple of seats with great agility.

Not all of the accused men were as light-hearted as Gould appeared to be. Of Allen, one newspaper wrote,

Poor Allen's dejected look has given place at times to a desperate rallying of his powers. When goaded by the calm and distinct evidence of witness after witness against him, he has turned like a hunted creature at bay.

It is impossible to avoid a strong feeling of pity for the youth, whatever degree of guilt may ultimately be brought home to him. On Tuesday he expressed a positive conviction that by next Friday night he would be in Dublin. Whether his insane hope is founded on the idea of a free dismissal, or on the yet wilder dream of a rescue, he does not precisely indicate.

To one of the officials having charge of him he has spoken sometimes with a gentleness opposed to his customary manner, of his father, who, strange to say, is governor of a gaol in the County of Cork.

Young Allen has shown himself to be by no means devoid of natural affection in the anxious inquiries he has made with a view to assure himself that his own position of shame and peril will not injure his father by depriving him of his appointment.

At seven-thirty the jury filed back and the prisoners were returned to the courtroom to hear their fate.

They had listened with apparent indifference to their own counsel's denunciation of the Fenian conspiracy, but paid much more attention to the observations of the Attorney-General and the judge. Now, with the verdict about to be announced, they looked pale and tense, despite the earlier show of bravado.

In an atmosphere charged with emotion, the foreman of the jury rose to his feet on being addressed by the judge and delivered the verdict to a hushed courtroom – 'GUILTY', against all five of the prisoners.

The words brought gasps from many of the onlookers, for it had certainly been expected after the evidence of the defence witnesses that Maguire at least would be acquitted, and possibly one or two others.

Although a great deal of public bad feeling had been in evidence following the outrage, it was clear also that the prisoners had evoked a certain amount of sympathy in many quarters, for it was realised that they had undoubtedly sacrificed themselves to allow Kelly and Deasy to escape. After all, if two men wearing handcuffs could get clean away, others, unencumbered and well-armed, could certainly have done so, had they not lingered at the scene to cover the flight of the two leaders. Even taking into account that Larkin's weakness had held them back, they had delayed too long at the bridge in holding the police and the crowd at bay, and this was surely the reason for their capture.

The Clerk of Arraigns now asked each in turn if he had anything to say why sentence should not be passed upon him.

The prisoners' masks of restraint now fell away completely, each man speaking out with great fervour and conviction. Allen, no more than a callow youth, was the first to be heard. The witnesses against him had been practically unanimous in their descriptions of his wild, impetuous behaviour at the scene of the affray. Now, as he looked around the court like a caged animal, he was slightly more subdued, yet from his manner it was clear that he was still very much obsessed with the cause of Fenianism.

In a quiet controlled voice he told the court that no one regretted the death of Sergeant Brett more than he – yet he was totally innocent of the charge brought against him. His name was not William O'Meara Allen, but William Philip Allen, of Omara, County Cork.

'Justice', he said, 'has not been done me at all, but I am not regretful to die for my country, its liberty and republican principles.'

Michael Larkin came next, saying that he had received a fair trial, but that although present at the scene of the attack on the van, he was totally innocent of the crime he had been found guilty of.

It was stated by many people at the time that Larkin delivered the frankest and most manly speech of all the prisoners. Perhaps the excitement of the moment, finding himself thrust under the spotlight, gave the little tailor a sudden rush of false courage, for not many days were to pass before Larkin would begin to go to pieces as the full realisation of his awful position dawned on him.

183

Closing his speech, Larkin declared in a firm, clear voice that he was quite willing to die for his country.

Gould, the next man to speak, contrasted very sharply indeed with Larkin. An aggressive, strong-looking individual of above average height and build, he was obviously shrewd and intelligent and a very determined character. A perfect choice, in fact, as the man to cover the escape route.

Glancing round the courtroom defiantly, Gould denied emphatically that he was guilty of murder. He now wished it to be known that his real name was Captain Michael O'Brien, formerly of the United States Federal Army, born in the County of Cork. He produced several sheets of foolscap paper and proceeded to deliver a lengthy and rather tedious address on the wrongs perpetrated by the British on Ireland. It was clearly of little interest to the majority of those in court, apart from the Irish contingent, a number of whom responded at intervals with grave shakes of the head and the occasional low moan. When he had finished, O'Brien handed the script over to his lawyer and sat down abruptly.

Maguire and Shore, who now admitted that his real name was Edward O'Meagher Condon, also addressed the court and similarly protested their innocence. Maguire was the less eloquent of the two. Condon's speech from the dock, delivered in a decidedly American accent, with a definite Irish brogue, made a profound impression on almost everyone present. It ended with the words 'God save Ireland!' a cry which the other prisoners fervently repeated after him.

Maguire, who appeared to hold himself aloof from the other prisoners, pointed out that if he, or any members of his family, had been disloyal it was hardly likely that he would have re-enlisted in the Royal Marines after twelve years' service. From his manner it was evident that he was a humble, down-to-earth individual, who, according to his sister's neighbours, was partial to hard liquor, but quiet and inoffensive. These same English neighbours, it will be recalled, had come forward in support of his alibi.

Mr. Justice Mellor then proceeded to pass sentence of death on all five men, and advised them not to entertain any hopes of mercy. Before the prisoners were removed from the dock they shook hands with their counsel and thanked them for their efforts. Then all except Maguire shouted again, 'God save Ireland!', before they were led out of court.

The five Irishmen were placed in separate cells in the New Bailey prison, Allen expressing the confident conviction that the sentences would never be carried out.

More information was coming to light concerning the prisoners' recent activities. It was clearly established that both Condon and O'Brien had, in the months prior to the attack on the van, been actively engaged in forming new Fenian circles in various parts of the country.

O'Brien had spent some time in Liverpool, where he was under surveillance by the police. When questioned on one occasion at his lodgings and asked to give an account of himself, he had produced a uniform and papers proving that he had held a commission in the United States Federal Army. He was allowed to remain at liberty at that time, though he was still viewed with suspicion.

Condon, it was discovered, was an American citizen, according to naturalisation papers issued by the State of Ohio. He also, like most of the top Fenians, had served in the Federal Army, and it now came to light that he had been involved in the Chester affair. Larkin also had been to America, but had not stayed for very long.

Allen's father had formerly been employed as a turnkey at the county gaol in Cork, later being transferred to Bandon, where he became keeper. Allen's grandfather had, many years before that, served as Parish Clerk of Ballymartle.

CHAPTER 21

Mistaken identity

T he country had been thoroughly shaken by the news of the Fenians' broad daylight attack and the death of Sergeant Brett. It was therefore only natural that feelings of revenge should be uppermost in the public mind. As far as some of the prisoners were concerned the death sentences were not unexpected. Whether they would ever be carried out was another matter. In the meantime there were other prisoners to be dealt with, including such men as big John Francis Nugent, who could certainly be described as dangerous. It was now a question of waiting to see if any others would be added to the list of condemned men.

Nugent, along with John Brennan, Timothy Featherstone, William Martin, Patrick Coffey and John Bacon, was brought up the morning after the five had been sentenced to die. They were charged with being involved in the attack on the van and the death of Sergeant Brett. All pleaded not guilty.

Mr. Digby Seymour and Mr. Ernest Jones defended Nugent, Martin and Coffey, while Mr. Sergeant O'Brien and Mr. Cottingham appeared for the other three. They were again faced by the formidable figure of the Attorney-General, Sir J.B. Kerslake, and his team.

The prisoners' counsel, between them, challenged over thirty jurists before twelve were eventually empanelled, while fifteen men who failed to answer were each fined £5. Some of the jurors, accepted by the defence, were then challenged by the prosecution, one of them, a member of the Society of Friends, causing Digby Seymour to remark, 'They challenge a Quaker because he is against hanging.'

Eventually all was settled and the case proceeded.

The Attorney-General said he would show that John Bacon had been one of a party of men seen near the bridge immediately before the attack. Nugent and Martin had used pistols and stones to repel the police and the crowd. The other prisoners had acted in concert with them with the same objective in mind.

Martin was identified by several witnesses. He had been captured over two miles away from the scene of the attack, yet under cross-examination, one witness, George Moorhouse, admitted that Martin, who was walking in the direction of Clayton when taken into custody, was not 'puffed', and did not appear to have been running.

The witness Kate Riley stated that Martin had stopped her as she was walking under the archway in Hyde Road just before the van had arrived at the bridge, and asked her where she was going. When she replied that she was on her way to see the Chaplain at Belle Vue prison, Martin had said, 'You don't stir from here.'

As she struggled to get away, she told the court, Martin pulled from under his coat what appeared to be a long carving knife with a brass handle and threatened to run it into her if she dared move.

'I was frightened. So I said I'd stay where I was. He left me then and joined the other Fenians.' The witness also identified Brennan.

'And I suppose', said Digby Seymour, cross-examining, 'that this terrible man took your word that you would not stir and went away.'

'Yes sir.'

'How often have you been convicted of felony?'

'I have not come here to tell that sir.'

'But you will tell it!'

'You must answer the question', Justice Blackburn told her.

'Twice', came the reluctant reply.

'And on the last occasion, were you not sentenced to twelve months' imprisonment?' asked Digby Seymour.

'Yes sir.'

'Then I do not ask you any more questions, madam.'

P.C. Shaw swore that Martin had been one of the men who drove back the police, and Inspector Gill said he had stopped the prisoner on the banks of the Ashton Canal near the gates of Philips Park. His boots were very muddy. Asked what he was doing, he replied, 'Nothing.' When the Inspector asked where he was going, his answer was, 'Nowhere in particular.' But when told that he was being taken into custody on suspicion of having been involved in the outrage, Martin said he had a brother who worked nearby, whom he was on his way to see, and that he knew nothing about the attack on the van. The Inspector said that Martin was 'flushed' when arrested, as if he had been walking fast, but was not out of breath.

Charles Schofield, a police constable who had travelled in the following cab, swore to having seen Martin at the scene of the attack.

'He was standing just behind Allen on the left hand footpath, when they were firing at the horses'. Schofield also recognised Nugent as one of the attackers.

Railway clerk John Beck took the witness stand next. He had about him a confident, positive air, and could hardly have anticipated the difficulties he was soon to get himself into.

188

Beck swore to having seen Martin throwing stones at both police and civilians. He had also seen Coffey.

Questioned by the defence, Beck admitted to having previously identified the prisoner Foley, who had later been discharged. The witness insisted, however, that he was quite certain about Martin.

Digby Seymour reminded him that he had not identified the prisoner in the Magistrates' Court.

'He certainly did', cut in Mr. Justice Mellor.

'No, my lord, he did not', insisted Digby Seymour.

'Is his name not John Martin?'

'No, my lord, it is William Martin.' Then, turning again to the witness.

'Did you not identify a man, before the magistrates, named John Martin?'

'I believe it was John Martin.'

'But this is not John Martin.'

'I'm certain I swore to this man before', insisted Beck.

'Did you see this man before?', asked Mr. Justice Blackburn, impatiently.

'Yes.'

'Did you swear to only one man named Martin?'

'Yes, only one of that name.'

'How many Martins did you point out before the magistrate?' Digby Seymour pressed him.

'One'.

Re-examined by the Attorney-General, Beck now insisted that he had identified the prisoner in the dock (William Martin) in the Magistrates' Court.

'He was the man. I gave no evidence against John Martin.'

'You say you saw the prisoner at the affray. Did you see two men there who resembled the prisoner, or only one?', asked the judge.

'Well... there were two men like him in the Magistrates' Court, and I saw them both. But I saw only one man at the bridge when the van was attacked. At the Magistrates' Court he wore a blue tie.'

'I believe', queried Mr. Justice Blackburn, 'there is a John Martin among the prisoners?'

'There is', replied the Attorney-General.

'Is he down at the gaol?'

'Yes, my lord.'

'Then I think it would be well for him to be brought up.'

'Your lordship has got it upon your notes', said Digby Seymour, 'that the Martin this witness identified was wearing a blue tie.'

189

'It seems to me desirable to bring forward the other Martin', answered the judge, 'then we shall see which of the two the witness now swears was the man.'

'As your lordship wishes.'

Two constables immediately left the court, Digby Seymour in the meantime pointing out that the prisoner in the dock was dressed as he had been on the day of the attack.

John Martin was eventually marched in and told to stand close to his brother while the witness scrutinised both very carefully.

'Well?' he was asked by the judge. 'Be very sure now. Was this or the other prisoner the man you saw at the van?'

'That's him!' Beck suddenly blurted out.

'Which do you mean?'

'The man behind.'

'Not the prisoner in charge, but the other?'

'Yes.'

'So you are now convinced, on seeing the two men together, that when you identified William Martin you made a mistake, and that the man you meant to swear to was John Martin?', the judge suggested.

'Yes.'

At this there was uproar in the courtroom.

'Meant to swear?' Digby Seymour almost shouted. 'Swore, my lord, swore!'

When the noise had subsided, Mr. Justice Blackburn addressed the court.

'Of course the evidence against William Martin is now completely disproved. It is an illustration of the possibility of a witness being mistaken in a case of personal identity'.

'And of the awful thought that William Martin might have lost his life because of it', added Digby Seymour. 'It makes one shudder. I should like to make a remark in regard to this witness -'

'Not at the present time', interposed the judge.

The spotlight was now on John Nugent. Three witnesses swore to having seen him throwing stones at the police, one to having seen him attempting to break in the side of the van with a large rock, and a fifth, Joseph Smith, who lived not many yards from the arch, was sure he had seen Nugent from his bedroom window, with a pair of revolvers. P.C. John Thompson also swore to having seen the prisoner battering at the side of the van with a large stone.

When witness John Griffiths stated he had seen Nugent under the arch with a pistol, the prisoner turned to his companions and laughed.

190

P.C. Joseph Hirst, the man who had taken O'Meagher Condon into custody, told the court that Shore [Condon], had been accompanied by another man when captured.

'They were walking fast and seemed excited and out of breath. When I went after them they started to run. I struck one of them a blow on the head, then arrested him. I believe the man sitting in the centre of the front row of prisoners to be the other one, but I wouldn't positively swear to it.'

The man indicated was Nugent.

Witness William Hughes said he saw Bacon, walking with the aid of a crutch, go into the Halfway House tavern some two-and-a-half hours before the attack started, and several other witnesses testified to having seen Coffey and Featherstone at the scene. Again the defence attempted to prove mistaken identity in Coffey's case, there apparently being some similarity between him and Larkin. This line, however, led nowhere, for the chief witness, Charles Thomas, a plumber, was quite positive in asserting,

'I think there is a slight resemblance between them, but I'm not mistaken, I saw Larkin at the bridge and Coffey as well. He was throwing stones at the police and the people.'

Digby Seymour, addressing the jury on behalf of his clients Nugent, Martin and Coffey, said he felt sure he would be able to satisfy them that the prosecution's case was extremely weak.

'Apart from a sense of personal responsibility, I regret that I have to appear for them at all, for I feel certain in my own mind that justice has been sufficiently vindicated. Five lives have already been forfeited for the constructive murder of one man.'

Seymour went on to comment in detail on parts of the evidence, dwelling at length on the matter of identification and in particular on the miserable performance of the witness John Beck.

Before witnesses for the defence were called, John Bacon was discharged for lack of any real evidence as to his actually having taken part in the attack.

Ann Brook claimed that William Martin had called at her house in Great George Street on the afternoon of September 18th, to ask the way to Clayton. Mary Jane, her young daughter, was sent outside to point out the road to him. The little girl gave evidence, saying she remembered the incident quite clearly, and also the fact that it occurred on the day of all the excitement.

William Saunders, plasterer, told the court,

'I've worked with Nugent. He's a joiner. I saw him in Buckley

Street on the 18th September. He was there between half-past-three and ten-to-four. He was working at the carpenter's bench repairing an old window sash belonging to Mr. Hadfield, the pawnbroker.'

James Ash, tailor, said he had seen Nugent at the workshop at least three times between 3-30pm and 5-15pm that day. So had John Smith, a labourer. Henry Hadfield, who superintended building work for his father, said that both Nugent and Nugent's father had worked for him since the previous Christmas.

'They've been working on new houses we're building in Burton Street. On the day the police officer was shot I was with the Nugents from 1-30 till ten minutes past two in Rochdale Road. Then they went off to Dr. Bedale's new building down in Miller Street. I know the time, because we also run a pawnshop, and I'm in the habit of going out during the dinner hour when it's closed.'

James Miller, who worked as a carter for the Hadfields, said he saw Nugent for most of the day until dinnertime, when he went away, coming back about three.

'He said he'd been to Dr. Bedale's. I was jumping at the time and I challenged him to jump against me for a quart of ale. We jumped till half-past-three. After that I never lost sight of him till half-past-five, because while I was loading the cart with bricks he was working near me.'

Further corroboration of Nugent's apparent innocence came from Michael Flynn, blacksmith, who said his business was about 50 yards from where Nugent had been working.

'He sent two lads down with a bar of iron he wanted me to piece. I took it back to him about a quarter-to-four.'

John Boyle said he was painting a window frame near to where Nugent was working.

'He was passing and I asked him to come and unfasten a window for me. It had stuck and the weights wouldn't work. He refused to do it. That would be sometime between three and four.'

Many more witnesses spoke on Nugent's behalf, including his father, Robert Nugent, who had himself been in custody and released. Nugent senior stated,

'I started work that morning at six and my son worked with me at the same bench. We were fitting window sashes and laying floors. During the day we left to go to Dr. Bedale's concerning a job for which I gave him an estimate. We had to wait, as he was engaged. It would be about twenty-to-three when we saw him. My son was with me all the time. It was about twenty-past-three when we got back to the job. My son changed his good hat and set to work at the bench again. I didn't leave till six o'clock, but John finished a few minutes before that. He has a watch, so I know the time. He wasn't out of my sight for more than a few minutes all day.'

A map was produced and passed around among the jury. It was ascertained that the distance from the workshop to Hyde Road was approximately two miles.

Finally, Dr. Bedale himself appeared, having been prevented from arriving earlier because of his work. The doctor's evidence tallied very closely with that given by Robert Nugent, although the Attorney-General did point out that when questioned previously he believed the events referred to had occurred on another date. Now he said.

'I did in the first instance say I did not think the Nugents came to see me on the 18th September, but subsequent reflection had convinced me that it was in fact on that day.'

Several witnesses came forward on Patrick Coffey's behalf. Coffey was also a joiner and lived in Bonsall Street, Hulme. Edwin Davis, his employer, gave him a good character reference, but could only account for his movements on the day in question until 1-30pm. At that time the prisoner had been laid off as there was no further work for him.

'The brick-setters were idle that day, and this stopped the joiners from working.'

Peter Powell and Roe Parker, clerk and manager respectively of the Co-operative Society's Downing Street branch, had both dealt with Coffey on 18th September.

'I changed £4 in clothing checks for him', said Parker.

Further evidence, given by Powell, was corroborated by an entry in a subscription book.

'Coffey's payment of three shillings was due on that day. And that's when he paid it.'

A little probing by the Attorney-General, however, revealed that the payment had actually been made at some time between six and seven in the evening.

The Co-op manager insisted that Coffey had not even known of the attack, let alone taken part in it.

'I saw him standing at the shop window and asked him if Kelly had been recaptured. He said he knew nothing about it. He was very surprised and ignorant of the matter until I mentioned it. In any case he's the last man I would expect to be involved in any breach of the peace.'

The witness was then questioned by the prosecution about a room in the Co-operative building which was sometimes hired out for

193

use as a ballroom, but denied that any function to raise Fenian funds had ever been held there.

Patrick Mc'Tigue, a tailor employed by Shirley's, of Market Street, Manchester, spoke on behalf of Brennan.

'I've known him four years. On the afternoon you speak of I saw him in Swan Street, Shudehill. He was walking past Mc'Kenna's Vaults. That would be about half-past-one. I kept him company for a while and we went into Crompton's Vaults. we played cards there for close upon an hour, then went into Smithfield Market. After a bit we went to the Crown and Kettle and had some biscuits and porter, then we loitered about the streets for a while. Later on we had another drink at the George Inn.'

Elizabeth Healey, a seamstress, said she had seen Brennan in Rochdale Road at about 4pm, then again at 4-30, in the vault of the George Inn. This was corroborated by a barman, William Brecken.

Witnesses were also called on Timothy Featherstone's behalf.

In summing up, Sir John Kerslake admitted that the evidence of John Beck and Kate Riley was utterly worthless and should be dismissed from the minds of the jurists. There were, however, at least eight other witnesses who had given evidence against the prisoners which could be thoroughly relied upon. He also felt that the Co-operative manager had not been as frank as he might have been regarding the use to which his ballroom had been put. He did not place much credence on the alibi set up for Brennan, and left it to the jury to decide whether or not they felt that the case against Featherstone was one of mistaken identity or not.

The jury had been out for nearly four hours when a message was passed to the justices from the jury room inquiring whether, if acquitted of murder, the prisoners could still be charged on the other indictments of felony and misdemeanour. The answer, in the affirmative, was quickly relayed to them.

Shortly after 5pm the jurists re-appeared and delivered a verdict of not guilty of murder in respect of all the prisoners.

As the acquitted men were led from the court, John Francis Nugent was given into the custody of Thomas Welby, Head Constable of the Irish Constabulary, who held a warrant issued by the Lord Lieutenant of Ireland, charging Nugent with complicity in the Fenian conspiracy in Ireland. He was escorted to Liverpool that afternoon and taken by boat to Dublin.

It was later revealed that Nugent had played a leading part in the rising at Drogheda in March earlier in the year, and had narrowly escaped from the police by leaping from a window when about to be arrested.

Later that day a third batch of prisoners was brought up. They were Thomas Scalley, Henry Wilson, Michael Joseph Boylan, Michael Maguire and William Murphy, all charged with murder.

Police-Constable Yarwood was again the chief witness. He told the court that he had seen the prisoner Henry Wilson on the Manchester side of the arch with Boylan.

'He was just standing on the footpath, as any pedestrian might be?' asked the judge.

'Yes.'

At this juncture the proceedings were halted for the day. Next morning, however, it was announced that the Attorney-General had been called back suddenly to London. Before leaving Manchester he and his associates had, on the previous evening, very carefully looked over the case against Wilson and decided that they did not now feel the evidence was strong enough to be relied upon for the support of such a serious charge. Therefore, in the exercise of their discretion, they had decided to withdraw it.

'Then there must be an acquittal', said Mr. Justice Blackburn. 'And as this particular case is not now going on it must result in the acquittal of all five prisoners.'

The five were therefore cleared of murder, though other charges would still be brought against them.

While these proceedings were in progress all sorts of rumours were circulating in the city regarding the intentions of the Fenian Brotherhood. Talk of a rescue attempt was being taken very seriously by the authorities, with large forces of troops standing by, just in case, some within the walls of the New Bailey prison itself. In addition, bodies of armed police constables guarded the approach to the gaol day and night.

Inside the prison, Royal Marine Thomas Maguire waited anxiously, along with the other condemned men, in the fervent hope that some word might be relayed from the Home Office regarding a reprieve.

Maguire's own case, in fact, was receiving much public attention. A petition, raised by members of the press, was forwarded to Mr. Gathorne Hardy, Secretary of State for the Home Department. It ran,

We, the undersigned members of the metropolitan and provincial press, having had long experience in courts of justice, and full opportunity of observing the demeanour of prisoners and witnesses in criminal procedure, beg humbly to submit that having heard the evidence adduced before the Special Commission on the capital charge preferred against Thomas Maguire, private in the Royal Marines, now under sentence of death, conscientiously believe that the said Thomas Maguire is innocent of the crime of which he has been convicted, and therefore pray that you will be pleased to advise Her Majesty to grant Her Most Gracious Pardon to the said Thomas Maguire.'

It was signed by 22 journalists from leading newspapers in Manchester, London, and many other parts of the country.

On Wednesday November 6th a letter was received by Mr. Digby Seymour from a Mr. Tours, former surgeon on the flagship *Princess Royal*, who stated that Thomas Maguire was well known to him, having been quite often on his sick list while serving on the *Princess Royal* 'on the China station', and had never previously been in any kind of trouble.

'I had no idea until last Saturday', wrote the ship's surgeon, *'that Maguire was one of the condemned. He was in my opinion an ignorant fellow, and could easily be led to drink by others when on shore. But he has not the brain to do what those Fenians did. Had he been a bad character he would never have been taken on again for a further period of service. On the ship he was always obedient and never gave any trouble. What could have induced him to fall in with such bad company I know not.'*

'I can assure you that none of his friends have contacted me on the subject, I have written on my own accord, believing the man to be innocent'.

Several days after this, Maguire was handed a letter from his headquarters, Stoneham Marine Barracks, Plymouth. It was his discharge, and was endorsed with the words,

'Condemned to death at Manchester for the murder of Charles Brett.'

Maguire was very upset on reading the letter. He had served 13 years and 147 days in the Royal Marines, a record of which he was extremely proud.

Of the remaining Fenian prisoners still in custody, seven only were ultimately found guilty, on various indictments, the most serious being that of assaulting police constables and causing actual bodily harm. The convicted men were: Daniel Reddin, John Carroll, Charles Moorhouse, Thomas Scalley, William Murphy, John Brennan and Timothy Featherstone.

Sentencing them, Mr. Justice Blackburn had this to say,

'Every one of you took part in the attack and is therefore partly guilty, in my view, of the murder of Sergeant Brett. I therefore feel myself bound to give you the maximum punishment which the law permits in such a case.

'The sentence upon each of you is that you be kept in penal servitude for five years.'

At this there were subdued moans from several women in court. William Murphy then spoke up from the dock.

'I wish to say, my lord, and to protest in the face of a liberal British public, that it is not for assaulting the police that I've been convicted. The papers handed in against me stated a charge of treason – felony… '

'Yes, yes', interrupted the judge impatiently, 'but I cannot go into that. The verdict of the jury has been passed. If any appeal is to be made it must be made to the Home Secretary.'

'As to the evidence', persisted Murphy, 'I hope the press will take notice of the papers handed in against me.'

The prisoners were then removed from the dock, shouting farewell to their friends and families among the spectators. As the convicted men were led out, some sort of commotion and a brief scuffle occurred at the rear of the court, but it was quickly suppressed and the area speedily cleared.

With most of those responsible for the Hyde Road outrage firmly dealt with, the authorities now had the further satisfaction of being able to announce that they had behind bars one of the most important Fenians known to be in England, Colonel Ricard O'Sullivan Burke, chief procurer of weapons for the Brotherhood, and the man responsible for arming the Manchester Fenians. Arrested in London, he gave the name 'George Berry', but his deception was soon discovered, thanks to the co-operation of the traitor Godfrey Massey. Burke, along with another prisoner calling himself Joseph Theobald Casey, was remanded in custody charged with treason, felony and assaulting the police while resisting arrest.

CHAPTER 22

Sweating it out

In 1867 Monsignor Gadd was a young curate of twenty-nine attached to St. John's Cathedral, Salford. In November of that year he was in Ireland, enjoying a vacation at Limerick Junction, when he received an urgent communication from the Cathedral informing him that he was required to return at once, *'as five Irishmen are under sentence of death in Salford gaol.'*

The New Bailey prison was just over the border in the City of Salford, and stood at the junction of New Bailey Street and Stanley Street. Until 1790, when the New Bailey was first opened, the House of Correction at Hunt's Bank had served as the City's main lock-up. The new gaol was packed to its maximum capacity within a very short time of opening its gates, with children, as well as men and women, incarcerated within its sombre high walls.

Though such innovations as workshops and a school master were introduced into the new prison, the old punishments – placing in irons, flogging and the treadmill, were retained, being considered a necessity, even in an up-to-date and supposedly enlightened, institution.

The five condemned men were housed in adjoining cells, two on one side of a passage, three on the other. The cells were small, bare, very damp and ill-lit. The men could not communicate with each other because of the strict silence rule, but were allowed to write to their families.

Arriving back in Manchester, Father Gadd immediately made his way to the gaol to meet 'his boys', as he would refer to them from then on. After talking to each individually he knelt down on the stone flags of the passage to say Mass. From there he could clearly hear the responses to his prayers coming from beyond the heavy, studded cell doors. This was repeated daily. The young priest made it his business to spend every available moment with the prisoners, for if the sentences were to be carried out they had precious little time left. The usual span between sentence and execution in those days was about two to three weeks. The five Irishmen were most receptive to Father Gadd's ministrations. The priest was later to say, 'My poor boys, how they did pray.'

This was, of course, hardly surprising, considering the position they were in. Yet Allen, at least, retained high hopes of a reprieve. He simply refused to believe that the extreme penalty would be carried out. Whether this belief was founded on his knowledge that he had not intended to kill, or whether he simply could not imagine the English authorities taking revenge in such a violent way, will never be known, but of all the prisoners, he, according to the evidence the most guilty of all, refused to accept that he was about to die.

Allen's mother was the first member of his family to visit the prison, and found him in good spirits. Later he was seen by his fiancée, Mary Hickey, who was very much affected and wept bitterly during their short time together. Also present was Allen's sister.

A curious incident, indirectly concerning Mary Hickey, had occurred about a week previously, when a young woman named Adelaide Noble MacDonald was noticed by a patrolling policeman as she peered into the window of a barber's shop in the Hyde Road, which happened to be the one kept by John Griffiths, principal prosecution witness in the Fenian trials.

'Them's nice looking pictures', the constable remarked to her pleasantly.

The girl replied by asking him, 'Are you an Irishman?'

'No, I'm an Englishman, why?'

'A sharp lot of policemen you are', said the girl insolently. 'How is it you can't catch Kelly and Deasy, and such a reward offered for them?'

The policeman turned away without answering, and was about to walk off when he was suddenly rocked by a loud report and blast close to his ear. Turning around sharply he saw that the girl was holding a pistol and was in the process of re-loading it, at the same time shouting,

'I mean to be hung. I came here to shoot Griffiths.'

A fierce struggle ensued, with the constable finally managing to wrench the weapon from her grasp – or at least a half of it, for it snapped in two, the barrel coming away in the policeman's hand, while the stock was retained by the girl. The arrest was then completed.

Before the magistrates, the prisoner, who did not employ any legal representative, would say very little. It was strongly rumoured, however, that she was an intimate friend of William Philip Allen, while another report had it that she was a close friend of Mary Hickey.

Miss MacDonald refused to give an address, though it was ascertained that she worked as a servant. All she would state was that she had no friends in Manchester, and that she had come from Liverpool.

200

She showed very little interest in the proceedings against her and frequently laughed aloud as evidence was given by various witnesses, one newspaper remarking that her levity was 'quite remarkable considering the seriousness of the charge.'

Miss MacDonald was described as being of prepossessing appearance and about 20 years of age. She was committed for trial to the Assizes.

Meanwhile, within the grim walls of the New Bailey, Michael Larkin's demeanour had undergone something of a change since his brave speech from the dock, when he had declared his willingness to die in the cause of Ireland. The true horror of his situation now seemed to have dawned on him fully. Of all the prisoners, he alone seemed in danger of cracking under the great mental strain.

In a letter to his wife, living in Hulme, Manchester, Larkin bemoaned his fate in being found guilty of a murder of which he knew himself to be 'innocent in the sight of God'. A rather curious and cryptic sentence followed,

'I was told that if I would say nothing about Kelly and Deasy in the dock I should have another trial.'

He explained to his wife in the letter that she had not been allowed to see him because she had not obtained the usual order from a magistrate, and finished by urging her to keep the children out of bad company.

The letter was poorly put together, badly mis-spelt, and clearly the work of an illiterate and very simple, though sincere, sort of man. There was no political allusion of any kind. The clear impression is gained that Larkin had been carried along by events rather than by design. Also, that he had come strongly under the influence of men fiercely determined to obtain their political ends, without serious thought of the cost to themselves or their companions.

The date of the execution had now been fixed by the High Sheriff, for November 23rd, a Saturday. The executioner would be William Calcraft.

On Thursday November 14th, Larkin's wife and family were allowed into the prison, and a long and painful reunion was witnessed by the gaolers. All the convict's four children were present, the youngest being about four years old.

Despite the sense of outrage felt by the general public at the daring rescue and the tragic death of Sergeant Brett, doubt lingered in the minds of many regarding the sentence. Possibly a charge of manslaughter might have been more appropriate in the first place, rather than that of wilful murder. Now that sentence had been passed, some held the firm conviction that commutation to life imprisonment would be the better course. It was certain that the carrying out of the executions would result in making martyrs of the condemned men, and Ireland could boast more than her share of these already.

A meeting was held on Monday evening November 11th at the Trevelyan Hotel, Manchester, for the purpose of discussing the possibility of sending a petition to the Home Office in favour of commuting the sentences. Those attending were not Fenians or even Fenian sympathisers. One speaker stated that his motive for supporting the meeting was his belief that the implementation of the full penalty, far from suppressing Fenianism, would serve only to fan the flames.

A Mr. J.D. Morton said he considered an execution would have no good effect on the city of Manchester, and would certainly have a very bad effect on Ireland and on the other side of the Atlantic. A motion was passed that the meeting should form itself into a committee for the purpose of organising a petition.

Thomas Maguire was visited by his sisters, who tried hard to lift his spirits by passing on news of the efforts being made on his behalf by people with no other interest than to see justice done.

Mr. Justice Blackburn refused to see a deputation of citizens who came to petition on behalf of all the prisoners. However, the communication was later presented to the Home Secretary by Mr. Watkin and Mr. Bazley, both M.P.s. As a result, the following letter from the Home Office was received at the prison on Wednesday November 13th.

Whitehall Nov. 12. 1867

Sir —— I am directed by Mr Secretary Hardy to acknowledge receipt of your letter regarding the case of the convicts now under sentence of death at Manchester, and to communicate to you that after careful inquiry instituted at the desire of the learned judges and the Attorney-General, there appears to Mr. Hardy good reason to believe that the defence of Thomas Maguire was true, and he has therefore recommended to Her Majesty an unconditional pardon.
I am sir, your obedient servant,
Adolphus F.O. Liddell.

After receiving this communication the Governor of the prison went immediately to Maguire's cell with the good news. The prisoner did not at first react in the way one would expect of a person who has just been given back, not only his life, but also his freedom. He simply stood there nodding rather vaguely, as though he could not understand the full significance of what he had just been told. But on hearing that the Governor did not intend to keep him in custody a minute longer, that he was to be 'turned out' at once, Maguire became very excited and almost wept with joy.

It was only eight o'clock in the morning when the gate was opened and he stepped out into the street alone. But despite the early hour, news of his release spread very rapidly. A boy driving his cart passed Maguire as he reached Chapel Street and recognised him. The boy shouted his name and soon a small crowd had gathered, some shouting, 'Look, it's Maguire.'

After the ex-convict had stopped briefly with some of the passers-by and told them of his pardon, a number of people gathered round and excitedly followed as he made his way to his sister's house, the mob growing at every step.

The short journey to the house in Preston Court, Greengate, took much longer than it would normally have done, as complete strangers stopped Maguire and shook his hand or shouted congratulations to him. By the time Preston Court was reached, the crowd numbered in excess of a hundred.

Mrs. Perkins, Maguire's sister, and also an unmarried sister, had only just come downstairs when they heard a knock on the door. Both wept with joy on seeing him, although taken completely by surprise.

Father Gadd, who arrived at the prison later that morning, was taken aback to be told that Maguire had already left, having been escorted to the gate by the Governor, who had placed a free pardon in his hands and told him to go.

On the day following, a letter of thanks from Maguire appeared in a local newspaper.

Sir – I don't know what to say or how to find words to thank all those kind gentlemen that have been so kind to me. Since I was released this morning I have been surrounded wherever I went with scores of people, shaking hands with me and all so glad to see me set at liberty that I have not had a minute scarcely to myself, and feel so much excited now not to know what I'm doing. But I am so wishful to thank, from my full heart, all the editors of papers and the gentlemen who got up the petition for me and anybody that signed it or took any

203

part in getting my pardon, may God bless and reward them all will always be my prayer. Since I was taken up I have prayed hourly to God to clear my innocence, and thought it hard to be charged with the crime I was, after serving my Queen and country faithfully between 13 and 14 years, and the Almighty answered my prayers. I have only one thing more to wish for, and that is that I may be allowed to return to headquarters and serve my time out in the Royal Marines. I never did anything to disgrace the service, but was proud to belong to it, and hope my discharge, which came to me on Sunday, will not be enforced as I shall lose 13 years' and 147 days' service if it is. I give my best thanks also to my late commanding officer, Captain Jones, of Her Majesty's ship Princess Royal, *for his kind letter. I cannot say more. My heart is too full to thank you all as I would like. So believe me, yours very gratefully.*

Thomas Maguire.

Maguire subsequently realised his wish – re-instatement in the Royal Marines.

Reports of Fenian activities continued to fill the newspapers, under such diverse headlines as 'FENIAN CRUISER SIGHTED OFF THE ERRIS COAST', and 'CAPTURE OF TWO FENIANS AT READING.' The latter referred to the case of two Irishmen who had allegedly attempted to induce an English Police Constable to take the Fenian oath, and also made indiscreet inquiries regarding the local militia barracks.

No doubt the above took place in or around public houses and could not have been viewed very seriously.

The plight of the Fenian convicts still held in the New Bailey Prison, however, was very serious indeed, and strenuous efforts were being made by responsible people all over the country to save their lives.

A public meeting was held on Clerkenwell Green in London to organise a petition. Over 2,000 people are said to have attended. The chief speaker was a Mr. Finlen, and several resolutions were agreed on, the main one being that the prisoners should be regarded, not as criminal malefactors, but as political offenders.

A memorial to the Home Secretary was drawn up, expressing the opinion that;

The clemency of the Crown in the case of the Fenian prisoners would be neither misplaced nor misconstrued, but would move the national conscience to respect the law, and compel the people of every grade to repudiate outrages such as were committed by the Fenians. It would obtain for the British Government the proud distinction of carrying civilisation to a higher point, and would teach the nation to regard with abhorrence acts of violence which the Crown mercifully declined to retaliate against.

A deputation of over 80 men arrived outside the Home Office at 2pm the following day. They were confronted by an underling, who informed them that Mr. Gathorne Hardy, the Home Secretary, had declined to grant them an interview. Although disappointed, the petitioners were determined, especially Mr. Finlen, who led his party into the building, and after some argument with officials, managed to commandeer an upstairs room, where an urgent consultation was held. Finlen read out a letter which had just been passed to him, confirming Mr. Hardy's refusal to meet the deputation. It ended:

Mr. Hardy has already declined to receive deputations on the subject and must equally decline to do so in this instance. He is, however, prepared to receive any memorial that may be sent for his consideration.

As Mr. Finlen attempted to address his followers he was interrupted by an official, and snapped. 'Keep quiet sir. Hold your tongue. You are only a servant here.' He went on to say that the Government would bring blood upon its own head if it did not receive the overtures for mercy which were now being made.

There were cheers at this and Finlen concluded:

'I say the Home Office has disgraced itself by refusing to see a body of working men who have sacrificed a day's wages to come here as we have done. I say here, under this roof, that I would throw all the Tory Governments that ever lived into the sea rather than see those glorious and plucky Fenians who rescued Kelly and Deasy, immolated on the scaffold in Manchester'. Again there were cheers. 'If they shed the blood of these men their lives should not be held sacred, or their positions as advisers to a good Queen rendered secure –by their paltry, bloody and miserable conduct.' There was more cheering, then the deputation trooped out into the street.

Commenting on the incident, one newspaper remarked:

Mr. Gathorne Hardy really must manage in some way to become master in his own house. The scene which Mr. Finlen and his friends were so strongly permitted to enact at the Home Office was one to make government in this country look ridiculous. There is a not a president of a petty republic in the world who would tolerate the invasion of the public offices by a set of disorderly persons, and their hostile occupation for a space long enough to hold a public meeting. If it had been reported that the Fenians were marching upon some ruined castle 200 miles away, Mr. Hardy would have been all activity; but people will never believe that he can protect the whole country if the very seat of authority can be usurped.

The tenor of Mr. Finlen's speech in the Home Office proved beyond doubt that his interest in the case did not stem solely from a desire to see justice done. Yet there were many who felt not the slightest sympathy for the condemned men. When it was made known that a large number of volunteers would be required to act as special constables on execution day, there was an immediate and unseemly rush of men to sign up, not just by the unemployed, but by men whose bosses had made it clear that no obstruction would be put in their way should they wish to take time off work on 'hanging day'. In addition to these, members of the Salford Rifle Volunteers were sworn in as 'specials' and issued with staves.

It was announced that all men taken on as special constables would be paid a reasonable sum for their services and provided with refreshments. Before one day was out, over a thousand extra men had been sworn in. It was estimated that they would be required from 4pm on the day before, until mid-morning of execution day, but in case of any emergency they were engaged for three days' service.

All this frantic activity followed instructions from Whitehall to the effect that it would be the duty of the civil authorities to deal with any riot or disturbance. However, should any kind of organised attack occur then the military forces would be standing ready to intervene.

Disturbances in various parts of the country were making the authorities distinctly apprehensive. A group of men in Crewe, Cheshire, who had been under police surveillance for some time were suddenly arrested. They were named as Bernard Lynagh, clerk, Daniel Gunning, fitter, John Hassett, shoemaker, and A. Murdock, school-master, and charged with being the organisers or 'centres' of a local Fenian circle which had been observed drilling in a field in the town.

Excitement was also created in York by a messenger galloping through the streets in great haste with a despatch for Colonel Crawley of the 6th (Inniskilling) Dragoons, stationed at York Barracks. Within a very short time the Regiment was standing by ready to entrain for Hull, Middlesbrough and Sunderland, where Fenian unrest had been reported.

206

Closer to Manchester, at Bacup, groups of Irishmen were seen drilling on the outskirts of the town. This caused some panic, the local authorities immediately ordering the removal of the volunteer arms from the armoury at Stacksteads to a place of greater safety. It was known that a large number of Fenian sympathisers lived in and around the little Lancashire town, for close on £20 had already been subscribed in aid of the Manchester Fenians' Defence Fund.

A case brought before the magistrates at Royton, near Oldham, shows how high feelings were running at this time.

James Kerney, described by the *Oldham Standard* as an '*illtempered looking Irishman*', summoned Samuel Sinkinson, David Hadfield, Peter Hodgkinson and William Carter, four local men, for assault.

According to Kerney, he and three others had been walking from Oldham to Middleton, when they decided to call at the Free Trade Inn, Chadderton.

While they were in the bar Kerney went to look through a newspaper which lay on the table. He had only just picked it up when Sinkinson, who was with two other men, asked in a loud voice, 'What Fenian news?' Kerney replied that he knew nothing about Fenians and was reading the parliamentary news. Sinkinson then called Kerney 'a bloody Fenian', and remarked that he wished they were all hung, after which the alleged assault took place.

Questioned in court by Mr. Charles Buckley, defending, Kerney, according to the *Oldham Standard's* reporter, answered 'very pettishly and in a defiant manner, which at times caused the audience to show signs of disapproval.'

However, a witness for Kerney, Samuel Williams, proved more acceptable, as he apparently gave his evidence in a '*straightforward and creditable manner.*'

According to Williams, he, Kerney and a third man had been to Oldham seeking work, and had called at the inn as they were tired and thirsty from tramping around. He corroborated Kerney's statement in almost every detail, saying that a man had placed himself at the door and held it while the row was going on, so that the Irishman had been obliged to fight his way out.

The defence, however, insisted that the plaintiff had come into the inn already drunk and had started the row himself. This assertion was supported by Peter Hodgkinson, the landlord, his wife, and Jackson B. Knott, described as a '*reputable tradesman*', who had been present when the strangers arrived. Knott said he had seen Kerney strike Sinkinson on the head. Hodgkinson said he had met the plaintiff in the lobby and had been struck by him. On learning that he had hit the landlord, however, Kerney begged his pardon.

The magistrates fined each defendant ten shillings. In concluding his article the *Oldham Standard's* reporter turned out to be somewhat 'pettish' himself.

The complainant called two other Irishmen as witnesses, his partners in the affair, and they, it appears, are more fit to be believed than respectable English witnesses. No evidence was given against Hadfield, one of the defendants, still he must pay the fine. The landlord must pay for keeping his house in order, and Sinkinson and Carter must also pay for protecting their lives. So much for Royton justice!

Several days before the date fixed for the executions, a serious disturbance took place in Birmingham at an open-air meeting held to organise yet another petition. A vast crowd turned out and several hundred signatures were obtained. But there were many dissenters present and consequently the speakers could not be heard for the interruptions and general disorder. Finally, an attempt was made to overturn the wagon on which the speakers stood. This put an end to the meeting, for a full-scale riot then ensued in which one speaker was knocked to the ground and trampled on. Squads of police quickly turned out and dispersed the crowd.

The next day brought a counter-demonstration organised by people with an obvious hatred of the Irish. Several thousand such people attempted to hold a meeting outside the Town Hall, but were prevented by the police. They then marched through the Irish districts, shouting and jeering, and even smashed the windows of the Roman Catholic Cathedral. Groups of Irish turned out armed with shovels, staves and anything they could lay their hands on, to defend their homes and churches, but the police arrived and drove the mob away, to enthusiastic cheering from the Irish.

Such terrible scenes clearly did not bode well for the coming executions. The authorities, having every reason to be alarmed, posted notices, earnestly requesting members of the public, in the interests of safety, not to attend the hanging, so as to reduce, as far as possible, the dangers likely to arise from the assembling of a large crowd.

At the previous Sunday's mass for the condemned men, held at Salford Cathedral, it was recommended from the pulpit that Catholics should keep away from the executions. In several churches, special services were to take place at eight o'clock on Saturday 23rd, the hour the Fenians were due to die. By Wednesday, more than 17,000 people had put their names to petitions. On Thursday evening a torch-lit meeting was held on Clerkenwell Green. It was claimed at the time to have been the biggest ever held in London, being attended by well more than 10,000.

With such a large crowd on hand the military were alerted, a detachment of men being under arms at the nearby Clerkenwell House of Detention. The meeting, however, turned out to be very orderly.

Mr. Finlen was again very much to the fore, stating that,

'The executions would be a grievous mistake. Mr. Secretary Hardy acted very unwisely in not receiving our deputation, and it will be a disgrace to put four men to death for the murder of one.'

After going over the familiar ground of Irish discontent, he told the meeting that if their efforts that night were unavailing they would approach the Queen herself. He proposed that if the sentences were still carried out, a funeral procession should march through London with black banners bearing the harp, the shamrock and the names of those who had been hanged. The procession would be headed by a band playing the *Dead March* from *Saul*, and funeral orations would be delivered over those who had themselves been murdered.

This resolution was unanimously carried and also the proposal to petition the Queen directly, imploring Her to exercise Her prerogative of mercy.

A well-known radical, Mr. Charles Bradlaugh*, expressed the view that the very fact that a pardon had been granted to Maguire was sufficient to suggest a doubt as to the guilt of those sentenced with him, and that the murder of Sergeant Brett might have been the result of accident rather than malice.

That day a dispatch was received at the prison from the Isle of Wight. It was a gift of £100 from the Dowager Marchioness of Queensbury, to be distributed by Father Gadd, at his discretion, among the families of the condemned men. A letter was enclosed in which the Marchioness expressed her deepest sympathy.

My Friends,

It may be that this letter may minister some consolation to you on your approaching departure from this world. I send you some help for your wives and children in their approaching irrepairable [sic] loss, with the assurance that as long as I live they will be cared for to the utmost of my power.

Mr. Mc'Donnell, the bearer of this letter, will bring me their names and addresses from the priest who attends you.

*A man of such radical and stubborn views that when elected M.P. for Northampton in 1880 he was unseated because he refused to swear on the Bible.

The writer then embarked on a lengthy religious tirade before signing herself

Caroline Queensbury, Ventnor, Isle of Wight.

Father Gadd took the letter into each man's cell and read it to him. All expressed their warmest appreciation for the message of sympathy and very generous gift – a large sum in 1867 – particularly Larkin, who was moved to tears, especially as it brought some relief for his large family, a worry which must have weighed as heavily on him as his own frightening position.

That night a further communication was received at the New Bailey Prison. It was a letter from the Home Office stating that the sentence of death on the convict Shore [Condon] had been commuted to penal servitude for life.

It was true that O'Meagher Condon had not actually been seen committing any act of violence, nor was it known for sure at that time that he was one of the ringleaders – the architect of the plot in fact. But the principal reason for his reprieve would appear to have been his American citizenship. Apparently, much pressure had been brought to bear by the American Embassy in London. In the case of Michael O'Brien, however, no such pressure was exerted, the reason being that he had been in custody once before and released after the intervention of the American legation.

The news of Condon's reprieve brought fresh hope to Father Gadd and 'his boys'. The priest later stated,

We began to believe that after all, perhaps the penalty of the law would not be carried out to its fullest extreme. There was a hope, and a strong one, that the remaining prisoners, if not pardoned, would at any rate be reprieved.

However, it was my duty to leave nothing to chance. Every day without intermission we carried on with our allotted spiritual exercises. My poor boys, how they did pray. I besought Canon Cantwell of St. Patrick's to come and attend to Allen, who was a member of his flock. I also asked Father Quick to perform a similar service for Michael Larkin, who lived in St. Wilfred's parish, whilst I undertook to attend to Michael O'Brien, who appeared to have neither kith nor kin in Manchester.

An article in the American press gave the opinion:

There appears to be no doubt that the Manchester Fenians will be executed. It is impossible to expect anything else. If such offences were passed over it would go a long way to dissolving society in

210

England, for it would put it within the power of any Irishman to knock anybody he pleased on the head and excuse himself by pointing to 600 years of wrongs endured by his native land. A Frenchman, who was informed not long ago that the Greek brigands who infest the roads around Smyrna and rob and murder all comers, regardless of nationality, were driven to it by the Turkish Government, replied very aptly that if his own throat should be cut by them it would be no use their telling him that it had been done to give a lesson to the Sublime Port.

The English police, who are hired to protect life and property in English towns, may fairly make the same reply to agents of the 'Irish Republic'.

Meanwhile, the Salford magistrates held a meeting to make plans for preserving the peace on execution day, now no more than 48 hours away. When details had been finalised, work was immediately begun on barricading the streets in the vicinity of the prison. A vast crowd had gathered to watch as New Bailey Street was closed at both ends. Guns were placed in Stanley Street near the prison gates, and preparations were made to block off the ends of lower King Street, Albert Street, Bridge Street, Gartside Street and Water Street. Work continued throughout Thursday night, while many people remained to watch, their main interest being in the erection of the scaffold, a specially-built affair protruding from the upper section of the prison wall and overhanging the street.

Those in the street stood about and talked of the coming executions and of various bits of gossip and rumours concerning the Fenians. One story going the rounds was that an acquitted prisoner had been heard to boast that not only did he take part in the rescue but had helped form one of the local Fenian circles and also led the Manchester contingent to Chester earlier in the year. This man also insisted, it was claimed, that the killer of Sergeant Brett was not among the prisoners under sentence of death, but was still at large. He also, apparently, confirmed that Thomas Maguire had never at any time had anything to do with the Fenian Movement and had certainly not taken part in the attack on the van.

Mr. Digby Seymour had not spared himself in his efforts on behalf of the condemned men. His work, however, finally came to nought when the judges concerned in the case, after much deliberation, made known their final decision regarding an appeal, through Mr. Justice Blackburn's communication,

Sirs,

I regret to say that the result has been to satisfy us that the law is too clear to justify us in considering an appeal. Entertaining that opinion, we have officially informed the Secretary of State for the Home Department that there will be no further appeal to a court of law and that it is now for Her Majesty's Government alone to determine what shall be done with the convicts. This decision of ours is final.

CHAPTER 23

'A crowd of inhuman ghouls'

F riday night, and the crowds in the vicinity of the gaol had grown to huge proportions. Local beerhouses did a roaring trade, with the jostling mob conversing about one subject only. Though the majority were men there were many women and children to be seen, even *'babes in arms'*.

There was much joking and levity, with people singing, laughing and shouting merrily, as if it were some sort of national holiday. It must have been a grotesque and sickening scene, and one which caused Father Gadd to write later,

A crowd of inhuman ghouls from the purlieus of Deansgate and the slums of the city had been gathered for hours in the streets abutting the gaol, and had made the night and early morning hideous with the raucous bacchanalian strains of Champagne Charlie, John Brown and Rule Britannia!

Many of the shops around the prison were reported to be doing an extraordinary business, especially Sidebottom's, the tobacconists, whose 'Albert mixture' was in great demand.

'The crowd', one report ran, *'were in a thoroughly good humour, and remained so throughout the long night.'*

This despite the fact that the night was an extremely cold one, with a damp November mist beginning to rise above the murky waters of the River Irwell. Still, as the 'ghouls' were obviously determined to enjoy themselves, the state of the weather was hardly likely to put them off.

The crowd around the barriers was thickening rapidly as many left the beerhouses to make sure of a good view when morning came. The police were very much on the alert, especially those patrolling within the barriers, for as the streets in which they were erected contained rows of houses, they could not be completely closed until almost the last moment. Every house in New Bailey Street was visited and the name of each person living there taken down. Anyone else having business in the street or at the prison was checked at the barrier before being allowed to pass.

Some residents, however, inevitably took advantage of the situation to make money by letting window space to outsiders keen to

*Story of The Old Faith in Manchester. John O'Dea.

213

get the best possible vantage point. No doubt these people were claimed as visiting relatives. A party from Oldham 'took' an upstairs window quite close to the scaffold for the sum of ten shillings.

At 10am the special constables were marched in and formed up in lines between the scaffold and the barricades. The police then cleared the street as far back as Albert Bridge. Like the police, the Specials were under the command of Captain Sylvester, and were recognisable by their armbands. The railway viaducts, over which trains passed close to the prison walls, were patrolled by the military, as were all streets at the rear of the gaol, where troops of the cavalry and artillery stood ready to act at a moment's notice.

Inside the walls, a guard, drawn up from men of the 57th Regiment, had been doubled, while further reserves of the 72nd Highlanders stood by at Albert Street police station on the Manchester side of the river.

In addition to the military, and the Manchester and Salford police forces, most neighbouring towns sent men, Oldham contributing twenty under the command of the Chief Constable. To help protect the town in their absence, no doubt as a precaution against the possibility of any Fenian activity, over ninety Specials were sworn in and spent most of the evening engaged in sword drill. They turned out to be rather a rowdy lot and before the evening was over one Special had been taken into custody for drunkenness.

Throughout the night the crowds around the prison grew steadily. Song after song was struck up and hundreds joined in. A contemporary report stated,

The choruses were taken up with great aptitude and must have been almost audible within the prison walls. There is perhaps nothing more out of harmony with the awful occasion than an execution mob. They are usually of a caste to be seen so often in the streets; largely composed of ruffians, devoid of sympathy, wanting in feeling and untouched by any religious sentiment. They are drawn together by the very inhumanity of their motives, and look upon a punishment which the law sets up as the most dreadful within its catalogue with no more respect than the devotees of the most commonly condemned sports regard their favourite pastimes.

By six o'clock in the morning the crowd had increased enormously, as had the clamour. Very few Irish people were to be found among the dense, swaying mass. They had obviously heeded the advice of their religious leaders, to stay away. Of course, many were already in church and many hundreds more would join them during the night and in the early morning.

214

There was though, at least one exception. For a brave, unknown Irishman did raise his voice in defence of his condemned countrymen. With a hostile, drunken crowd gathered around him, this man stood alone near the barricades in Chapel Street and spoke out forcibly and fervently on the plight of Ireland and the very bad effect that would result from the hangings. He was shouted down, his voice being drowned by the derisive, obscene shouts and laughter of the mob, before they broke again into another bawdy song.

There was no apparent sign of any Fenian activity, but a rumour that threats had been made against the life of Calcraft was confirmed when the hangman handed a note to the authorities, which read,

If you hang any of the gentlemen condemned to death at the New Bailey prison, it will be the worse for you. You will not survive afterwards.

Calcraft apparently took the threat very seriously, for he wrote to the justices,

I have received the enclosed letter. It seems a serious job. I hope you will look into it, and that I shall get home safe and sound again.
Yours respectfully
William Calcraft.

On O'Meagher Condon's reprieve coming through, the hopes of the remaining three convicts were naturally raised for a time, but as Friday wore on with no further development, the possibility of a favourable communication from the Home Office became more and more remote and they seemed gradually to resign themselves to their fate.

In the morning, a large number of the relatives of Allen and Larkin turned up at the prison, but found difficulty in gaining admittance. As they stood in a group outside the gates they were quickly identified and pointed out by passers-by, and an inquisitive mob soon gathered to stare at them. Fortunately, Superintendent Gee was on hand and escorted the relatives to the Albert Street police station. Some time later a message was received that Allen's mother would be allowed in to see him, and she returned to the prison accompanied by his uncle, John Hogan, his brother-in-law, and two young women, one his sister, the other a cousin. Both had travelled from Ireland.

At first only his mother was allowed inside the prison, and she was forced to endure a long wait in the corridor before being shown into her son's cell. Later the other members of Allen's family were allowed a brief visit, but Mary Hickey, the condemned man's fiancée, not being a relative, was now excluded.

215

Also waiting was Michael Larkin's wife, Sarah, a young child in her arms, and the other three children standing beside her, along with Larkin's mother, who appeared extremely agitated and repeatedly voiced the opinion that her son would not be executed, saying, 'The rope is not spun that will hang my boy.' Larkin also had two female relatives who had made the journey from Ireland, but were refused admission.

The warders standing guard in Larkin's cell witnessed a pathetic and heart-rending scene as the humble little family, which had not long before settled in Manchester with high hopes of a better life than they had known in Ireland, was united for the last time.

Father Gadd met the excluded visitors and assured them that the condemned men were preparing themselves in a becoming manner to meet their deaths.

These final partings must have been a harrowing sight indeed and would no doubt be vividly etched in the minds of those who witnessed them.

Michael O'Brien received no visitors. Like O'Meagher Condon he had no close relatives in England, their families being in America.

Father Gadd had been a tower of strength, particularly during this very difficult time. In these last lonely hours the condemned men would lean on him even more heavily, for though they had shown great strength of character, there can be no doubt that they must have been filled with dread at the thought of what was about to happen to them.

Father Gadd would not leave them at all on the day prior to their executions. At ten o'clock that night a final communication did arrive from London. It stated simply that no clemency could be exercised in their cases, and that they must die. It was the last hope gone.

That night Father Gadd, as usual, led the prisoners in prayer, then they all retired, having asked to be awakened early in the morning.

In his book *Story of The Old Faith in Manchester,* John O'Dea wrote that the condemned men were aroused at a quarter-to-five from *'tranquil and profound slumbers.'*

Certainly it is recorded that they rose early, about five-thirty. That they slept peacefully is doubtful indeed.

They were now attended by three priests, Father Gadd, Canon Cantwell and Father Keating. Father Quick had not yet arrived. A mass was held at which they received their last Communions, their Confessions having been heard on the previous day.

Father Gadd, an extremely resolute man himself, continuously exhorted 'his boys' to try to remain calm and strong, to show no fear. In

216

Allen and O'Brien he had two excellent subjects, for despite the horror of it all, they were so far standing up very well under the strain. Poor Larkin was a different proposition. He was beginning now to show signs of cracking, and who could blame him? He was a sick man with a large family to worry about, and was not physically strong to begin with. If, perhaps, he appeared less courageous than the others he is certainly not to be condemned for it.

Most of the time that morning was spent in prayer. At about a quarter-to-eight the tramp of feet was heard in the corridor. It was the Governor and his party, including the hangman and his assistant. Armstrong, a man described as *'a strong, powerful, manly fellow, upwards of six feet high.'*

Calcraft set about the job of pinioning each prisoner in turn, passing quickly from one cell to the next, the entire business being completed within minutes. Apart from Larkin, who appeared very shaky, the prisoners stood up very well to the first part of their ordeal. Allen and O'Brien seemed quiet and reasonably calm.

One can hardly imagine what the feelings of the reprieved O'Meagher Condon must have been. Probably a mixture of relief, pity, and intense mental anguish, as he sat there in his cell and listened to all that was going on.

When the thick leather straps had been passed around each man's waist, their elbows held by smaller loops and their hands strapped together in front of the body, all was ready. Last farewells were then exchanged between priests and prisoners.

The crowd outside the gaol had now grown to tremendous proportions, yet ironically, few would actually see the hangings, for the fog had thickened and now hung heavily over the grim fortress, a dense yellow haze, adding still more eeriness to the gruesome scene.

The mob, their spirits dampened somewhat by the chilly grey of early morning, were not nearly so noisy and boisterous as they had been a few hours earlier. They now seemed restless and anxious to see the event for which they had waited all night.

Through the fog the tramp of marching feet could be heard all around, both outside the prison and also within the walls, where a company of the 72nd Highlanders was assembled with fixed bayonets. Detachments of these were then ordered to climb ladders to a platform built along the inside of the prison wall to the same height as the scaffold. On reaching it they were just visible to the spectators in the streets below and were immediately ordered to keep out of sight, which they did by kneeling down.

217

The tiny procession was now moving through the prison. Warders stood with bared and bowed heads as it passed them, the intonations of the priests being answered by the condemned men as they walked slowly, trance-like, along the dim stone passages.

'Lord have mercy upon us. Christ have mercy upon us.'

Allen, with Canon Cantwell at his side, came first. The young Irishman's face was white as a sheet, and to those in attendance it must have been obvious that he was trying desperately to conceal any outward manifestation of weakness. He seemed to be praying earnestly, yet though his lips moved rapidly, no sound came from them. Close behind him came Michael O'Brien, a stronger-looking, more powerful figure than either of the other prisoners. In his hands was a crucifix, which he grasped firmly as he uttered the responses to the litany. The words came quite loud and clear. 'Christ hear us. Christ graciously hear us.'

Larkin, a slight, undersized figure, came last, his short straggly beard appearing unkempt against the pale, strained face. His physical strength had already begun to leave him, for he was supported by a warder on either side. The fervency with which he now prayed made his voice clearly audible for some distance.

The condemned men reached a flight of wooden steps which Allen began to mount slowly and laboriously, yet with still the same determined expression on his face. O'Brien followed him in similar fashion, but Larkin had to be helped up, stumbling uncertainly and painfully with every step, at the same time still repeating desperately: 'Lord have mercy upon us. Christ have mercy upon us.'

Outside on the platform, close to the scaffold, the kneeling soldiers shivered in the damp early morning air, their eyes nervously shifting from the three nooses swinging above the drop, in a macabre manner, towards the door leading onto the scaffold, then back again.

At precisely five minutes to eight o'clock the door swung open. First to appear was Calcraft. Close behind him came Allen. Though he seemed deliberately to avoid looking directly at the three ropes, he appeared composed enough and stood very erect, with head held high and long flaxen hair wafting gently in the breeze around his pale features. He was barely twenty years of age and at this moment looked even younger.

The three prisoners shook hands with each other. One contemporary report states that the hangman also shook hands with each prisoner in turn. This is possible, but doubtful, for it is recorded that as Calcraft approached him holding the white cap, Allen gave him a contemptuous look. The young Irishman stood aloof, almost proud, as his head was covered and the rope adjusted around his neck.

218

O'Brien stepped forward and walked to the rope at the other end of the beam, but Calcraft moved him to the centre. Before the white cap was placed over his head, O'Brien again took hold of Allen's hand and kissed him. Calcraft stood by, waiting. Then, as O'Brien resumed his place, upright and unwavering, the hangman covered his head and placed the noose around his neck.

Larkin had watched all this, his face contorted as a result of his great mental anguish. He was brought forward by the two warders, almost stumbling onto the drop. Before his head was covered each man had no more than a moment or two to cast a glance over the vast sea of faces below. The last glimpse they would ever have of the world.

The spectators, few of whom could clearly see in any sort of detail what was happening, because of the fog, had now fallen into a breathless, awed silence.

After his head had been covered and the rope placed around his neck, Larkin appeared to faint, falling first to his right. Then, after being held up by a warder, he slumped to the left, almost falling against O'Brien. The little tailor seemed to have lost the power to control his limbs and lurched forward just as Calcraft pulled the lever. The drop went down with a heavy thud and the three young Irishmen plunged out of view.

At almost that exact moment a further loud report was heard which had the effect of startling everyone present and bringing the riflemen to the alert. It was quickly realised, however, that the explosion had been a fog warning signal from the railway, which passed close by.

The rope supporting Allen swayed for only a short time, then hung still, a strong indication that his neck had been broken instantly. Unfortunately, this was not so in the cases of Larkin and O'Brien, for the ropes from which they hung suspended continued to jerk and swing about violently for many minutes afterwards.

A skilled executioner such as John Ellis* for example, who of course came later, would seldom fail to ensure that the victim died instantly. For if the drop was correctly measured – the weight of the body being one vital factor to be taken into account – it was usual for the neck to be broken, thus eliminating the possibility of slow strangulation. When this occurred the hangman was considered to have bungled his job and would receive an unfavourable report from the prison Governor.

The entire operation had taken no more than three minutes. Now the Governor and the rest of the officials, accompanied by the priests, returned to the interior of the prison – all that is, except Father

* The subject of *The Rochdale Hangman and his victims* by Jack Doughty. Jade 1998.

Gadd – who remained on the scaffold, clearly horrified at the thought that two of the prisoners were still alive, being slowly choked to death – and an old warder named Kirkland, who must himself have harboured some humane feelings. To Calcraft, of course, who now descended into the pit below the drop, this was not a unique situation. In the old days, if a victim still struggled after several minutes had elapsed it was not unknown for the hangman to finish the job by tugging at the wretched man's legs until he became limp. According to the account of historian John O'Dea, written in 1910, from information given to him by Father Gadd, this is precisely what Calcraft did, quickly, if horrifically, putting an end to the suffering of Michael Larkin.

Before he could turn his attention to O'Brien, however, Father Gadd came quickly down the ladder and fiercely forbade the executioner to lay a finger on him. Calcraft sullenly withdrew, leaving the priest alone in the pit with his charge, who still somehow clung to life. Father Gadd stayed with him, clasping O'Brien's hands in his own, which held the crucifix, and quietly praying, until finally the poor man's body ceased to twitch and the long-drawn-out agony was mercifully at an end.

Unaware of the drama being enacted below the scaffold, the majority of spectators began to turn and drift quietly off to their homes. It was as if the horror and terrible finality of it all had silenced even the most stony-hearted among them.

Inside the gaol Calcraft and his assistant, Armstrong, waited for the customary hour to elapse before the doctors could examine the corpses and officially pronounce them dead, after which they could be taken down.

The hangman's fee would total £20 plus expenses; £10 for the first victim and £5 each for the other two.

———————————

Each of the three executed men left a last 'declaration', written just a few hours before they were to die.

Allen again protested his innocence of the murder of Sergeant Brett. His letter reads;

I state this to put juries on their guard for the future, and to have them inquire into the characters of witnesses before they take away the lives of innocent men. But then, I ought not to complain. Was not our Saviour sold for money, his life sworn away by false witness?

Later in the letter Allen wrote:

I confess I nobly aided in the rescue of the gallant Colonel

220

Kelly and Captain Deasy. It is known to the whole world what my poor country has to suffer, and how her sons are exiles the world over; then tell me where is the Irishman that can look on unmoved and see his countrymen taken prisoner and treated like murderers and robbers in English dungeons?

May the lord have mercy on our souls and deliver Ireland from her sufferings. God save Ireland!

William Philip Allen.

The declaration of Michael Larkin ran;

Men of the world – I, as a dying man going before my God, solemnly declare I never fired a shot in all my life, much less the day the attack was made on the van, nor did I ever put a hand on the van. The world will remember the widow's son's life that was sworn away, by which he leaves a wife and four children to mourn his loss.

I am not dying for shooting Brett, but for mentioning the names Kelly and Deasy in the court. I am a dying patriot for God and my country, and Larkin will be remembered in time to come by the sons and daughters of Erin. Farewell dear Ireland for I must die a martyr for your sake. Farewell dear mother, wife and children, for I must leave you all for poor Ireland's sake.

After more in a similar vein, Larkin's letter ended:

Father in heaven, forgive those who have sworn my life away. I forgive them and the world.

Michael Larkin.

Michael O'Brien wrote;

I have only a few remarks to make. I did not use a revolver or any other firearms, or throw stones, on the day Colonel Kelly and Captain Deasy were so gallantly rescued. I was not present when the van was attacked.

I say this, not by way of reproach, or to give annoyance to any person, but in the hope that witnesses may be more particular when identifying, and that juries may look more closely into the character of witnesses before they convict a person to send him before his God. I trust that those who swore to seeing me with a revolver or throwing stones were nothing more than mistaken. I forgive them from my heart.

Later in the letter O'Brien referred to the rift between the Fenians in America.

I sincerely beg my countrymen in America to heal their differences and to unite in God's name for the sake of Ireland and liberty.

With reference to Colonel Kelly, I believe him to be a good, honourable man, unselfish, and entirely devoted to the cause of Irish freedom.

Michael O'Brien.

221

O'Brien left a second letter, addressed to his brother, in which he again maintained his innocence. In this rather lengthy document, O'Brien wrote of several other Irish martyrs and mentioned Peter O'Neill Crowley, a Fenian, who, during the rising in Ireland in March that year, had found himself, along with a comrade named John Mc'Clure, surrounded in Kilclooney Wood, Tipperary. The two of them, although on their own and heavily outnumbered, made a fight of it. In the end Mc'Clure was taken prisoner and Crowley shot.

O'Brien ended his letter,

...Give my love to my father and mother, to Mary Ellen, John Phillips, Tim, Catherine, uncles, aunts and cousins.

Farewell from your affectionate brother,

Michael O'Brien, alias William Gould.

This letter is to be found, in a good state of preservation, at St. Patrick's Church*, Livesey Street, off Oldham Road, Manchester, where I spent some time in discussing it with the parish priest, Monsignor Richard Earley, in March, 1979. At this time the Monsignor was over eighty and in poor health. He told me that O'Brien's letter had previously been kept at the Shamrock Hall in nearby Rochdale Road, an Irish club. When the club closed down, the secretary (also named O'Brien), kept the letter, eventually passing it on to Monsignor Earley.

The Monsignor, who joined St. Patrick's in 1947, told me that when Mr. Eamon DeValera paid a visit to Manchester in 1948 he asked if he might be allowed to take O'Brien's letter back to Dublin for the national archives. His request was politely refused, the Eire premier having to settle for a photograph of the original.

It was claimed in a contemporary newspaper that each of the condemned men had planned to make a speech from the scaffold, but that they were persuaded by Father Gadd to give up the idea.

Not long after the crowds had dispersed, the other seven convicted men, Daniel Reddin, John Carroll, John Brennan, Timothy Featherstone, William Murphy, Charles Moorhouse and Thomas Scalley, were removed from the New Bailey prison in a police van on the first stage of their journey to Millbank convict prison in London, where they would spend the next few years. The operation was carried

* It is interesting to note that a number of past pupils and parishioners of St. Patrick's have distinguished themselves in the world of entertainment, the most famous being the great Leslie Stuart, who wrote many hit songs, including *Lily of Laguna, Little Dolly Daydream* and *Soldiers of the Queen*; his brother Lester Barratt, the comedian; the Dalton Brothers; Mary Sheridan and Vincent Robinson, better known as 'Enoch', comedy star of stage, screen and radio in the 1940s.

out in the strictest secrecy and with perfect co-ordination as the streets abutting the gaol were now all but deserted. With a strong escort made up of warders and police armed with revolvers, the van was driven to London Road railway station, where the convicts were transferred to the London train only minutes before it pulled out.

Daniel Reddin, a Dubliner, was described later by Condon, as *'one of the bravest and coolest men I ever met.'**

According to Condon, Reddin became paralysed while in prison as a result of the punishment he received, and, believing him to be shamming, doctors persisted in prodding the soles of his feet with long needles. He died shortly after his release.

* Condon's account. (*Irish World*, 1908)

CHAPTER 24

Repercussions

That the executions had left many people highly perturbed, irrespective of nationality, there can be no doubt. Various bodies, as well as individuals, spoke out strongly against the Government's extreme action. At a meeting of the Reform League a member named Mote proposed that the following resolution be forwarded to the Prime Minister,

This council emphatically condemns the hanging of Allen, Larkin and O'Brien as judicial murder for political reasons only, by Her Majesty's Government; and this council therefore expresses heart-felt sympathy for their bereaved relatives.

Mr. Mote went on to accuse the authorities of having put the three men to death for the purpose of terrifying the Fenians, and not as a punishment for the pretended [sic] crime.

Although the resolution was seconded, several members asked Mr. Mote to withdraw it on the grounds that it would place in an invidious position those who sympathised deeply with the plight of Ireland but would have to vote against it.

Having established that the council, by and large, sympathised with the motion, the proposer then withdrew it.

The *Cork Examiner*, of November, 1867, gave the opinion that,

The Irish people will believe that three of their fellow countrymen were offered up on the scaffold as a sacrifice to the spirit of hatred and brutal revenge. We at least will not attempt to persuade them to accept injustice as one of the inevitable decrees of providence.

By way of contrast the *Northern Whig*, also of November, 1867, stated,

A stripling of nineteen and two other Fenians have died for Kelly and Deasy, and of course much Kelly and Deasy care. Stephens is in Paris, avowing himself with specious ostentation to be in great poverty, and borrowing money from his friends to pay even the expenses of the advertisements he issues for pupils as a teacher of English.

Kelly and Deasy are skulking in places best known to themselves, evidently not disposed to run the slightest risk.

The challenge has been openly given for this Fenian organisation, if it possessed one vitality worthy of acknowledgement by its enemies, to show itself. It slunk away to its fitting home; the slums of

Salford, Manchester and Liverpool, and allowed its wretched dupes to die a felon's death.

It is capable of midnight assassinations, of the most atrocious threats and the vilest bombast. When, however, it is resolutely confronted, whether it be by a dozen Irish policemen, or openly braved as it was in Manchester, it, like the bully and coward it is, thinks nothing of its solemn pledges and is only anxious to save its own skin.

Compare this conduct with that of Garibaldi and his volunteers near Rome. And yet we read in Irish organs, which abuse the liberty of the press, and which are themselves a proof that never before did a government tolerate so much, that Garibaldi, for whom the whole Italian people have such a passionate veneration, it is [sic] *mere filibust, while Kelly and Deasy are heroes.*

The persistent Mr. Finlen, determined to fulfil the promise made on Clerkenwell Green, did in fact lead his procession through the streets of London on Sunday November 24, the day following the executions. More than 2,000 people took part, including a small fife and drum band.

A meeting was afterwards convened in Hyde Park, when Finlen was again the most prominent speaker, delivering what he termed a 'funeral oration.'

At the conclusion of the speeches all the Roman Catholics present knelt down on the grass and offered a prayer for the three Manchester Fenians. The meeting then broke up with a dignity befitting the solemnity of the occasion, the mourners moving quietly away and heading for home.

At around three o'clock on the same afternoon more than 2,000 people congregated on the slopes of St. Joseph's Cemetery, Nechells, Birmingham, the majority of them wearing green ribbons on their hats. A young man began to read the Litany, whereupon the entire assembly knelt, some on the grass, others on the rough gravel. The scene was singularly impressive, not in the context of a religious service, but as a demonstration of the deep feelings of the Birmingham Irish for their three dead countrymen.

When the service was over, the police, who had kept a watchful eye on the scene, requested the mourners not to leave the cemetery in any sort of organised procession. The request was ignored. By the time the Irish had formed themselves up four deep on the gravel paths, the long green-flecked line stretched for almost a quarter of a mile. Solemnly, they filed out of the cemetery. The procession marched to Gosta Green, where an attempt was made by Inspector Kelly of the

226

Birmingham Police to break it up as several of the leaders began to make speeches. The meeting was eventually dispersed, but others were taking place at the same time in various parts of the city. At one of these, held at the gates of St. Mary's Church in Whittal Street, a serious incident occurred. About 10pm a Dr. Suckling, of St. Mary's Row, hearing a great volume of noise in the street, went outside. Standing at the corner of St. Mary's Row, the doctor listened for a few minutes to the speaker. At this juncture someone yelled out 'Order!' and immediately the mob began rushing off in all directions, probably under the impression that the police had arrived. A large unruly pack ran at the surprised doctor and proceeded to knock him about. Dr. Suckling attempted to get back into the house but his frightened wife had unfortunately bolted the door. He was struck about the head and knocked unconscious, but though very seriously injured, he eventually recovered.

The same mob, apparently in a frenzy, attacked two other people in a nearby street, while a ferocious clash between two Irishmen and a bunch of locals occurred at the Rose and Crown Inn, Whittal Street, and resulted in the Irish pair being turned out. They went away cursing, but returned later and hurled a large stone through the window. The landlord, a man named Baxter, unwisely thrust his head out and was struck a glancing blow from a hatchet, sustaining a severe, though not dangerous wound.

Several other meetings were convened in Birmingham that night. The Irish listened to the harangues and shouted their approval of the sentiments expressed. A man named Andrew Turvey was conveyed to the lock-up when he was found with a long-bladed carving knife in his possession, and was joined early the following morning by another named Welsh, described as a 'rough-looking fellow', who was apprehended roaming the streets with an axe.

The executions had been carried out without the slightest hitch. Good planning and tight security measures had ensured that there would be no further rescue attempts. The Manchester police and the City's magistrates were well pleased. It was over, and all was calm again. The hunt for Kelly and Deasy would go on, and rumours of 'sightings' would continue to come in from almost every part of the British Isles during the following months.

Meanwhile, the threat of Fenianism had been put down with a heavy hand, and it was the firm belief of the authorities that the hangings at Salford Gaol would prove such a powerful deterrent that in England, at least, serious Fenian activity would effectively cease.

They could not have been more wrong, for in hanging the three young Irishmen, they had given the Fenian Movement that which it had hitherto lacked – martyrs. Allen, Larkin and O'Brien were now in the illustrious company of Emmet, Fitzgerald, Wolfe Tone and all the others who had laid down their lives in the fight for Irish liberty. As the Manchester Martyrs, they passed into the realms of folklore, to be sung about and revered as *'the boys who smashed the van'*.

For the time being the threat of Fenianism had been quelled to some extent, effectively subdued even. But within a matter of weeks the whole business would again explode in the faces of the authorities when it was least expected.

As well as those who had been shocked and appalled at the carrying out of the death sentences, there were many who applauded the event. This is clear from reports of various incidents occurring up and down the country around this period. At Kirkham, Lancashire, an Irishman named Patrick Tracy was set upon by a mob outside the Swan public house, dragged inside, beaten and kicked, then 'put on trial' for Fenianism, various members of the company acting as barristers, judge and jury. After being found guilty he was sentenced to be thrown into a pit filled with water, and drowned.

Seized again by his tormentors, Tracy was carried bodily to the rear of the premises and flung without further ado into the pit, which contained more sludge, however, than water. Although badly shaken, he was able to crawl out on the other side and escape across the fields. No doubt the perpetrators had never intended to carry out their 'death sentence', but the Irishman had been given a very rough time and the affair inevitably ended up in court.

The defendants, William Bennett, Edward Birch, William Parkinson, James Porter and William Shorrocks denied that Fenianism had anything to do with it, insisting that they had merely questioned Tracy regarding an attack on a young man named Sanderson outside the Swan earlier the same evening. They claimed they had not laid a finger on the plaintiff, were obviously believed, and escaped any punishment whatsoever, the magistrates, astonishingly, dismissing the case.

The people of the town of Warrington were thrown into a panic some two months after the executions when rumours of an attempt to blow up the town's gasworks began to circulate. A lad of 13 turned up at the home of an Irishman living in Mersey Street, close to the gasworks, and told him to leave the house before the end of the week. When questioned, the boy said he had been sent by a woman named Finnerty, who lived at Town Hill, but police could not trace such a person and concluded that he had invented the tale.

228

However, just after 11pm on the following Sunday night, a police constable passing by Gas Street noticed a cloud of smoke rising from the gasworks and was all but overcome by the strong smell of gas. The policeman immediately alerted two gasworks employees who were on the far side of the yard. It was then discovered that a plug had been removed from the purifier, causing gas to escape at a rapid rate. The furnaces had just been drawn, and a huge heap of red-hot coke lay in the yard. If the gas had reached this a tremendous explosion would have resulted, which would no doubt have destroyed the works and many adjacent properties. Fortunately, the calamity was averted owing to the alertness of the constable.

Four men, one a noted Fenian and brother of the keeper of a beerhouse, a well-known Fenian haunt, were subsequently taken into custody. They were John Burns, Thomas Cloran, Michael Mulkearn, of Town Hill, and Edward Griffin of Tanner's Lane. All were employed at the gasworks and were in the yard at the time, which, if they were implicated, was somewhat surprising in view of the danger to them-selves. On being charged, three of them claimed they knew nothing, while the fourth said the plug had been blown out.

After the case had been heard it was announced that the magistrates were of the opinion that the removal of the plug had been a deliberate and malicious act. Yet although several witnesses had been called, including the gasworks manager, not enough evidence was produced to connect any of the prisoners with it. They were therefore discharged.

Several Irishmen were also arrested in the Welsh town of Merthyr Tydfil, where it was revealed that a man named William Casey had had the Fenian oath administered to him by one Patrick Coffey. Others arrested were Patrick Doran, said to be a local Centre, Captain Thomas Reardon, Captain William Holland, Patrick Casey and Robert Barrett.

CHAPTER 25

The horror of Clerkenwell

L ondon's Clerkenwell prison had a long history behind it even in 1867. In 1615, the Middlesex justices purchased a stretch of open countryside and built on it a House of Correction, the land and prison costing a total of £2,500. Between then and 1650 many religious and other allegedly dangerous people were imprisoned for such crimes as blasphemy. In 1668, the renowned diarist Samuel Pepys, visited a friend of his wife there.

Towards the end of the seventeenth century a new prison was erected on the south side of the old Bridewell and for many years both gaols remained in use. In 1769, fire destroyed the greater part of the new prison. It was believed at the time that the man responsible was a Papist who had started the blaze on the inside and then escaped in the confusion. In 1774–5, a new prison was built on a much larger scale.

During riots in 1780 a party of the insurgents approached the gates and insisted on the release of the prisoners. They brought wood shavings to start a fire, but some, realising that the flames might easily spread to nearby houses, as the street was so narrow, persuaded their companions to abandon the plan. So, although the gates were smashed open with pickaxes and many prisoners set free, no damage to life or private property ensued.

The old prison was demolished in 1804 and in 1818 was entirely rebuilt on more extensive lines. The walls were thick, solid and very high.

When Colonel Ricard O'Sullivan Burke was imprisoned there in the latter part of 1867, no one could have imagined they would be dynamited in a daring attempt to release the Fenian leader.

When Burke, along with fellow prisoner Joseph Theobald Casey, was brought up in court in December, 1867, he came face-to-face with the traitor Godfrey Massey, who was the prosecution's star witness. Massey stated that he knew Burke well, having first met him in New York in 1866. He told the court,

'James Stephens had an office at 19, Chatham Street. It was there I met Burke along with Stephens, Colonel Kelly and Captain John McCafferty. I knew him then as *Captain* Burke.

'I attended a meeting at Stephens' lodgings at East Thirteenth and West Eleventh Street, when the names were taken of those officers who had volunteered to go to different parts of England. Colonel Kelly it was who took the names.

'Some days after this Stephens was superseded, as he was insincere and grossly incompetent from a military point of view. Kelly then acted in his place.

'I left New York for England on 11th January, 1867. Burke had already sailed in advance of me. I landed in Liverpool, then proceeded to London, where I again met Burke and afterwards stayed with him in lodgings he'd taken at number seven Tavistock Street. He went by the name of Wallis and I by the name Cleburne.

'At this time Kelly was head of the organisation in London. General Cluseret was Commander-in-Chief of the Fenian armed forces, and I, as his deputy, had the job of organising in Ireland. I therefore gave instructions to Burke, appointing him to Macroom in the County of Cork. I told him to make himself acquainted with the resources of the district, and when the rising commenced to destroy the means of communication so as to force the regular army to march on an equality with us.'

Massey alleged that Burke told him he had been up to Birmingham and obtained credit for £900 worth of firearms, to be shipped to Ireland for the rising.

George Kylock, percussion cap and ammunition maker, and general dealer in firearms at 45 Littlehampton Street, Birmingham, followed Massey into the witness box and told the court,

'I know Burke, though not by that name. I first saw him in my office when he gave the name of Edward C. Winslow and said he was staying at the King's Head. I supplied him with 250,000 percussion caps and 40 Lemait and Girard's ten-shooter revolvers. The cost was £385–7–6d and he paid the money on the spot. He said he'd need a lot more revolvers and I got them for him from different makers. He examined them in my office.

Altogether I sold him 657 revolvers. The gross amount was £1,972, all of which is paid but £18, which was for some cases. There were also rifles and various other such items as bullet moulds and keys for locking the guns. There was once when I gave him credit for £698–1–6d and delivered the rifles to a place he had in George Street. Some of them were signed for by a man named Mullidy, who came to my office once with Burke, as his servant.'

Casey gave the witness a sharp look and laughed, whereupon Kylock said,

'I believe that is Mullidy. Now I see him laugh I believe that is the man, although I could not swear to him.'

232

The witness was in fact quite wrong, as was ascertained later when the real Mullidy was produced in court.

William James Hill, gunmaker, swore to having seen Burke in the company of Kylock, who had brought him to his shop at 9 St. Mary's Row, Birmingham,

'I was asked what quantities I could supply and told them 100 a week, which I did, and received payment from Mr. Kylock. I didn't know what the guns were for, but I remember hearing something mentioned about the Southern Confederacy.'

As the American Civil War had been concluded long before the period in question, the witness's last remark was possibly a lame attempt to justify his own actions.

Corroborating Massey's testimony, Mrs Eliza Lambert of Tavistock Street, Bedford Square, London, identified Burke as the man who had lodged with her.

'This gentleman is Wallis', she said, pointing to the prisoner, 'and that is Cleburne, his companion.' At this she indicated Massey, who had been brought back into the courtroom. 'They lodged together in the front room on the third floor of my house.'

William Greeny, employed by a firm of carriers, testified to having delivered 25 heavy wooden cases to 24, George Street, Parade, Birmingham, while Thomas Wakemen, foreman in the goods yard at Birmingham's Curzon Street Station, recalled having sent a consignment of similar boxes to an address in Park Lane, Liverpool. In each instance the name E.C. Winslow was mentioned as the recipient. Samuel Marriot, employed at Waterloo Station, Liverpool, said he thought the man who had signed for them was Burke.

The prisoners were remanded in custody and placed in the House of Detention at Clerkenwell.

Inevitably, a rescue plan was soon afoot. It was rumoured later that Burke himself planned his own escape. This could well have been the case, for the prison authorities very unwisely allowed both Burke and Casey to receive visitors, among them a young woman named Anne Justice, whose part in the terrible tragedy which was to follow would place her in the dock along with several fellow conspirators.

Two of the most prominent members of this ill-assorted band of London Fenians were the brothers William and Timothy Desmond, shoemaker and tailor respectively. The Desmonds, along with Nicholas English, also a tailor, and several other Irishmen, were kept in touch with the situation inside the prison by Anne Justice, a close friend of Timothy Desmond. They met frequently at various houses, where lengthy discussions took place on the subject of a rescue attempt, the

233

main concern being for Colonel Burke, who was facing an extremely stiff sentence.

The would-be heroes were undoubtedly inspired by the successful Manchester rescue, and at first serious consideration was given to the feasibility of mounting a similar operation. However, inept as they ultimately proved to be, the London Fenians at least had enough sense to realise that a second 'smashing of the van' while the prisoners were being transported either to or from court, would never work.

A few revolvers had been procured, mostly in poor condition, and also a quantity of percussion caps and flasks of powder.

It was stated subsequently in court that messages written in invisible ink had found their way out of prison via Anne Justice and into the hands of the plotters. It was also stated that when arrested Colonel Burke had in his possession the materials for writing such messages. To render the lettering readable a substance called cinnabar* is used. This Burke also had. Presuming that these things were taken away from him on his arrest, it is still conceivable that further supplies could have been passed to him by Anne Justice during the course of her visits. He would also, of course, have instructed her in the use of cinnabar. The result of all this was that a scheme for blowing a hole in the prison wall was conceived between Burke and those on the outside.

Having scraped together as much finance as their modest circumstances would allow, the plotters purchased a quantity of gunpowder and managed to obtain an empty barrel. The final details of the plan were worked out at the house of William Desmond. Present at this meeting were the Desmonds, Anne Justice, Nicholas English, James O'Keefe, James O'Neill, Jeremiah Allen, and a young man calling himself Jackson, whose real name was Michael Barrett. He could not have known it then, but Barrett was destined to play the leading role in yet another Fenian tragedy.

O'Neill told the meeting that he could get hold of a costermonger's barrow to transport the powder keg, which was to be placed against the prison wall while the inmates were at exercise on the other side. When the hole was blown, Burke and Casey would be standing by to race through the gap to freedom.

On the following day, 12 December, the Fenians met again at Desmond's house at twelve noon. All were present except Jeremiah Allen, whose absence, however, did not unduly worry the others, as he had intimated that he might not be able to attend at the agreed time. In fact, Allen did not appear at all that day and only learned that the attempt had failed when he met Michael Barrett in the evening.

* Of oriental origin, A mercuric sulphide, vermilion in colour.

234

It was to come to light later that Allen had at some earlier date been in communication with the police, but at what stage he first made contact was never clearly established. It must have been sometime prior to the first rescue bid on 12 December, for it was later stated in court that Allen had given information to an Inspector Thompson regarding a possible attempt to free Burke and Casey by attacking the police van on its way from the Magistrates' Court to the prison. After this plan was abandoned it may be assumed that the Inspector kept in touch with his informant. Yet, although Allen himself stayed well away from the action on 12 December, it would appear that he did not give the game away on that occasion, for nothing was done to interfere with the plotters.

On that day, while the prisoners were at exercise, a warder named Richard Maskell noticed Colonel Burke drop out of the line and retire to a far corner of the yard, where he removed one of his side-spring boots and slowly wiped the sole of his foot.

While Burke was leaning against the wall, apparently getting rid of a stone, the Fenians were on the outside with their keg of gunpowder, which they had somehow managed to convey to the prison virtually unnoticed.

The fuse was lit and the Fenians retreated to the shelter of a nearby alley, where they held their breath and waited. Nothing happened. After a time they cautiously returned to the barrel to find that the flame had gone out. Becoming aware of curious eyes upon them, they hastily hoisted the barrel onto the truck again and made off with it up a side street. They had not, however, attracted as much attention as might be imagined, only a few small boys having watched their weird antics.

By the following day, the authorities had been informed by Dublin Castle that an attempt to blow down the prison wall and release Burke and Casey was imminent. Surprisingly, however, it would appear that very little was done, apart from making sure that the prisoners themselves would not be in the exercise yard if and when the explosion occurred. The times of exercise were now varied and Burke exercised in one of the female yards. The only other precaution taken was to place a handful of policemen on patrol in the streets around the gaol.

Friday 13th was to prove extremely unlucky for many of the residents of Corporation Lane, Clerkenwell. The day began quietly enough with people coming and going in their usual neighbourly way. Everything appeared normal. Beneath the surface, however, things were stirring.

At 12–20pm. Anne Justice visited Casey, telling the warder at the gate that she was a relative. She was seen by George Ranger, a policeman in plain clothes on duty outside the prison. Ranger was still there when she left, and watched her cross the road to the Prince of Wales beerhouse. Later, at around 2pm, he saw her again, loitering near Short's Buildings. Thinking the woman's movements suspicious, Ranger went back inside the gaol and consulted with a warder named Moore.

Around this time a stranger knocked at the door of Mrs. Holder, a widow, of 4 Corporation Lane. Her son answered it to a man who asked if he might be allowed to go to the top storey of the house to try to get a look at his cousin who would be at exercise in the prison yard. The widow refused and shut the door in his face. Some time afterwards one of the warders noticed a man at the upper window of a house in Woodbridge Street, overlooking the exercise yard. He called a colleague, but when they looked again the man had disappeared.

After making inquiries about the prison visitor, Anne Justice, George Ranger left the gaol and immediately spotted the woman again. She was standing with a man outside the Prince of Wales. The man was Timothy Desmond, and from his manner he appeared to have been drinking. At about 3-20pm Jeremiah Allen and another man came down Stratton's Ground and spoke to Justice and Desmond.

All this occurred on the opposite side of the prison from where the explosion was to take place. The yard where the plotters believed Burke and Casey would be exercising ran parallel to Corporation Lane on the gaol's northern side. It was a densely-populated area, a fact apparently not taken into account by the dynamiters. There is no doubt that in handling explosives they were dealing with something about which they understood very little.

The prison wall was 25 feet high and two feet, three inches thick at its base, narrowing to about 14 inches at the top. It would soon become clear that the wreckers had not the vaguest idea of the amount of explosive necessary for the breaching of the wall. A 36-gallon beer cask, containing a mixture of petroleum and gunpowder, was to be the means of freeing Burke and Casey.

When Anne Justice visited Casey at mid-day, he could not have known then that the exercise arrangements were to be altered, for on leaving the gaol she made no attempt to interfere with the Fenians' plans.

At about twenty minutes to four that afternoon a man entered Corporation Lane pulling a costermonger's barrow. On it was the barrel,

236

covered by a piece of sacking. Having stopped and looked around to make certain he was not observed, the man removed the covering and tilted the truck, allowing the barrel to roll onto the ground. Two other men then appeared from a court opposite and set it upright against the prison wall.

One of the three then attempted to light the fuse, while the other two retired to the safety of a nearby passage. On seeing the light flicker, then go out, one of them tossed a box of matches across to his colleague, who again lit the fuse, which appeared to be a thick wad of tightly rolled paper thrust into the barrel's bung-hole. This time it flared up like a squib and was seen by several people nearby. One, a milkman, immediately ran off to look for a policeman and almost bumped into one just around the corner.

The dynamiters had already taken to their heels, scurrying up a nearby alley like rats along a sewer pipe.

P.C. Moriarty raced to the spot, but on seeing the fuse so well ignited he backed away rapidly. At that moment Frederick Dimmock, a boy on his way to Clerkenwell Green with a parcel of newspapers under his arm, approached the scene. He had seen 'a man in a light coat' set the fuse alight, and very foolishly went to get a closer look. Fortunately, before he could get too near to it, the barrel went off with an almighty roar. The newsboy was thrown to the ground and showered in sparks and broken glass. Amazingly, he escaped serious injury, as also did P.C. Moriarty, who was knocked flat on his back. The metal plate was torn from his helmet and the skirts of his greatcoat ripped away as cleanly as if they had been cut by a pair of shears. Apart from being very badly shaken, neither of the two suffered any permanent damage, which was something of a miracle, as several people some distance away were killed outright, others maimed for life.

Had the affair not turned out so tragically, it might have been almost laughable, for the would-be Fenian heroes, in attempting to blow a hole in the wall large enough for two men to get through, had succeeded in destroying over forty feet of it.

John Abbot, aged thirteen, who lived in the Lane with his parents at number five, told this story,

'I was standing outside the front door when I saw a big barrel close to the prison wall. A man left the barrel and crossed the road. Shortly after he came back and lighted it. He stood for a while till he saw the squib start to burn. Then he ran off. He was dressed something like a gentleman, with a long brown overcoat and a black hat. He had light coloured hair and whiskers.'

237

The boy saw no more after the stranger ran off, as he was thrown down and covered in bricks and mortar.

Mr. Thomas Young, also of 5 Corporation Lane, said he was standing at his door at the time.

'Little Johnny Abbot was beside me and called attention to what was going on. Two men were near the barrel when it was lit. Something began to fizz and they both ran off up St. James's Place. Then it blew up.'

The explosion rendered Young insensible and threw him about a dozen feet up the passage of his house, with Johnny Abbot clinging round his neck. After a few minutes Young's head cleared somewhat. He then discovered that his thumb had been blown off and was hanging by a bit of skin. Stumbling to his feet he took no more than a couple of steps before falling into the cellar, as the floor of the house had been torn up by the explosion.

Climbing back up, Young got Minnie Abbot, Johnny's eight-year-old sister, out of the building. She was very seriously injured and died later. He also got his wife and sister out before going to the hospital and having his own wounds dressed. Johnny Abbot was detained in St. Bartholomew's Hospital, but was not in a serious condition.

The house was completely shattered, there being very little left but the walls. Every room was wrecked and every single item of furniture smashed beyond repair. In all, eleven people were inside at the time, including relatives and lodgers. All were taken to St. Bartholomew's, some seriously injured. Two other houses, numbers seven and nine, also owned by Young, were similarly destroyed.

After watching Anne Justice and her companions for a while George Ranger had again returned to the prison. At about 3-45 he heard the explosion on the opposite side of the gaol and immediately ran out to look for the suspects. He later related,

'I went across to Short's Buildings, where I met P.C. Sutton. We soon spotted Timothy Desmond, Jeremiah Allen and the woman Justice. I knocked Allen down, then took him into custody along with Justice. P.C. Sutton arrested Desmond as he attempted to run off. We took the three of them back to the prison. When we got there a scuffle started in the yard and we put Allen and Desmond on their backs.'

The explosion was heard for miles around and alarmed people as far away as Brixton. As well as the massive breach in the wall, most of the prison windows were shattered and marks of the impact could be seen against the side of the building itself, where bricks had been hurled by the sheer force of the blast.

238

Practically every house in Corporation Lane was devastated. Windows were blown in, furniture destroyed and walls badly damaged. Even part of the roadway had been torn up for a considerable length close to the wall. Many adjoining streets also suffered badly from the effects of the explosion. Babies in their cradles, mothers and young children, were tossed against the walls of their humble dwellings, and workmen at their benches thrown to the floor.

At the moment the keg blew up, William Clutton was standing at the door of his stable in Davies Street attending to his horse. He was struck dead on the spot. Later examination showed that his breastbone bore the appearance of having been completely crushed.

For at least a quarter of a mile around the gaol the muddy streets glistened brightly because of the great quantity of splintered glass which was strewn about. As people cried and moaned among the rubble, willing hands rushed to help get them clear and to dig for their relatives. The victims had lost just about everything. Men, women and children covered in blood were dragged out of the ruins. A child named Minnie Thompson had her face completely destroyed by fragments of glass, while other wounds were caused by glass being driven through her clothing. She died later in St. Bartholomew's.

The shrieks of the women, the shrill screams of the children and general moaning added greatly to the horror of the scene.

Within a short time the Fire Brigade arrived on the spot, but the only fire to be seen was that in a grate high up in a wall of one of the devastated houses. It had been burning before the explosion, was still alight, and appeared to have suffered very little disturbance from the tremendous blast.

The firemen were informed that at least one person was believed to be still buried among the debris of one of the worst-hit houses. They immediately set about clearing away the rubble.

Some of the victims were taken to the Royal Free Hospital at Gray's Inn Road. At St. Bartholomew's a senior doctor said he had never seen such fearful wounds nor so much blood. To make things worse almost all the injured were covered from head to foot with black grime. Within a matter of hours it was established that at least four deaths had occurred. Apart from William Clutton and the two children, a Mrs. Hodgkins was also killed. Those made homeless were housed in the local workhouse.

The scene of devastation was visited by the Duke of Cambridge, Lord Barrington, Lord Colville, Home Secretary Gathorne Hardy and Mr. Liddell, the Under-Secretary, while the Prince of Wales and Queen Victoria sent messages of sympathy.

239

The sum of £500 was allocated by the Chancellor of the Exchequer for the relief of the distressed, and Inspector Potts of C Division received a further £50 from the authorities for immediate distribution among the worst hit. Sums varying from £2 to £5 were given out.

A collection was taken at the Catholic churches in the dioceses of Westminster and Southwark for the Clerkenwell victims, and a deputation of Irishmen waited upon the Home Secretary to present an address signed by 22,603 London Irish, expressing their loyalty to the Crown, and their determination to support the Government in suppressing conspiracy and sedition. Meanwhile, the authorities had posted notices offering a £400 reward for information leading to the apprehension and conviction of the perpetrators.

It was around this time that the defence counsel for Burke and Casey, Dr. Kenealy, withdrew from the case. He subsequently received several threatening letters from Fenian sympathisers.

The irony of the whole affair was that if the prisoners had been exercising in the yard at the time, it is highly unlikely that there could have been a single survivor, so great had been the impact and damage on both sides of the wall.

CHAPTER 26

Who fired the barrel?

S everal more suspects were soon dragged in, including William Desmond and Nicholas English, while the police also found themselves another traitor in the shape of one James Vaughan, who admitted in court that he had been a member of the Fenian Brotherhood right up until the day he saw the reward notices.

At the magisterial hearing of the case against Desmond and English, Vaughan was questioned by Mr. Lewis, who appeared on behalf of the prisoners, and was asked,

'I understand you were aware of what was to be done at the prison?'

'Yes', he replied, 'but I didn't believe it would be carried out to cause such a deal of bloodshed.'

In attempting to show the witness in as bad a light as possible, Mr. Lewis asked him,

'Have you been in the army?'

'Yes.'

'Are you a deserter?'

'Yes.'

'You admit it?'

'Yes.'

'What regiment were you in?'

'The 58th.'

'Were you ever court-martialed?'

'Yes.'

'How many times?'

'Once.'

'Only once? Are you sure of that?'

'Yes, I didn't come here to tell lies.'

'If you knew about the plot, why did you not communicate with the police sooner?'

'Because I thought only the wall would be blown down.'

Vaughan then told the court that there had been a meeting at a house in St. John's Square, which a Roman Catholic priest named Father O'Connor had attended. The priest, however, was not ultimately implicated in the plot.

Vaughan was directly questioned by the prisoner William Desmond, who asked him,

'How long have you known me?'

'About eighteen months?'

'During that time have you ever had reason to suppose I belonged to the Fenian Brotherhood?'

'Certainly I have.'

'Who do you say you saw at the meeting in St. John's Square?' Nicholas English asked.

'I saw you there.'

'And I saw you there', snapped back English, 'and a fine fellow you are.'

'You must not make such comments', the magistrate told him. 'Only ask questions.'

At the conclusion of the hearing, William Desmond and English were added to the three persons already charged with murder, these being Timothy Desmond, Jeremiah Allen and Anne Justice. Soon to join them were James O'Neill, James O'Keefe, Patrick Mullaney and Michael Barrett.

On hearing his fate, William Desmond brazenly laughed out loud, but English turned pale and appeared extremely upset.

Late on the night of 21 December, Anne Justice made a determined bid to strangle herself in her cell, but was stopped just in time. To prevent a repetition she was handcuffed, and warders were posted to watch her day and night. As well as a heavy guard of police, Grenadier Guards patrolled the corridors of the prison. There would be little opportunity for further rescue attempts.

Jeremiah Allen was soon freed, as also was James O'Neill, who protested strongly that he could bring a score of witnesses to say he had been in Glasgow on the day in question. Despite the fact that witness Thomas Young swore O'Neill was the man who fired the barrel with matches thrown to him by Michael Barrett, the prisoner was set at liberty.

The following were finally charged with murder at the Central Criminal Court in April, 1868. William Desmond, aged 38; Timothy Desmond, 46; Nicholas English, 56; Michael Barrett, 25; Anne Justice, 22 and James O'Keefe. All pleaded not guilty. The remaining prisoner, Patrick Mullaney, was not in the dock with the rest, having turned Queen's Evidence.

A number of witnesses claimed to have seen several 'roughs' hanging around Corporation Lane on the fateful day, among them Nicholas English, who had been in and out of the local beerhouses all day. However, the witnesses were far from unanimous in identifying the man who had actually fired the barrel.

242

Johnny Abbot swore that William Desmond was the man responsible. Another witness stated,

'William Desmond is very much like the man who stood by the barrel, but he had a lighter coat on, and a tall hat.'

A female witness, in naming Desmond, was quite certain that he had worn a white hat. This was probably correct, for when arrested, Desmond was wearing a black hat, but the white one was discovered stuffed inside his waistcoat.

Michael Barrett was also identified by a number of witnesses as the man who applied the match to the barrel, including a young boy, Charles Mosley, and eleven-year-old Thomas Wheeler, who was brought from the hospital to give evidence.

Another boy, Henry Morris, told the court that he was apprenticed to Patrick Mullaney, and that several months previously his master had been visited on more than one occasion by two men calling themselves Brown and Jackson. They had in fact turned out to be Colonel Ricard O'Sullivan Burke and Michael Barrett.

After Burke was arrested 'Jackson' continued to visit Mullaney's premises, and on the day of the explosion he and another man came in by the back door. Jackson's companion had a piece of his ear hanging off and was bleeding badly, Morris told the court.

'One of the workmen asked my master what had happened. Mr. Mullaney said that the man had been fighting and had his ear bitten off. I went into the back room for an ironing pad and saw Jackson trying to wash his neck. It was all black. He had shaved his whiskers off. He still had them on his cheeks, but the beard and moustache were gone. I think he'd changed his trousers too, as I saw Mr. Mullaney folding them up.'

Mullaney corroborated the boy's evidence regarding the whiskers, saying that Barrett had removed them because he was afraid he would be identified. Barrett had told him he was getting out of London as quickly as possible.

He was, in fact, later apprehended in Glasgow, which in itself could have had some significance, for both Barrett and the discharged James O'Neill had Glasgow connections, and during the course of the trials a strong rumour prevailed that Captain Murphy, Head Centre for Scotland, was implicated in the plot. But, as in the case of Father O'Connor, no concrete evidence was obtained by the police.

According to Mullaney, the man whose ear was damaged was not involved in the rescue attempt, and no further arrests were made.

Mullaney also confirmed that Colonel Burke had sent a letter in invisible ink out of the prison. Mullaney stated,

243

'I know that Michael Barrett was a spectator in court when Colonel Burke was brought up. I heard English talk about Greek fire on two occasions, and I know it was being mixed up at his house. It was kept in black bottles with corks to keep the air out. He asked me to store some at my place, but I refused.'

Michael Barrett was identified by several more witnesses as the man who fired the barrel. In the dock he was by far the most striking of the prisoners. His fellow conspirators were a rather ragged-looking bunch, their clothes being dirty, greasy and almost threadbare. Barrett, young and good-looking, was quite neatly dressed, in a well-cut coat and clean white shirt. Anne Justice presented a pathetic figure indeed, and seemed to have suffered more than the others from her imprisonment. During the trial she was allowed a seat.

Later in April, Anne Justice was acquitted of the charge of murder. On hearing the court's decision she turned to Barrett and kissed him, shook hands with the other prisoners and whispered something to Timothy Desmond, then left the dock in a very excited state. Before she could leave the court, however, she was reminded by the judge that she would remain in custody to answer other charges.

After all the evidence had been heard, Michael Barrett alone was found guilty of murder. The other prisoners were held on charges of treason-felony, but all were ultimately discharged, the Attorney-General having decided not to proceed with the remaining indictments against them. Michael Barrett was sentenced to death.

With Barrett awaiting execution, the case against Burke and Casey proceeded. They had made a second court appearance some weeks earlier, charged with assaulting Inspector Thompson, who was later rewarded for his bravery in apprehending them with the sum of £10, awarded by the Home Secretary. P.C. Fordham, who assisted in the arrest and 'displayed great firmness, though ignorant of the desperate character of the suspects', was awarded £2.

On their next appearance in court, in April, 1868, Burke and Casey were joined in the dock by a good-looking man of about thirty, who gave his name as Henry Shaw, but was said to have been known also as Mullady, Mullidy or Malady. The three men were charged with treason-felony.

The notorious John Joseph Corydon was called to the witness box. He was twenty-six years old and had served in the United States Federal Army, first as a private, but finishing as a lieutenant. He had taken the Fenian oath in 1862. Up to the time of his appearance in court to testify against Burke and Casey, he had received a total of £300 for betraying his friends.

Corydon immediately identified Shaw as Harry Malady, a Fenian who had lived in Salisbury Street, Liverpool, at the house of a Mrs. Blackmore.

'He lodged there with several other Fenians, including Thomas Farrell, a Centre, Harry Byrne and John Lennon.

'I saw him at meetings in Liverpool and Birmingham in the company of Burke and Casey. I was aware that they were buying arms. After the seizure of some guns they were storing, Farrell and Malady left for America. That was in 1866. Malady came back at the beginning of 1867 with Captain Rogers and nine or ten others, including Captain John McCafferty.

'A few days before the Chester affair I was at a meeting in Liverpool and saw Malady there. We all had orders to be at Chester on the Monday night. A week after this we were given orders to go to Ireland. This was at a meeting in the Zoological Gardens in Liverpool. Malady was there again. Captain Beecher, the paymaster, was in charge, and he gave us the money to travel. I next saw Malady in County Mayo.

'I knew Colonel Burke in America. He'd been a sergeant and later became a Captain in the 15th New York Engineers.'

Amelia Tye, assistant to Mr. Kylock, the Birmingham arms dealer, identified Burke as the mysterious E.C. Winslow, and Malady as a man who had given her a letter addressed to her employer. John Devany, another Fenian traitor, also gave evidence against Colonel Burke.

In early April, 1868 an application was made under the Copyright Act to restrain a London photographer from selling copies of a picture of Burke, at that time lodged in Newgate prison.

Apparently, Burke had consented to sit for it in the prison yard on condition that no copies were sold. He had been led to believe that the picture was wanted for purposes of public justice only, but the photographer soon began disposing of them for his own profit. Burke then took the step of making over his own copyright to a Mr. O'Halleran, in consideration of that gentleman's undertaking to defray a portion of the Colonel's legal expenses. An order nisi was granted.

Henry Shaw, alias Harry Malady, received a sentence of seven years' penal servitude. Burke got fifteen years, while Casey was discharged.

The gallant Colonel, in his address to the court, admitted that on the evidence produced no jury could have acquitted him. He declared, however, that as an alien he owed no allegiance to Her Majesty the Queen 'beyond respect', and that therefore he could not be held guilty of the crime of treason-felony.

In December, 1867, two other gun-runners had been picked up by the police. They were William Phearson Thompson, alias Patrick Lennon, who was apprehended at London Road Station, Manchester, while in possession of more than forty revolvers, and William Hogan of Bradford Street, Birmingham, local secretary of the St. Patrick's Assurance Society. The former was charged with being involved in the attack on the van in Hyde Road, Manchester, and the latter with being an accessory before the fact.

The execution of Michael Barrett was fixed for Tuesday 12 May, 1868, to be carried out in front of the gaol at Newgate, where many notorious murderers had been finally dispatched.

Because much doubt had been expressed regarding some parts of the evidence against him, a stay of execution was granted for seven days, during which time Commissioners were sent to Glasgow to take further evidence on the spot. As it turned out, the time allowed proved insufficient and a further seven days was agreed upon. It was all to no avail, for when the investigation was complete it was announced that no new evidence had been produced to warrant a re-opening of the case, and that Barrett must go to the gallows.

As usual the morbidly curious were there in force to see the wretched young Irishman despatched. From midnight several hundred people loitered in the streets, idly lounging against the barricades. Most of them had come straight from the beerhouses, bringing bottles of liquor, which they consumed steadily throughout the night, an extremely mild one. Some found themselves a good vantage point, set-tled down, and had a nap while awaiting the 'show'. To break the monotony the usual bawdy songs were sung, while occasional quarrels broke out, to be settled with fists and foul language.

Around 3am, as the clear darkness of a fine spring night gradually began to give way to the greyness of dawn, those slumbering on the pavements, or in doorways, were aroused by a heavy rumbling from

246

within the prison yard. The huge gates slowly opened and the scaffold, a ponderous contraption, was drawn forth to its place in front of the great walls.

At 4am the beerhouses re-opened and steadily filled with bleary-eyed men and women still suffering the effects of the previous night's drunkenness. By six o'clock most of the drinkers were back on the streets, anxious not to lose their places. Among them could be seen the odd respectably-dressed person and a number of apprentices.

Though there was little evidence of any Irish representation in the crowd, the police were there in force, armed with revolvers and cutlasses, every lane, court and alley leading to Newgate being well covered. The undercurrent of excitement seemed to increase as the early hours passed, until, by 8am, it had reached fever pitch.

Shortly before this, the hangman went into Barrett's cell, where the priest, Dr. Hussey of Moorfield church, was praying with the condemned man. Calcraft, the hangman, at once pinioned the prisoner, who did not attempt to resist in any way, but held himself erect in a quietly dignified manner. He was taken by a side passage to the northern part of the gaol and onto the scaffold. The young Irishman took his last walk with a firm, determined step. He was asked by the executioner to take his place on the drop, which he did without the slightest sign of fear or hesitation. Calcraft quickly drew the cap over his head and placed the rope in position.

At this point the hangman seemed to fumble a little over his work. He adjusted the rope several times more before he was satisfied with the position of the knot, then moved the condemned man a foot or so to get him directly under the beam. The final operation of pinioning the victim's legs was then carried out. During all this the priest held Barrett's right hand as the prisoner joined quietly but earnestly in the prayers.

Before Calcraft left the drop he took hold of Barrett's free hand and shook it very feelingly, whispering a few words to him as he did so. When the drop fell Michael Barrett appeared to die very quickly, without too much suffering. From the moment Calcraft entered his cell he made no remark of any kind.

Dr. Hussey told reporters that no last statement had been made by the dying man which he could pass on to them. He added that during the course of his attendance at the gaol he had never met a prisoner who was as sincerely repentant or one who died in a more devout frame of mind. The prison officials also spoke very highly of Barrett's conduct.

247

After hanging for an hour the body was cut down and buried within the precincts of the gaol.

Michael Barrett was the last person to be hanged publicly in this country.

Only one month later, at a Fenian club established in Paris on one of the City's most frequented boulevards, William Desmond was to be seen in the company of several Fenians, including James Stephens. He was heard on a number of occasions to declare openly that Michael Barrett was innocent and that he himself had fired the barrel. Desmond admitted that Barrett had been involved, but claimed that he was certainly not guilty of the specific crime for which he had forfeited his life, and should be avenged by a series of systematic executions throughout England. Fortunately he was not taken seriously.

CHAPTER 27

Another Fenian hero

In the months following the smashing of the Fenian forces in Ireland, the entire organisation was in a state of absolute chaos. Prominent Brotherhood leaders were arrested almost every week, their despatch to gaol in most cases being no more than a formality. This was due to the help of traitors, among whom Massey and Corydon were the most notorious, though there were a number of others, such as Devany and Talbot.

One man, however, continued to evade capture, while still carrying out raids on military installations in Ireland throughout 1867.

He was an extremely bold Irish-American named William Mackey Lomasney, better known as Captain Mackey, who had been present at the meeting in New York when Stephens was relieved of command.

Mackey had originally arrived in Ireland in 1865 and was arrested at Queenstown on suspicion of being a Fenian. On the strength of certain documents found on him he was committed for trial towards the close of that year, and, like Captain John McCafferty around the same period, was released on a technicality. Being an alien and not having been convicted of any crime, he was allowed to go, on condition that he leave the country, which he did. Embarking on an Inman steamer that winter he was not seen again in Ireland until the beginning of 1867.

On 5 March that year, Mackey, then calling himself Francis Lomas, commanded the second division of the Cork Infantry of the Irish Republic, which attacked and burned the barracks at Ballyknockane.

After the rising had been put down, nothing more was heard of Mackey, and it was supposed that he had escaped to America. Some months later, however, a series of daring raids, obviously calculated to cause panic, took place around Cork. These continued throughout 1867.

In the early part of February 1868 the police came into possession of information – again the result of traitors in the Fenian ranks – to the effect that the man responsible was none other than Captain Mackey, who had made Cork City his headquarters. In addition to carrying out these raids he also made periodic visits to Fenian circles in other districts, and was playing a big part in attempts to re-organise the shattered remnants of the Brotherhood.

On receipt of this intelligence the police made searches in various parts of Cork City, but without result. In one instance they were furnished with the street, if not the exact house, where Mackey was said to be hiding. Every dwelling was thoroughly searched, but the fugitive, having got wind of the raid, had quietly changed his quarters only a couple of days before.

At the time the search was made Mackey had not long returned from Macroom, where he had gone to organize one of the most daring raids he had ever planned in Ireland, the seizure of Macroom Castle. The Castle was the headquarters of the West Cork Artillery Militia, as well as being the private residence of Colonel White Hodges, and the Fenians supposed that it contained the arms of the regiment.

With 50 men armed with revolvers, Mackey planned to over-power the militia guard and carry off as many of the weapons as possible. But when the men were all gathered together ready for action a quarrel developed among them which Mackey was unable to quell. At the last moment the operation had to be abandoned. Disgusted at the unmilitary behaviour of the men, Mackey denounced them as cowards. Then, after dismissing them, he set off and walked all the way back to Cork City the same night, a distance of over 20 miles. An astonishing feat by modern standards, but no doubt quite commonplace in 1868.

Having changed his address, Mackey felt safe enough, but the police picked up his trail more quickly than he had anticipated. On Thursday morning 15 February they received definite information as to where he could be found, and a plan for his capture was quickly formulated. Knowing their man to be an elusive customer, the police were determined to spread a net that even Mackey would be unable to slip through.

That evening several groups of policemen, numbering almost a hundred, moved quietly into position at the furthest extremity of every avenue leading from Market Street, a thoroughfare connected by a number of narrow lanes, with North Main Street on one side and the quays and a quarter inhabited by the very poor, on the other. At one end, near Patrick Street, was a narrow opening, easily guarded, with the gaol commanding the approach at the other end. Each and every one of these points was well covered, and most of the policemen involved carried firearms.

At 9am Head Constables Geale and Walsh, with Constable Casey, all three in plain clothes, strolled casually into a public house kept by a man named Cronin, in Market Street, close to Portney's Lane, while three other constables took up their positions outside the front door with several others going to the rear.

250

The two Head Constables walked straight through to the back parlour where they found four men, the proprietor, two customers and Mackey, who was immediately seized by Geale. The Captain's companions were also arrested and offered no resistance, but Mackey, after being momentarily taken aback, suddenly wrenched himself free and made for the stairs. Before he could mount them, Geale had pounced on him again and a violent struggle ensued. Both were muscular men, and though Geale was the bigger of the two, he was a good deal older than Mackey. He succeeded in pinning the American against a wall. Constable Casey came to his assistance, while the third policeman held the other prisoners at gunpoint. But before he could be handcuffed Mackey made one last desperate effort to break away. Getting one hand free he drew a revolver from his breast pocket. Geale saw the danger just in time and grabbed the weapon. The two men went down in a heap and as Mackey fought to regain control of the gun it suddenly went off. The ball missed Geale but struck Constable Casey, inflicting a severe wound. Geale finally got the revolver away from Mackey, then held the Captain firmly on his back as the other constables entered the premises and helped to secure the prisoners.

By this time at least 50 policemen had surrounded the building, with a large crowd also in attendance. Cries went up that the police were arresting a Fenian, and as the crowd pressed closer the constables were forced to drive them back.

Mackey and his companions were brought out. The Captain seemed greatly agitated and quite breathless after his struggle, but though handcuffed and heavily guarded, he was still not subdued and kept glancing around while being led through the crowd, as if still searching for some means of escape or possible rescue. Surrounded by so many armed police, he must surely have realised that there was no hope of getting away.

When taken into the Bridewell Mackey was in such a state of excitement that passion overcame discretion. After first giving his name as Murphy, he began to taunt the police and boast of all he had done to annoy and perplex them. He also demanded to know who had sold him and bitterly denounced the traitor.

That same week a further incident in Cork led to a minor riot, when several men were arrested for shooting at a policeman. A larger mob, assailing the police with stones, attempted to free the prisoners, but were driven off by mounted constables armed with swords and others on foot with fixed bayonets. The rioting and attacks on the police continued all that day until after midnight. Many constables and

251

rioters were badly injured, and a man named O'Leary died in hospital the following morning.

The authorities had more than enough against Mackey to put him away for a very long time, but worse was to follow. Two weeks after the shooting in Cronin's bar Constable Casey died, and Mackey found himself facing a charge of wilful murder, a crime of which he was almost certainly innocent.

In the dock at Cork Assizes the prisoner looked much younger than his 27 years. Unusually for those days he was clean shaven, with neither moustache nor side whiskers. Not very tall, he was slim but muscular, carried himself with a proud military bearing, and had a look of keen intelligence about him. Though his clothes were well worn and lacking several buttons, his appearance was nonetheless that of a tidy, well-turned-out gentleman.

During the proceedings, Mackey was busily engaged in taking notes and conferring with his counsel. At other times he would glance around at the faces in court, which was always densely crowded. A large number of ladies packed themselves into the Sheriff's box and the galleries. The appearance of the dashing Captain in the dock was the attraction of course and his smiling, courteous manner and the way in which he conducted himself generally did not disappoint them.

A squad of constables was placed strategically around the courtroom and along the corridors outside. In the hall was posted a strong body of soldiers and constabulary armed with rifles. It was the same in the surrounding streets, with both mounted and foot soldiers standing by in case of any further disturbance. In all more than 500 policemen were on duty, forty of them mounted. A large proportion of these had been brought in from other districts and were billeted in private houses taken over by the authorities. In case of emergency, troops of the 9th Lancers, 10th Hussars, the 62nd and 81st Foot, were standing by under the command of Major Campbell. Over the barracks the Union Jack was kept hoisted at all times. The lowering of it would be the signal to turn out the troops.

During the examination of the first witness the Grand Jury came into court with a true bill against the prisoner for robbery of arms from the martello tower at Foaty.

The trial for murder then continued, the jury eventually bringing in a verdict of "Not Guilty". Mackey was now tried on the less serious charges, found guilty, and on Saturday 21 March was brought up for

252

sentencing. When asked if he had anything to say why sentence should not be passed on him he replied that he was satisfied with the verdict, but explained,

'It is fair and just – according to British law, but I do not consider it so in accordance with right and justice. I would like to thank the jury for their recommendation of mercy, but, with every respect to the court, I regard the recommendation with utter indifference. I want no mercy.

'Tonight I shall sleep in a prison cell; tomorrow I shall wear a convict's dress. But to me it will be a far nobler garb than the richest dress of slavery. It is as impossible to subdue the soul animated with freedom as it is for England to crush the resolute will of this nation, determined as it is to be free or perish in the attempt.

'According to British law these facts proved against me – fairly proved I acknowledge – may be crimes, but morally, in the eyes of free men and in the sight of God, they are more ennobling than disgraceful.

'It is surely not a crime to assist our fellow men to acquire those rights which no man, no nation, can justly deprive them of. If devotion to Ireland and love of its faithful, honest and kind people is a crime – then I proudly and gladly acknowledge my guilt.

'Much has been said in these trials regarding the objects and intentions of Fenianism. I know that the motives which prompted me were purely patriotic and unselfish, and the same can be said of most members of the organisation. I know of very few persons, with the exception of such contemptible wretches as Corydon, who have profited by their connection with Fenianism. My own friends lost all they ever possessed by it. Talbot and Corydon I believe have sworn at previous trials that it was the intention of the Fenians to have divided the lands of Ireland amongst themselves in the event of success. Though a humble member of the organisation I have had the honour of being acquainted with the majority of the Brotherhood's leaders on both sides of the Atlantic, and I never knew one of them to have any desire other than the satisfaction of seeing Ireland free. That was the only reward they ever wished for.

'I may say that liberty, if worth possessing, is worth struggling and fighting for. The Government of England think they have seen the end of the struggle, but I tell them they have not even seen the commencement.

'Therefore my lord, I say I was determined and quite ready to sacrifice my life if necessary to gain that liberty for Ireland, and I am not now going to be so mean-spirited, so cowardly, or so contemptible, as to shrink from my share of the general suffering. I am ready then for the sentence of the court, satisfied that I have acted right, committed

253

no wrong, outrage or crime whatsoever, and that I have cast no disgrace upon my parents, friends, my devoted wife or upon myself. I am ready to meet my fate, and I rest in the calm resignation of a man whose only ambition throughout life has been to benefit and free – not injure – his fellow man.'

After reviewing the evidence brought against him, Mackey concluded his lengthy speech with the inevitable cry of 'God save Ireland.'

It had been an impassioned and very moving address, having about it the unmistakable ring of truth and sincerity. Even the judge was touched by it, as could be detected by the gentle way he now spoke to the man in the dock.

'I am very sorry for you, and for your poor young wife, who must suffer in your suffering, and I shall not aggravate the pain of your position by useless argument to alter the opinions you hold. You will have time enough in the dreary hours of seclusion to reconsider those opinions and modify them by calm reflection, and I have no doubt that you will yet mourn for the mis-spent energy and criminal folly of the past.

'But I will say a word to those with whom you have been associated, or who may be disposed to imitate your conduct, to their own destruction and to the great detriment of the country to which many of them, I don't doubt, have a sincere attachment. I would ask them to note the lesson that secret conspiracy brings ruin, swift and sure, to all who engage in it.

'I would ask them to listen to the warning voice which has come to them across the Atlantic – the voice of a man of high ability, and they will hear John Mitchel* expose with courageous truthfulness the gigantic delusion by which they been fooled, the fatuity with which they have obeyed leaders who lured them to destruction.

'I would entreat men of honest minds and pure intention, who have been wretchedly misled, to relinquish this insane struggle against the irresistible power of a mighty empire, which can only end in disaster to themselves.

'The sentence of the court is that you be detained in penal servitude for the term of twelve years.'

Mackey stood up and said that he wished, before being taken away, to remove an impression, quite unintentionally conveyed by his counsel, that it was the soldiers in the martello tower who might have stolen gunpowder themselves and made the charge against him to cover up their own crime.

* John Mitchel, the former Young Irelander, and a man much respected among Irish rebels, in his newspaper, published in New York, denounced Stephens as a liar and a humbug.

254

'I wish to say that no charge of this sort could be made against these men, who had done their duty as well as they possibly could.'

'Very good', replied the judge. 'Very proper.'

The prisoner continued, 'And with reference to what your lordship had to say regarding... '

'I'm sorry', interrupted Mr. Justice O'Hagan, 'but I cannot hear anything more now that sentence has been passed.'

Mackey nodded, looked up in the direction of some female friends in the gallery, smiled and blew kisses to them in a rather theatrical manner, then retired from the dock.

Mackey's career had been colourful, if somewhat brief, and as the judge had so eloquently put it, he would now have plenty of time to reflect on the error of his ways. Surprisingly, however, the long years spent behind bars apparently did nothing to temper the Captain's fanatical feelings, for on his release he immediately resumed the fight.

At a time when Charles Stewart Parnell was striving to achieve the same result by more peaceful means, the impetuous Mackey joined up with a bunch of characters as reckless as any of the old Fenians.

In 1884 he finally paid the penalty, blowing himself up while attempting to dynamite London Bridge.

CHAPTER 28

The last remnants

The quarterly return of 'Births, Marriages and Deaths' registered in Ireland at the end of September, 1867 clearly illustrates a tremendous decrease in the population. A total of 18,475 persons (9.851 males and 8,624 females) emigrated, mainly to America. In the previous year the corresponding quarter had seen 19,640 leave the ports of Ireland for foreign parts. So it would be quite correct to say that the Irish were by this time scattered all over the world.

Some, in fact, were forcibly shipped overseas. In October, 1867 for instance, the convict ship *Hougoumont* was loaded with a cargo of several hundred prisoners at Portland. At around mid-day, ninety Fenians, chained together, were marched down to the pier under an escort of the 13th Light Infantry and put on board.

Also making the long journey to Australia was Captain Young, Governor of the penal settlement at Freemantle, who was returning from leave.

Some time after the ship departed an extraordinary story found its way back to England via a Sydney newspaper, in which it was stated that a Fenian ship had sailed to intercept the *Hougoumont*, those on board intending to rescue the Irish convicts. This foolish rumour was taken seriously by the Admiralty, which promptly dispatched Her Majesty's ship *Brisk* to run down the phantom enemy vessel.

The *Hougoumont*, however, arrived safely at her destination on 10 January, 1868. Her master, Captain Cozens, later wrote to a friend in Adelaide,

For the information of yourself and all the good folks of South Australia I inform you of the arrival here of the 'floating hell' the Hougoumont. *I was surprised and vexed to see newspapers printing such trash. The fellow who wrote it ought to be kicked. He knows nothing at all about the discipline of a convict ship.*

We were supposed to have a bad lot on board, and yet no attempt was made to take the ship, nor were the prisoners kept below like wild beasts. On the contrary, they were on deck every day from daylight till dark, and gave not the slightest trouble. The Fenians conducted themselves in the most satisfactory manner, and only two of the other fellows had to be flogged.

257

Few Irish-Americans now remained in England or Ireland. Mostly, they either went back home or found their way over to France, where they hung around with revolutionaries of various nationalities in Paris.

Under the heading *'Fenianism, a bad speculation'*, the Paris correspondent of the *Irishman* had written, some time late in 1867,

I have met three Irish-American officers of distinguished service here in Paris during the last year. I will give an example of the luxury in which they are living.

Their breakfast costs them nothing, as they lie in bed till dinner hour. Their dinner costs 5 sous, which is about 2½d. Their suppers are left-overs from dinner.

The last time I saw Captain C—— formerly of Corcoran's Legion, he was leaving for London on money lent by a friend. The last time I saw of Captain K—— of the Irish Brigade, he was seeking employment as a common labourer at the Exhibition. And on the last occasion I met the gallant Captain B—— of the Federal Engineers, his earthly goods were wrapped up in a sheet of newspaper under his arm, and he had no idea where he would lay his head that night.

The New York correspondent of the *Cork Herald* reported that a circular had been sent to all Fenians in America calling for *'the exercise of redoubled energy in putting the Brotherhood in a respectable state of organisation again'*, and added,

The aspect of the present day is not at all gloomy after the stormy past. On the contrary, the prospects are even brighter than before and augur well for a brilliant termination of our struggle against the power of a mighty nation.

The Massachusetts Fenians have recently been in council in Boston. The Fenians of California and Nevada are also bracing themselves for a long pull, a strong pull, and a pull together.

Following these stirring words there were further forays into Canadian territory in 1870 and 1871, but these, predictably, fizzled out in much the same manner as the earlier raids.

That the Fenian Movement was rapidly deteriorating there was no doubt. Its high point had been reached and was now far behind it, despite the fact that a number of its leading lights still retained their freedom, notably Colonel Kelly and Captain Deasy. Both would now have to content themselves with becoming figures of legend; heroes of Irish folklore. For many months, however, they would continue to be hunted men. 'Sightings' would be constantly communicated to the authorities, but no trace of them would ever be discovered, at least not on this side of the Atlantic.

258

Some reports stated that the fugitives had never left Manchester and were still hiding in the City weeks after their rescue. One such report, in the form of a letter which appeared in an Irish newspaper in November, 1867, stated that immediately following their escape, Kelly and Deasy took refuge in the house of an old Irish woman, where Kelly disguised himself, slipped out of the back door, and mixed with the crowd. The report went on;

An omnibus passed at that moment and Kelly got into it in the presence of half-a-dozen policemen who were in the act of arresting two men on top of the vehicle, believing them to have been involved in the rescue. Further on he encountered another batch of policemen and waited to learn full particulars from them. Later in the evening of the same day, Kelly and Deasy returned to Manchester and took up their quarters at the house of a tried friend.

This cannot be true. No mention is made of the handcuffs or of their being removed. There is clear evidence, however, that Deasy's were knocked off at the house of Daniel Rider in Taylor Street, Bradford, Manchester, at around 4-30 on the afternoon of the outrage. This much at least would appear to have been borne out by O'Meagher Condon, who later stated that he had attempted to cut through the links of the handcuffs by means of a large knife and a brick soon after Kelly and Deasy got away from the van, but without success.

Of the three men seen in Taylor Street that afternoon one was in handcuffs (Deasy), while another answered Kelly's description. At that time this man wore no handcuffs, which supports the claim that they had been smashed with a stone in the brickfields soon after the rescue, presumably by the third man.

Although it was O'Meagher Condon's responsibility to escort the two escaping Fenian officers out of the city, he most certainly was not the third man, for by the time the three strangers were seen in Taylor Street, Condon had already been apprehended. Nor does he appear to have been one of the men subsequently arrested. On the other hand, not all of the rescuers were captured. Some undoubtedly got clean away. The third man could well have been one of them.

A article published soon after the turn of the century stated,

In 1893 there were seven rescuers still living in the United States. Peter Ryan, who struck the 'cuffs from Kelly's wrists, Joseph Keeley (sic), John Stoneham, Michael Clooney, James Lavery, James Bellew and Edward O'Meagher Condon.

If this is accurate then it is more than probable that Peter Ryan was the third man, and the last rescuer with whom Kelly and Deasy had contact before leaving Manchester and disappearing completely. Ryan may, in fact, have escaped with them to America.

Another persistent rumour was that Kelly had been seen in the country district of Saddleworth, an outpost of Yorkshire on the Lancashire side of the Pennine hills, but on being checked out by the police the rumour proved groundless. The *Oldham Standard* reported,

Probably this rumour was got up by some wag in order to relieve the monotony of that romantic, but otherwise dull locality.

A further report claimed that Kelly had travelled only as far as Liverpool, where he decided to remain, having secured a remunerative position as an Inspector of shipping and commerce, *'until such time as Irishmen in America form a consolidated body for the overthrow of the British oligarchy.'*

In April, 1868, a man who boarded the steamship *Oriana* at Leghorn behaved in such a way as to lead some of the other passengers to suppose that he might be a Fenian. Though travelling under the name Lionel Glanville, he appeared to answer the description of Captain Deasy, and his conversation seemed to indicate that he might well be a prominent member of the Brotherhood.

At London Bridge the *Oriana* was met by two boats carrying Thames police officers and escorted up the river. As she anchored, several detectives went on board. Glanville was immediately arrested and taken to Leman Street police station in Whitechapel, where he was closely questioned. At the same time a telegram was dispatched to the Manchester police and detectives from that city arrived by the next train.

However, it turned out to be yet another disappointment, the Manchester officers failing to identify the suspect, who was at once freed. It was pointed out to the angry traveller that his own conduct and conversation had been the cause of his arrest.

The *New York Sun* printed the following ludicrous article,

Captain Timothy Deasy, who was arrested in Manchester and rescued by the Fenians of that place, arrived in this city on Sunday. He will be tendered a public reception on Tuesday.

Captain Deasy gives a humourous account of his escape from Liverpool. Having packed his trunks with the aid of Colonel Kelly and disguised himself to defy detection, he proceeded on board the steamship City of Paris *in company with the Colonel. The latter, dressed as a porter, carried the traps on his back in the most approved manner of the fraternity.*

They passed the long line of detectives and reached the deck of the vessel without attracting any attention. Deasy then handed Kelly a shilling for his trouble, but the assumed porter, playing his part to the

full, refused to accept such a paltry sum for so much work. The regular porters were then called upon to act as referees and decided that their ill-used 'colleague' was entitled to eighteen pence at least. Kelly was so demonstrative that the police threatened to arrest him if he did not accept the shilling and go away, which he thought it better to do, exchanging a knowing look with his 'employer'.

At Queenstown the Captain put on a careless exterior and passed among the detectives, discoursing freely about the emigrants and making enquiries generally respecting the objects of the wretched Fenians in keeping up such a hopeless crusade against Her Britannic Majesty. During the course of the conversation the rescue of Kelly and Deasy was alluded to and condemned. One of the detectives remarked that he'd be damned if they would get away from him if he had them in his clutches.

This story seems highly improbable to say the least. Still, Kelly and Deasy did somehow contrive to leave the country. That fact is beyond question, although it is not known to this day how they accomplished it. Perhaps the fact was more colourful than the fiction.

They did eventually reach America, where they continued, no doubt, to plan for another tilt at the old enemy. Neither, however, lived to see Ireland gain independence.

Timothy Deasy died in 1880. Kelly, who worked at the Custom House in New York, died on 5 February, 1908, and is buried in Woodlawn Cemetery. His grave bears the inscription: Thomas J. Kelly, Civil War Veteran 1861–66, Grand Army of the Republic, New York City.*

Most of the other veteran Fenians also spent the latter part of their lives in America. John O'Mahoney died in New York in 1877, Kickham, Luby and the rest surviving him by a good many years. John Devoy lived until 1928, when well into his eighties.

Edward O'Meagher Condon was released from prison after serving eleven years of his sentence, and returned to America, where he was to meet up again with Ricard O'Sullivan Burke, who had also completed his sentence, less remission.

Jeremiah O'Donovan Rossa, after years of severe punishment in English gaols, largely on account of his own stubbornness, was freed in 1871 under a general amnesty. In 1869 Rossa had been accorded the unique distinction of being elected Member of Parliament for Tipperary while still a guest of Her Majesty. As there was not the slightest possibility of his release at that time, the election was declared void and a fresh ballot taken. Rossa died in America in 1915.

Manchester Martyrs by P. Rose.

261

James Stephens continued to live in Paris, where most of his time was spent in the company of others of his kind; would-be revolutionaries, ineffectual idealists and dreamers. The failure of the men who had deposed him gave Stephens a new credibility for a time, but nothing was to result from it. Several times he visited America, ostensibly on Fenian business. Meetings were convened, usually consisting of no more than a handful of staunch followers from the past. Although many hours were spent in futile discussion, with Stephens being as flowery and verbose as ever, it was, as always, just talk. No Fenian ships loaded with arms would ever sail again for the west coast of Ireland. The promises of support from France were never to materialise either. The Fenian flame was all but extinct during this period.

In the eighteen-eighties, Stephens, now no longer a threat to anyone, was allowed to return unmolested to Ireland, where he lived out his life in retirement. The old warrior was to be accorded one last honour, however, in 1897, when a memorial to commemorate the Manchester Martyrs was erected in Moston Cemetery, Manchester, paid for, according to the inscription, by the Irish people.

Thirty years after the execution of the three young Irishmen, James Stephens was invited to England to lay the foundation stone. Stephens, who must have relished the great honour bestowed upon him, died in Dublin in 1901.

A Manchester newspaper at the time described the monument thus,

The memorial is in the form of a Celtic cross placed on a pedestal. The foundation stone is from the Hill of Tara, the base being composed of sixteen* stones representing the counties of Ireland, the cornerstones its four provinces. In front of the cross is a figure of Erin armed with sword and shield, and on the reverse side a miniature copy of an Irish round tower. At each corner is the figure of an Irish wolfhound and the portraits of the three men are to be given. This very impressive memorial was designed and put together by Mr. J. Geraghty of Bootle.

The laying of the stone was made the occasion of a public demonstration in the City, deputations of Irishmen from most of the towns of Lancashire and Yorkshire being present. After the ceremony a meeting was held at St. James's Hall in the City centre, Mr. E. Griffiths presiding.

* This is an exact quote, but there are, in fact, 32 stones representing the 26 counties in Eire and the six in Northern Ireland. The four provinces represented are Munster, Ulster, Leinster and Connaught.

For many years after this, on the Sunday nearest to 23 November, the anniversary of the executions, a procession through the city and on to Moston Cemetery took place, culminating in a service around the memorial.*

In 1974, following the Birmingham bomb outrage, the memorial was daubed with paint by persons unknown. The traditional march was called off by the organisers, a very wise decision as things turned out, for the cemetery was crawling that day with members of the National Front party under their chairman Mr. J. Kingsley Read. As they waited in vain for the Manchester Martyrs Committee and their supporters, a close watch was kept on them by a large force of police, while a number of mounted policemen patrolled the fringes of the cemetery and made sure that members of the public entering to visit the graves of relatives were not impeded by the chanting, flag-waving mob at the gates.

To visit the cemetery now is most depressing. The monument is badly disfigured and in a very poor state generally. Due to acts of vandalism it no longer matches the description given at the time of its erection. The figure of Erin and the wolfhounds are gone. The round tower remains, but the 'portraits' of the martyred three have been badly daubed with paint. Yet though the monument's present drab state most certainly detracts from its former imposing grandeur, the very forlornness of its appearance somehow endows it with a greater poignancy.

So long as this memorial remains, regardless of its condition, it will, in the words of the ballad, serve '*to keep the memory ever green of the boys that smashed the van*'.

* This ceremony has now been discontinued.

CHAPTER 29

Controversy

There is no doubt that the dramatic events of 18 September, 1867 caused a great sensation on both sides of the Atlantic. In Manchester the outrage was endlessly discussed and argued about for many months afterwards and the story passed down from father to son, particularly in Irish families, which by now accounted for a very large part of the City's population. Even today, many older Manchester Catholics claim to know something about the Hyde Road bridge incident. When questioned they will invariably tell you that a bunch of local Fenians rescued two of their leaders from a prison van, and that during the confusion a policeman was accidentally shot and killed.

Where historians are concerned there is much more to it than that, although it must be mentioned here that some writers have obviously accepted the uncorroborated accounts of such people as John Devoy, for example, without investigating further themselves, and this has resulted in the perpetuation of certain inaccuracies regarding some of the more controversial aspects of the case.

In fact, ever since Allen, Larkin and O'Brien were executed the whole affair has been surrounded by controversy, the main points at issue being:

(a) Did the rescuers set out with the intention of gaining their objectives by whatever means were found to be necessary, even to the extent of taking life?

(b) Was the shot that killed Sergeant Brett fired to break the lock or was the gun deliberately thrust between the bars of the grille and discharged directly at the custodian of the van's keys?

(c) Who fired it?

My own reconstruction of the rescue itself is based entirely on the sworn testimony of witnesses in court, both at the magisterial hearing and at the trial. The witnesses were not totally in agreement on every point, (they seldom are), but when the evidence is carefully scrutinised an overall picture does emerge, and it is thereby possible to piece together the story of the attack on the van as seen through the eyes of those who were actually present when it took place.

Regarding the first question: Constable Yarwood was quite sure that Michael Larkin had deliberately tried to shoot him. However,

265

it is clear that Yarwood, who dashed away quickly from the scene, panicked, as did Larkin, who fired wildly in the air. So it seems unlikely that there was any intent to kill in this instance.

Constable Shaw estimated that upwards of forty shots had been fired by the Fenians during the attack, most of them hitting the railway arch. Shaw added, however, 'I don't think the men were much experienced at shooting, or we should not be here to tell the tale.'

This, of course, was just one witness's opinion, which should be viewed with a degree of scepticism, for even bad marksmen would be unlikely to direct most of their shots against the railway arch, unless they intended to fire high above the heads of the police and public. Also, when Allen was being chased across the brick-field, he had, according to the witness Thomas Barlow, fired at the ground 'so as not to hurt anyone'.

On the other hand, what cannot be overlooked is the fact that Allen shot Sprosson in the foot and that Constable Seth Bromley was wounded in the thigh after Allen had pointed the gun 'straight at him'. The same policeman also testified that Constable Trueman had been chased by Gould [O'Brien], who fired a shot at him, the bullet just grazing his back.

So what becomes apparent from the evidence is that while the majority of the attackers probably did not intend to kill or maim, there were at least two among them who were reckless enough for anything. It must also be stated that even the actions of the less guilty endangered life.

The question of whether the fatal shot was fired to kill Sergeant Brett or merely to smash the lock is the most controversial. Was the gun fired at the lock, or was it simply thrust between the grille bars and trained on Sergeant Brett, then fired? Let the evidence of the various witnesses on this point now be examined.

At the magisterial hearing, Mr. Higgin, for the prosecution, claimed that Allen had fired 'with deliberate aim' after Sergeant Brett had been threatened. Mr. Woodcock, house surgeon at the Manchester Royal Infirmary, stated that the bullet entered Brett's head at the roof of the right orbit and passed out again at the crown of the head:

'It must have passed upwards at an angle of 45 degrees.'

Damning as the evidence appears, it is not conclusive proof that Brett's killer poked the pistol through the grille and pointed it upwards at Brett's head before firing, because according to one of the women prisoners, the gun went off just as they attempted to drag Sergeant Brett away from the door. This could conceivably have brought Brett's head into the path of the bullet. The witness Emma Halliday stated that she had seen a pistol placed between the bars of the grille. She had pulled Sergeant Brett away from the ventilator and his head had 'come on a level with the pistol, which was discharged and Charlie fell.'

Witness Thomas Patterson said he saw the prisoner place two pistols in the grille, though he thought only one shot was fired. George Pickup, however, said Allen fired half a dozen shots into the ventilator. John Griffiths, one of the prosecution's most important witnesses, said he thought that Allen had fired 'at the van's lock'. Police Constable Shaw also felt that this was the case, stating at the trial,

'I gained the impression that Allen fired only to burst open the lock'.

So evidence of intent, with regard to the fatal shot is, perhaps, inconclusive. This brings us to the final question. Who fired the shot? Of that there would appear to be very little doubt; unless of course, one chooses to believe that the many witnesses who testified against Allen either perjured themselves or were all mistaken.

It has been argued many times over that the killer was not Allen, but Peter Rice, described as a short but sturdy Dublin man, who was involved in the rescue but never apprehended. Condon himself claimed that Rice was responsible. Could he, however, have been really certain? In all the confusion, with bullets flying about and men battering at the van with stones and axes, how could Condon have been sure just who did fire at the lock? After all, unlike most of the witnesses, he himself was heavily involved in the skirmish.

It has been said that one of the rescuers, who later escaped to America, claimed to have fired the shot which killed Brett, and the inference is that this man was Peter Rice. But then, others, apart from Condon, later claimed to have organised the rescue. The claim of the mysterious 'confessor' must therefore be regarded as dubious. Once out of the reach of the English law Rice would have little to lose and possibly much to gain in the way of notoriety by purporting to have been the assassin, the man who shot Brett undoubtedly being a hero in the eyes of some. It is possible, of course, that another Fenian, not Allen, also fired at the lock. If so, no clear description of him was given in court, while a whole stream of witnesses swore to Allen.

The possibility of mistaken identity must be considered. Marine Thomas Maguire, it will be remembered, although sworn to by a number of witnesses, was definitely not at the scene of the affray. Obviously, a Fenian who was never caught bore a strong resemblance to him, possibly James Lavery, a local Centre, who, according to Condon's account, was on the roof of the police van. But it is unlikely

267

that anyone could have mistaken Allen for Peter Rice, one being tallish and slender, the other small and stocky. Allen, with his long flaxen hair and pale features, would be very difficult to confuse with anyone else. All who saw him on that day, including the landlady of the Halfway House, remembered him very clearly.

So the claim that Sergeant Brett was shot by someone other than Allen, probably the elusive Peter Rice, does not hold up in the face of the evidence, any more than did O'Brien's insistence that he was not at the bridge when the van was attacked (a claim supported by several defence witnesses and later by Condon), when he was seen to fire his pistol at Constable Trueman and was caught running away across the railway yard. Or Larkin's statement, contradicted by his own counsel, that he had never fired a shot during the attack.

Although Condon organised the rescue Allen was clearly the ringleader when the time for action came. It was stated in evidence,

'Allen was the most prominent man there', and 'Allen was inciting the others the whole time.'

So it would not be unfair to say he was as guilty as any, and more guilty than most of the others. Under the law all who took part in the attack were equally guilty, so it might be considered fortunate that only three rescuers paid with their lives. On the other hand, it could be argued that if the law was not to be followed to the letter, why were three lives forfeited while others were spared? The law does state that all who aid and abet are guilty.

There is certainly an uncomfortable inconsistency about this which would seem to support the argument that the hanging of the unfortunate three was nothing less than an act of political reprisal, also calculated, to use the words of the judge at Captain Mackey's trial, to persuade others 'to relinquish this insane struggle against the irresistible power of a mighty empire.'

An interesting point is that all three men proclaimed their innocence throughout the trials and maintained this position even in their last letters. Yet each man was a God-fearing Roman Catholic. It is difficult to believe that any one of them would be prepared to die with a lie on his lips.

After writing the letters they made their last confessions and took communion on the following morning. It will never be known if any admission of guilt was made during those confessions, for such things are never allowed to go beyond the priest concerned.

The prison van, around which the drama had been so violently enacted, was to serve for a few years more before becoming redundant.

Some years ago a newspaper reported that '*the battered Black Maria ended its days as a bowls hut on the Corporation Cleansing Department's land at Chat Moss.*' In his book '*The Manchester Martyrs*', Paul Rose mentions a rumour of the van rotting away in a garden in Eccles, Salford, but goes on to say that those interested had been unable to track it down.

The Hyde Road bridge, which spans one the City's busiest thoroughfares, is, perhaps surprisingly, still in existence. And though it has undergone a good deal of reconstruction, a large part of the original brickwork remains. In more recent times a memorial has been placed close to the bridge, which bears the inscription:

Fenian Ambush
(September 1867)
Site of the rescue of two Fenian prisoners.
Following the shooting of a policeman
three of the rescuers were executed
at the last public hanging in
the Manchester area.
(November 1867)

Some yards further up the road is Toll Bar Street, in the vicinity of which the old Toll Bar, mentioned in newspaper reports of the rescue, once stood.

The New Bailey prison was demolished in 1871, by which time the new gaol at Strangeways, opened in 1868, was fully operational. When the old prison was taken down to make way for a railway goods yard, the bodies of those buried within its precincts were exhumed and re-interred at Strangeways, among them those of the three young Irishmen.

In a sense it could be said that the three Manchester Martyrs did not die in vain. Their drastic action and tragic end certainly helped to sow the seeds from which the rising of 1916 and final independence grew, for their names and daring exploits proved a source of inspiration to those who were to follow.

Yet one wonders exactly what the true sentiments of their families must have been. To Mrs. Larkin, for example, left with four

269

young children, the stirring speeches and talk of martyrdom would have meant very little. Perhaps she and others like her were the real martyrs.

Heroes there may have been that day in 1867 at the Hyde Road bridge, but none more heroic than Sergeant Brett, whose body lies beneath a plain, unpretentious headstone in Harpurhey Cemetery. The inscription reads:

Faithful unto death
In affectionate remembrance of
Sergeant Charles Brett
of the Manchester Police Force,
who died in the discharge of his duty at
Hyde Road, September 18th, 1867
in the 52nd year of his age.
'I dare not. I must do my duty.'

The last words of a very brave man.

Selected Bibliography

Newspapers
Banner of Ulster,
The Citizen,
Clare Journal,
The Cork Examiner,
The Cork Herald,
Drogheda Argus,
Freeman's Journal,
Irish People,
The Irishman,
The Irish World and American Industrial Liberator,
Kilkenny Journal,
Lancashire Free Press,
Limerick Chronicle,
Manchester Evening News,
Manchester Guardian,
The Nation,
The New York Sun,
The New York Times,
The Northern Whig,
The Oldham Standard,
The Times.

Books
The Manchester Martyrs, by Paul Rose.
Story of the old faith in Manchester, by John O'Dea.

INDEX

A

Abbot, John: 237–238, 243.
Abbot, Minnie: 238.
Accomb, John: 143.
Acts and Bills of Parliament:
    'Soup Kitchen' Act: 3.
    Act of Union: 39.
    Copyright Act: 245.
    Emancipation Bill: 3.
    Habeas Corpus Act: 25–26.
Admiralty: 257.
Allen, Jeremiah: 234–236, 238, 242.
Allen, William O'Meara: 111, 118, 129, 149, 167, 169, 183.
Allen, William Philip: 88, 95–96, 183, 200.
Allen: 97, 100–101, 103–105, 107–108, 116, 130–131, 133–140, 142–146, 168, 170–176, 180, 182–183, 185, 188, 199, 210, 215, 217–220, 225, 228, 265–268.
Ambler, Mr.: 146.
American Embassy: 210.
Anderton, Superintendent: 118.
Anderton, William Ince: 167.
Andrews, Mr.: 154.
Ardwick Industrial School: 93.
Armstrong: 217, 220.
Frances Armstrong: 93, 143.
Inspector Armstrong: 27.
Ash, James: 192.
Ashworth, James: 170.

B

Bacon, John: 124, 129, 131, 146, 167, 187, 191.
Barlow, Thomas: 175, 266.
Barnes, Mr. Robert: 163.
Barrett, Michael: 234, 242–244, 246–248.
Barrett, Robert: 229.
Barrigan, Patrick: 112.
Barrington, Lord: 239.

Battle of Hastings: 46.
Battle of Limestone Ridge: 34.
Batty, William: 176.
Baxter, James Henry: 93, 102–103.
Baxter, Mark: 104.
Baxter, landlord of the Rose and Crown, Birmingham: 227.
Bazley, Mr.: 202.
Beal: 179.
Beck, John: 161, 174, 188–191, 194.
Bedale, Dr.: 192–193.
Beecher, Captain: 245.
Bell, Inspector: 72.
Bellew, James: 88, 259.
Bennett, Mr. W.: 116, 129, 132–133, 142–143, 165.
Bennett, William: 228.
Berger, Jack: 171.
'George Berry': 197. *See Burke, Captain Ricard O'Sullivan.*
Birch, Edward: 228.
Blackburn, Elizabeth: 179.
Blackburn, Mr. Justice: 166–170, 172, 177, 181, 188–190, 195, 197, 202, 211.
Blackmore, Mrs.: 245.
Blanes and Sons, Messrs.: 161.
Bond, Oliver: 2.
Boulger, Matthew: 124.
Bourke, General Thomas F.: 62, 68. 73, 75–76.
Bourne: 64.
Bowman, Dr.: 93.
Boylan, Michael Joseph: 112, 116, 167, 195.
Boyle, John: 192.
Bradlaugh, Mr. Charles: 209.
Bradshaw, Sub-Inspector: 43.
Brears, Sergeant: 84.
Brecken, William: 194.
Brennan, John: 88–89, 104, 112, 129, 140, 143, 147–148, 167, 187–188, 194, 197, 222.
Brennan, Miles: 104–105.
Brereton, Sir William: 46.
Brett, Edward: 118.
Brett, Mrs.: 163.
Brett, Sergeant Charles: 90–91, 93, 101–103, 107, 116, 118, 127, 129–130, 136, 142, 149, 159, 162–163, 166, 168, 179, 181, 183, 187, 196–197, 202, 209, 211, 220, 265–268, 270.

274

Brierley: 73.
British Government: 12, 18, 25, 42, 64, 108, 166, 205, 212, 225.
Broadhurst, Henry Tootal: 167.
Bromley, Police Constable Seth: 93, 101, 175, 266.
Bromley, Richard: 98.
Brook, Ann: 191.
Brook, Mary Jane: 191.
Brophy, Hugh: 19.
Brophy, William Joseph: 88, 159, 161–162, 167, 174.
Brown, William: 20–22.
Brownrigg, Inspector: 60.
Brunslow, Henry George: 167.
Bryan, Michael: 124, 129, 139, 143.
Buckley, Mr. Charles: 207.
Burke, Colonel Ricard O'Sullivan: 38, 59, 71, 81, 87–90, 92, 197, 231–236, 240, 243–246, 261.
Burn, Mary: 148.
Burns, John: 229.
Butler, John: 112.
Butt, Isaac: 75, 165.
Butterworth, John: 170.
Byrne: 59.
Byrne, Harry: 245.
Byron, Lord John: 46.

C

Cahill, James: 88.
Calcraft, William: 76, 201, 215, 217–220, 247.
Cambridge, Duke of: 239.
Campbell: 122.
Campbell, Major: 252.
Cantwell, Canon: 210, 216, 218.
Carey, Martin Henley: 5.
Carlisle, Detective-Inspector: 50.
Carrington, William: 144.
Carroll, John: 88, 112, 129, 144, 167, 197, 222.
Carroll, Louisa: 179.
Carter, William: 207–208.
Casey, Constable: 250–252.
Casey, Joseph Theobald: 197, 231–236, 240, 244–246.
Casey, Patrick: 229.

Casey, William: 229.
Cassidy: 63.
Cavanagh, a defector: 66.
Central Criminal Court: 169, 242.
Chambers, James O'Brennan: 88, 159, 160–162, 167.
Chancellor of the Exchequer: 240.
Cheetham, John, M.P.: 167.
Christian, Mr. Justice: 67.
Civil War (American): 11–12, 22, 32, 34, 45, 48, 60, 76, 80–81, 233.
Civil War (English): 46–47.
Clark, Captain: 114.
Clarke: 122.
Clarke, George: 37.
Cleary, Dr.: 64.
Cleburne: 232, 233. *Alias Massey, General Godfrey*
Clent: 139.
Clooney,Michael: 88, 259.
Clooney, Patrick: 112.
Cloran, Thomas: 229.
Cluseret, General Gustave: 38, 59, 232.
Clutton, William: 239.
Cody, James: *See Cody, Michael.*
Cody, Michael: 76.
Coffey, Patrick: 122, 129, 138, 167, 187, 189, 191, 193, 229.
Coghlan, Head Constable: 55.
Colville, Lord: 239.
Condon, Captain Edward O'Meagher: 38, 80–81, 83, 86–90, 95–99,
    104–105, 107, 155, 184–185, 191, 210, 215–217, 223, 259,
    261, 267–268.
Patrick Condon: 60. *See Massey, Godfrey.*
Condon (Bantry): 23.
Connell: 93.
Considine, Owen: 6.
Cooper, Ellen: 93, 142, 161.
Cooper, Lieutenant-Colonel William: 153.
Coper: 23.
Corcoran, Michael: 112, 129, 143.
Cornwallis: 2.
Corridon: 82. *See Corydon, John Joseph below.*
Corydon, John Joseph: 48, 50, 60, 67, 74, 86–87, 244–245, 249,
    253.
Cosgrove, William: 62, 72–73.
276

China: 196.
Eire: 222.
England: 2–4, 10, 15, 17, 20, 25–26, 28, 30, 40, 45–48,
54–55, 57, 59–60, 72, 77, 79–81, 85, 88, 115, 126,
152, 197, 211, 216, 227, 232, 248, 253, 257–258,
262.
France: 2, 4, 17, 258, 262.
Ireland: 3–8, 10–12, 14, 16–17, 20, 24–30, 37–38, 41–48,
54–55, 57, 59–60, 63, 65, 67–69, 71–72, 75–76, 79,
82, 89–90, 94–95, 108, 122, 150, 154, 179–180,
184, 194, 199, 201–202, 215–216, 221, 225, 232,
245, 249–250, 253–254, 257–58, 261–262.
Italy: 19.
Japan: 30.
Mexico: 11.
New Zealand: 150.
Russia: 69.
Scotland: 47, 81, 87, 243.
Wales: 46.
Cozens, Captain: 257.
Crawley, Colonel: 206.
Crimean War: 40.
Cronin: 250, 252.
Crowley, Peter O'Neill: 222.

D

Daley, Patrick: 129, 143.
Darragh, William: 87.
Davis, Edwin: 193.
Deasy, Captain Timothy: 81, 83–87, 89–93, 95, 101, 103–105, 108,
113, 123, 126, 136, 144, 157–158, 176–178, 181, 183,
200–201, 205, 221, 225, 227, 258–261.
Denieffe, Joseph: 6, 7.
Desmond, Timothy: 233, 236, 238, 242, 244.
Desmond, William: 233–234, 241–243, 248.
DeValera, Mr. Eamon: 222.
Devany, John: 245, 249.
Devoy, John: 11, 19, 76, 95, 261, 265.
Dicconson, Mr. T.: 155.
Dimmock, Frederick: 237.
Doheny, Michael: 6.

Doran, Patrick: 73, 75–76.
Doran, Patrick (a Local Centre in Wales): 229.
Dowling: 27.
Drabble, Detective: 123.
Duffy, Edward: 19, 66, 75.
Dunne, Captain: 64, 68.

E

Chester, Earl of: 46.
Mayo, Earl of: 94.
Earley, Monsignor Richard: 222.
Eaton: 113.
Edwards, Captain: 47.
Egan, John: 55.
Egerton, The Hon. A.F., M.P.: 167.
Elgee, Captain: 163.
Ellis, a witness: 125, 149.
Ellis, John: 219.
Emmet Monument Association: 6.
Emmet, Robert: 2, 7, 228.
English, Nicholas: 233–234, 241–242.

F

Fariola, General: 59.
Farrell, Matthew: 6.
Farrell, Thomas: 245.
Kenyon, Father: 7.
Patrick Lavelle, Father: 7, 17.
Featherstone, Patrick: 148.
Featherstone, Timothy: 88, 146, 167, 187, 191, 194, 197, 222.
Federal Government: 25.
American Government: 26.
Fee, Isobella: 178.
Fee, Joseph: 178.
Fegan, James: 55.
Fenian Conspiracy: 18, 27, 44.
Fenian Movement: 1, 17–18, 20, 37, 41, 45, 59, 65, 67, 79, 80, 88, 211, 228, 258.
Roberts–Sweeney faction: 28–29.
Fenian: 10, 12–15, 18, 20, 37, 42, 44, 46, 50.

Fenian Brotherhood: 11, 14–16, 18, 22–23, 25, 33, 41, 43, 45, 54, 60, 68, 74, 76, 82, 87, 124, 149, 151, 195, 197, 241–242, 249, 253, 258, 260.

Roberts Fenians: 25.

O'Mahoney Fenians: 25.

Fenian War Bonds: 28.

Fenian Sisterhood: 10.

Fenian Senate: 16, 25–26.

Fenians: 1–2, 11, 13, 16, 19–20, 22–23, 26–27, 30–34, 36, 38, 43, 46, 48, 51–52, 54–56, 59–69, 71–72, 76, 79–81, 87–88, 96–97, 100–101, 103–104, 108–109, 114, 118, 122–124, 136, 144–145, 149–150, 152–155, 158, 166, 179, 185, 187–188, 196–197, 202, 205–208, 210–211, 221, 225, 233–236, 245, 248, 250, 253, 255, 257–258, 261, 265–266.

Fenton, Thomas: 54.

Fielden, Sir William Henry , Bart.: 167.

Finlen, Mr.: 204–206, 209, 226.

Fitzgerald, Lord Edward: 2, 228.

Fitzgerald, Mr. Justice: 75.

Fitzpatrick, a shoemaker: 61.

Flanagan, Mrs. Mary: 177, 180.

Flood, John: 55, 74–75.

Fluett, Mr.: 76.

Flynn, Michael: 192.

Foley, Hugh: 122, 125, 129, 146, 149.

Foley, James: 125, 149, 189.

Foley, Mary: 125, 149.

Fordham, P.C.: 244.

Forrester: 64.

Fowler, Mr. Robinson: 115–118, 124–125,129–135, 137, 139, 142–144, 146–148, 162.

G

Monsignor Gadd: 199, 203, 209–210, 213, 216, 220, 222.

Gallagher, Mr.: 32.

Gallagher, a ship's pilot: 71.

Gaols and prisons:

> Belle Vue Gaol: 88, 91, 93, 103, 107, 111, 118, 122, 137, 177, 188.
>
> Bridewell (Cork): 251.
>
> Clerkenwell House of Detention: 209, 231, 233.

Dartmoor: 44.
Dublin Castle: 62, 235.
House of Correction (Manchester): 199.
Kilmainham: 40, 76.
Longford Gaol: 152.
Millbank: 150, 222.
Mountjoy Prison: 56, 60, 71.
New Bailey Prison (Salford): 166, 185, 195, 199, 201, 204,
    210, 215, 222, 269.
Newgate prison: 2, 245–247.
old Bridewell (Clerkenwell): 231.
Oldham Town Hall: 73.
Richmond Bridewell: 19, 29.
Salford Gaol: 227.
Strangeways: 269.
Garibaldi: 226.
Garner, Inspector: 92, 123.
Gavin, Lucy: 162.
Geale: 250–251.
Geary: 14–15.
Gee, Superintendent: 92, 116–117, 121, 124, 178, 215.
Geraghty, Mr. J.: 262.
Gerrard, Sir Robert Tolver, Bart.: 167.
Gibbons: 52.
Gill, Inspector: 188.
Glanville, Lionel: 260.
Gleeson, John: 112, 129, 138–139.
Gleeson, a U.S. Army officer: 38.
Glifferson, Mr. Hugh: 32.
Goode, P.C.: 122.
Gould, William: 111–112, 129, 131, 133–138, 143–144, 148, 167,
    169, 174–175, 177–178, 180, 182, 184, 222, 266.
    See O'Brien, Captain Michael.
Grand Jury: 167–169, 252.
Grant, James: 179.
Greek fire: 61, 73, 153, 244.
Greenall, Sir Gilbert, M.P.: 167.
Greeny, William: 233.
Grey, Philip: 4, 6, 9.
Griffin, Edward: 229.
Griffiths, John: 97, 139, 190, 200, 267.
Griffiths, Mr. E.: 262.

Grosvenor, Earl, M.P.: 51.
Grosvenor, Lord Richard, M.P.: 51.
Groves, John: 151.
Gunning, Daniel: 206.

H

Hadfield, David: 207–208.
Hadfield, Henry: 192.
Hadfield, William: 148.
Halliday, Abraham Parker: 171.
Halliday, Emma: 93, 102, 141, 160, 267.
Halpin, General: 12, 38.
Haltigan, John: 6, 9.
Handcock, Martha: 179.
William Harbinson: 59, 62–63.
Hardy, Mr. Secretary Gathorne: 196, 205–206, 209, 239.
Harrison, Thomas: 47.
Harrop: 113.
Harvey, Bagenal: 2.
Hassett, John: 206.
Hayes, John: 103–104, 136.
Healey, Elizabeth: 194.
Henderson: 139.
Hepburn, Colonel H.P.: 51.
Hibbert, John Tomlinson, M.P.: 167.
Hickey, Mary: 200, 215.
Hickley, Mr., Chief Superintendent of Police: 53.
Higgin, Mr.: 129–131, 138, 143, 266.
Higgins, John: 55.
Hill, William James: 233.
Hirst, P.C., Joseph: 105–106, 191.
Hodges, Colonel White: 250.
Hodgkins, Mrs.: 239.
Hodgkinson, Peter: 207–208.
Hoey's Bar: 27.
Hoey, Mary Ann and Annie: 27.
Hoey, Peter: 88.
Hogan, Congressman: 25.
Hogan, John: 215.
Hogan, Patrick: 112.

Hogan, William: 246.
Holder, Mrs.: 236.
Holland, Captain William: 229.
Hollows, James: 171.
Home Office: 94, 121, 165, 195, 202, 205– 206, 210, 215.
Home Secretary: 125, 165–166, 197, 202, 204–205, 239–240, 244.
Hopper, Charles: 5.
Hopper, George: 13.
Hospitals:
 Arbour Hill Military Hospital: 27.
 Manchester Royal Infirmary: 118, 176, 266.
 University College Hospital: 151.
Howard, Warder Joseph: 104.
Hughes, Acting-Inspector: 27.
Hughes, William: 174, 191.
Hulley, William: 98, 176.
Humbert, General: 2.
Hunter, Robert: 103–104, 145.
Hussey, Dr.: 247.

I

Ingram, Elizabeth: 179.
Ingram, Mary: 179.
Irish Constabulary: 72.
Irish Republic: 249.
Irish Republican Brotherhood: 1, 5, 10.
I.R.B.: 7, 8, 9.

J

Jackson, William: 56.
Jeffreys, a pavior: 148.
Jenman, a witness: 151.
Johnson, President Andrew: 25, 76.
Johnson, Thomas: 146–148, 167.
Jones, Captain: 204.
Jones, John: 171.
Jones, Mr. Ernest: 87, 90, 129–134, 139, 169, 187.
Joule, Mr.: 85–86.
Jourdan: 65.
Justice, Anne: 233–234, 236, 238, 242, 244.

K

L

Lavery, James: 86–88, 259, 267.
Lecomb, Mr.: 177.
Lees, Cyrus: 171.
Lennon, John: 245.
Lewis, Mr.: 241.
Liddell, Adolphus F.O.: 202, 239.
Lomas, Francis: 249. *See Mackey, Captain.*
Lomasney, William Mackey: 249. *See Mackey, Captain.*
London and North-Western Railway: 89.
Long, William: 73. *See Cosgrove, William.*
Loomey, Mr. James: 32.
Lowe, Inspector: 72.
Luby, Thomas Clarke: 4, 7, 9, 13, 22, 261.
Luther, William: 112.
Lynagh, Bernard: 206.
Lynch: 44.
Lynch, Daniel: 146.
Lynn, Peter: 124, 125.

M

MacDonald, Adelaide Noble: 200–201.
Mackey, Captain: 38, 68, 249–252, 254– 255, 268.
Maguire, Michael: 112, 117, 129, 142–143, 145, 167, 195.
Maguire, Thomas: 112, 129, 131, 135, 139–140, 144, 167, 169, 171, 174, 178–179, 183–184, 195–196, 202–204, 209, 211, 267.
Maher, a cooper: 22.
Maher, Walter: 27.
Mahoney: 59.
Manchester Detective Force: 90.
Manchester Fenians: 226.
Manchester Martyrs: 12, 228, 262–263, 269.
Manchester Police Force: 91.
Manchester Watch Committee: 163.
Marriot, Samuel: 233.
Martin, John: 124, 167, 189, 190.
Martin, William: 88, 111–112, 116, 129, 136, 139–140, 143–145, 167, 187–191.
Maskell, Richard: 235.
Massachusetts Fenians: 258.
Massey, General Godfrey: 67–69, 74, 158, 197, 231– 233, 249. *See Condon, Patrick.*

Maybury, Superintendent: 90, 121, 123.
Mc'Clure, John: 222.
Mc'Donnell, Mr.: 209.
Mc'Namara, Francis: 159.
Mc'Tigue, Patrick: 194.
McAuliffe, John Francis: 52–53, 92–93, 113, 116–118, 139, 157–158.
McCafferty, Captain John: 14, 38, 45–48, 50, 52–53, 55–56, 73–76, 231, 245, 249.
McCann: 2.
McCarthy, Lieutenant: 51.
McConnell, William: 147.
McDonnell, Edwin: 151.
McHale, Captain: 48, 50.
McKane, Mrs.: 161.
McLaughlin, Thomas: 55.
McManus, Terence Bellew: 4–5, 7–8.
McMurdo, Brigadier-General: 66.
McNeil, Colonel: 63.
McWilliam, Robert: 112, 115, 129.
Mead, General George: 34.
Meany, Stephen Joseph: 39, 40–42, 74.
Mellor, Mr. Justice: 155, 166, 169, 184, 189.
Melvin, William: 82–83.
Merthyr, a defector: 66.
Miller, James: 192.
Millin, General: 12, 19.
Mitchel, John: 4–5, 254.
Molloy, Lawrence: 161.
Monaghan, Michael: 148.
Monarchs:
>William the Conqueror: 46.
>Edward I: 46.
>William III: 47.
>George I: 47.
>Queen Anne: 47.
>Charles I: 46.
>King Henry III: 46.
>Prince of Wales: 239.
>Queen Victoria: 239.
>William the Third: 75.
Moore, Louis: 112.
Moore, Michael: 5.

Moore, a warder: 236.
Moorhouse, Charles: 88, 112, 129, 167, 197, 222.
Moorhouse, George: 187.
Morgan and Molloy: 161.
Moriarty, P.C.: 237.
Morris, Henry: 243.
Morris, John: 129, 131, 143.
Morris, Michael: 113, 129, 143.
Morton, Mr. J.D.: 202.
Mosley, Charles: 243.
Mote, member of Reform League: 225.
Mulholland, George: 97, 140, 171–174.
Mulholland, Thomas: 103, 136.
Mulkearn, Michael: 229.
Mullaney, Patrick: 242–243.
Mullidy, Mullady or Malady: 232, 244, 246. *Alias Shaw, Henry*
Munn, Josiah: 144.
Murdock, A.: 206.
Murphy, an official in American War Dept.: 13.
Murphy (Bantry): 23.
Murphy, Captain James: 81, 87, 243.
Murphy (Dublin): 61
Murphy, P.J.: 81.
Murphy, William: 88, 146–147, 167, 195, 197, 222.

N

Nagle, Pierce: 12–13, 22.
National Front: 263.
Neary, John: 86–88, 97.
Neill, Mr. Robert: 121.
Newspapers:
    Banner of Ulster: 40.
    Clare Journal: 39.
    Cork Examiner: 225.
    Cork Herald: 258.
    Drogheda Argus: 40.
    Freeman's Journal: 39–40.
    Irish People: 9, 12–13, 18.
    Irish World and American Industrial Liberator: 80.
    Irishman: 258.
    Kilkenny Journal: 6.

Ballinrobe: 7.
Ballyknockane: 249.
Ballymartle: 185.
Bandon: 185.
Bantry: 23.
Bay of Fundy: 28.
Bermuda: 28.
Black Rock: 32.
Blarney: 64.
Bodenstown: 2.
Bradford, (Manchester): 259.
Bradford Moor: 54.
Brixton: 238.
Brooklyn: 30.
Bryan: 167.
Buffalo: 31–34.
Burnfort: 64.
Buttevant: 60.
Cahir: 60.
Carrick-on-Suir: 22.
Carrickmacross: 6.
Castle Martyr: 64.
Castleton, near Rochdale: 171.
Chat Moss: 269.
Cholmondley: 51.
Clayton (Manchester): 187, 191.
Clerkenwell Green: 204, 209, 226, 237.
Clerkenwell: 235, 240.
Clonkilla: 10.
Clonmel: 12, 60.
Curragh: 63.
Davyhulme Hall: 167.
Delamere Forest: 51.
Donnelly's: 5.
Drumcondra: 75.
Dublin Castle: 12–13.
Dublin-in-the-Green: 63.
Dundrum: 62, 72.
Eastport: 28.
Eccles: 269.
Erris coast: 204.
Fermoy: 60.

Foaty: 252.
Fort Erie: 33–34.
Fort Porter: 33.
Glasnevin: 7.
Glencullen: 62, 65, 72–73.
Gosta Green: 226.
Hamilton: 35.
Harpurhey Cemetery: 127, 270.
Hill of Tara: 262.
Holborn: 151.
Hollinwood, Oldham: 167.
Inishmurray: 71.
Irwell House, Prestwich: 167.
Island Bridge: 60.
Island of Campobello: 28.
Isle of Wight: 209–210.
Jones's Wood: 74.
Kilkenny: 4, 6, 9.
Killala Bay: 2.
Killaloe: 43.
Killarney Mountains: 55.
Kilclooney Wood: 222.
Kilmallock: 62, 64.
Kilteely: 63.
Kirkham, (Lancashire): 228.
Leixlip: 9.
London Bridge: 255, 260.
Macroom: 11, 232, 250.
Macroom Castle: 250.
Mallet's Folly: 37.
Mallow: 60, 63, 64.
Mallow Junction: 55.
Malone: 34.
Manhattan: 3.
Merthyr Tydfil: 229.
Michelstown: 64.
Middleton: 64.
Millstreet: 81.
Milltown: 62.
Morley: 54.
Mullinahone: 9.
Nenagh: 6.

Waterford: 60.
Werneth Park, Oldham: 167.
West Gorton: 161.
Westminster: 240.
Windy Arbour: 72.
Worsley Old Hall: 167.
Platt, John, M.P.: 167.
Police Court: 90.
Pollitt, Charles: 93, 99.
Porter, James: 228.
Potts, Inspector: 240.
Powell, Captain: 76.
Powell, Peter: 193.
Price, Mr.: 76.

Q

Queensbury, Caroline, Dowager Marchioness of: 209–210.
Quick, Father: 210, 216.

R

Ranger, George: 236, 238.
Read, Mr. J. Kingsley: 263.
Reardon, Thomas: 61.
Reardon, Captain Thomas: 229.
Reddin, Daniel: 88, 159–162, 167, 197, 222–223.
Redhead, Richard Milne: 167.
Reeve, P.C.: 153–154.
Reform League: 225.
Regiments etc.:
10th Hussars: 252.
10th Regiment, North Lincoln: 143.
13th Light Infantry: 257.
14th Illinois: 33.
15th New York Engineers: 71, 245.
1st Battalion, Scots Fusiliers: 51.
20th Massachusetts: 81.
21st Foot, the Royal Scots Fusiliers: 65.
2nd Dragoons (Royal Scots Greys): 62.
48th Foot, the Northamptonshire Regiment: 63.
52nd Regiment: 61.

Robinson, Elizabeth: 144.
Robinson, John: 171.
Rodgers, Congressman: 25.
Captain Rogers: 68, 245.
Rossa, Jeremiah O'Donovan: 9, 13, 22, 44, 150, 261.
Rossiter, Mrs. Esther: 162.
Royalists: 46.
Royds, Clement Molyneux: 167.
Russell, Harry: 40.
Ryan: 152.
Ryan, Patrick: 148.
Ryan, Peter: 88, 259–260.
Ryan, Thomas: 113, 129, 167.

S

Saunders, William: 191.
Scalley, Thomas: 88, 129, 140, 167, 195, 197, 222.
Scanlon, a farmer: 43.
A. Schofield and Sons: 73.
Schofield, Charles: 188.
Scotland Yard: 90.
Secretary of State: 212.
Sencott: 37.
Seymour, Mr. Digby, Q.C.: 168–171, 174–177, 179–180, 187–191, 196, 211.
Shandley, Inspector: 107, 139.
Shannon, John: 162.
Shaughnessy, Garrett: 6.
Shaw, George, Constable: 92–93, 116, 118, 131, 139, 171, 180, 188, 266–267.
Shaw, Henry: 244–246.
Sheares, a United Irishman: 2. *See United Irishmen.*
Sheriff, Medwin: 161.
Sherry brothers: 174.
Sherry, James: 122, 124, 143.
Sherry, Joseph: 122, 124.
Ships:
      Brisk: 257.
      Caledonia: 65.
      Canadaigua: 23.
      City of Paris: 260.

Erin's Hope: 71.
Hibernia: 126.
Hougoumont: 257.
Jacknell: 71.
Mitchegaw: 32.
New Draper: 55.
Nightingale: 23.
Oriana: 260.
Princess Royal: 196, 204.
Racer: 23.
Coleen Bawn: 55.
Simoom: 23.
Trafalgar: 65.
Shore, Edward: 106, 129, 133–135, 137, 139, 167, 169, 176, 178, 184, 191, 210. *See Condon, Edward O'Meagher.*
Shorrocks, William: 228.
Sinkinson, Samuel: 207–208.
Slack, Henry Wilson: 144, 160.
Smith, Captain: 7.
Smith, John: 192.
Smith, Joseph: 146, 190.
Society of Friends: 187.
Southern Confederacy: 233.
Special Commission: 169.
Speed, James: 34.
Sperry, Thomas: 143, 160.
Sprosson, Henry: 97, 101, 131, 138–140, 174, 176, 180, 266.
St. Patrick's Assurance Society: 246.
St. Patrick's Brotherhood (Ireland): 7.
St. Patrick's Brotherhood (Manchester): 88.
Stenston, Sergeant-Major: 51.
Stephens, James: 4–9, 11–13, 15, 16, 19–20, 23, 28–30, 37–39, 41, 45, 53, 66, 69, 74, 76, 124, 225, 231–232, 248–249, 254, 262.
Stephenson, Captain: 51.
Stephenson, Henry: 171.
Stoneham, John: 88, 259.
Strathnairn, Lord: 61.
Stuart, Charles Edward: 47.
Stuart, James Edward: 47.
Sublime Port: 211.
Suckling, Dr.: 227.
Sullivan: 23.
Sutton, P.C.: 238.

Sweeney, Edward: 148.
Sweeney, General Thomas: 16, 26–27, 29–30, 36–37.
Sylvester, Captain: 166, 214.

T

T. Taylor & Sons: 141.
Talbot, a Crown witness: 249, 253.
Talbot, Mr. W.H.: 160, 162.
Taylor, P.C., John: 93, 99, 146.
The Provisional Government: 57.
Thomas, Charles: 146, 191.
Thompson, Inspector: 235, 244.
Thompson, Minnie: 239.
Thompson, P.C. John: 190.
Thompson, Samuel Henry: 167.
Thompson, William Phearson: 246.
Thornhill, Dr.: 76.
Tone, Wolfe: 1, 2, 228.
Toole, Patrick: 122.
Torr, Detective-Sergeant: 161.
Tours, Mr.: 196.
Townfield Police Station: 73.
Towns and cities:
    Adelaide: 257.
    Aldershot: 65, 153.
    Ashton-under-Lyne: 49, 72, 89, 113, 115, 146, 153, 155, 171.
    Athlone: 11.
    Bacup: 207.
    Bangor: 48.
    Barnsley: 141.
    Bedford: 127.
    Belfast: 15, 59, 62–63.
    Birkenhead: 21, 48.
    Birmingham: 54, 59, 87, 208, 226–227, 232–233, 245–246, 263.
    Bolton: 171.
    Boston: 33, 258.
    Bradford (Yorkshire): 54.
    Bremen: 38.
    Burnley: 152.
    Bury: 153, 171.

Carlisle: 153.

Chadderton: 207.

Chester: 46–55, 64, 74–75, 80, 92, 153, 185, 211, 245.

Chester Castle: 46–48, 74, 117.

Chicago: 10.

Cork: 7, 13–15, 55, 59, 61–64, 74–75, 108, 185, 249, 250–252.

Crewe: 206.

Detroit: 14, 56.

Dover: 126.

Drogheda: 55, 61, 64, 195.

Dublin: 2, 4, 6, 9, 11–13, 15, 20, 23–24, 27, 37, 42, 44, 55, 59–62, 64–66, 73–75, 77, 121, 182, 194, 222, 262, 267.

Dundalk: 44.

Dungannon: 15.

Edinburgh: 90.

Ennis: 39.

Fleetwood: 15.

Freemantle: 257.

Galway: 12, 67.

Glasgow: 51, 54, 87, 242–243, 246.

Halifax: 48, 152.

Holyhead: 48–49, 52.

Hull: 38, 206.

Killarney: 55, 63, 79.

Kingstown: 23.

Le Havre: 45.

Leeds: 15, 54–55, 114.

Lees: 49.

Leghorn: 260.

Leicester: 126–127.

Limerick: 4, 60–65, 74–75.

Limerick Junction: 61–62, 74, 199.

Liverpool: 4, 15, 20, 41, 45, 47–52, 54–55, 59, 74, 85, 108, 126–127, 147, 152, 159–162, 185, 194, 200, 226, 232–233, 245, 260.

London: 2, 38, 40–41, 45, 51, 53–54, 59, 68–69, 74, 79, 85–87, 90, 151–152, 169, 195–197, 204, 209–210, 216, 222, 226, 232–233, 243, 245, 258.

Londonderry: 15.

Loughrea: 39–40.

Manchester: 4, 47–48, 50–51, 54, 77, 79–81, 83, 86–90, 95, 109, 111, 113–114, 117–118, 122–123, 126, 130–132,

298

138, 140–141, 150, 152–155, 157, 161–162, 165–166,
170, 177–178, 194–197, 199–202, 205, 207, 210–211,
214, 216, 222, 226–227, 234, 246, 259–260, 262,
265, 269.

Wheeler, Colonel: 35.
Wheeler, Thomas: 243.
Whitty, Mr. M.J.: 40.
Whitworth, Benjamin, M.P: 167.
Williams, Inspector: 41, 90.
Williams, Mrs. Esther: 161.
Williams, Samuel: 207.
Wilson, Henry: 83–84, 88, 112, 114, 116, 129, 133–135, 137, 167, 177–178, 195.
Wilson, Mrs.: 177.
Wilson, Richard Mayor: 167.
Winslow, Edward C.: 233, 245. *See Burke, Captain Ricard O'Sullivan.*
Withington, Thomas E.: 167.
Wolstenholme, John: 171.
Wood, William Raynor: 167.
Woodcock, Mr. John Robertson, a house surgeon: 118–119, 176, 266.
Woods, James: 114–115.
Wortham, Benjamin: 171.
Worthington, James: 93.
Worthington, Nathan: 167.
Wright, Mrs. Hannah Maria: 161.

Y

Yarwood, Police-Constable : 93, 99, 103, 116, 131, 171, 195, 265–266.
Yorke, Mr.: 15.
Young Ireland Movement: 1, 4, 7.
Young Ireland: 40.
Young Irelanders: 4, 9.
Young Irelander: 254.
Young, Captain: 257.
Young, Mr. Thomas: 238, 242.